# Praise for *The Forgotten 500*

"The daring rescue effort to save hundreds of downed airmen in dangerous enemy territory is an amazing but unknown WWII adventure story. Told in riveting detail for the first time, *The Forgotten 500* is a tale of unsung heroes who went above and beyond." —James Bradley, *New York Times* bestselling author of *Flags of Our Fathers* and *Flyboys*

"The operation's story is an exciting tale. . . . Evoking the rescuees' successive desperation, wild hope, and joy, and their gratitude to the Serbians who risked their lives to help, Freeman produces a breathtaking popular account." —*Booklist*

"Fascinating . . . full of romance, action, and adventure . . . this untold story of World War II has finally been told with skill and grace." —*America in WWII* magazine

"Gregory A. Freeman has written a riveting account of the greatest escape during World War II. It is a remarkable adventure story of courage and daring that is superbly told." —Tony Zinni, General, USMC (Ret.)

"Freeman's *The Forgotten 500* is a literary and journalistic achievement of the highest order, a book that illuminates, thrills, and reminds us that heroes sometimes do live among us. It will take your breath away." —Gregg Olsen, *New York Times* bestselling author of *The Deep Dark: Disaster and Redemption in America's Richest Silver Mine*

"This is an exciting, powerful story of escape and rescue. It has been buried for too long." —Tony Koltz, *New York Times* bestselling coauthor of *The Battle for Peace*

"A gripping true-life narrative of one of the most heroic and inspiring—but virtually unknown—military operations of World War II. . . . Freeman chronicles it with a master's touch for detail. Although this book reads like a fast-paced novel, it is based on scores of probing interviews and meticulous archival research. *The Forgotten 500* is destined to become required reading for serious students of the Second World War." —Malcolm McConnell, #1 *New York Times* bestselling coauthor of *American Soldier*

D0052621

# THE
# FORGOTTEN
# 500

## THE UNTOLD STORY OF THE MEN
## WHO RISKED ALL FOR THE GREATEST RESCUE
## MISSION OF WORLD WAR II

# GREGORY A. FREEMAN

NAL
CALIBER

NAL Caliber
Published by New American Library, a division of
Penguin Group (USA) Inc., 375 Hudson Street,
New York, New York 10014, USA
Penguin Group (Canada), 90 Eglinton Avenue East, Suite 700, Toronto,
Ontario M4P 2Y3, Canada (a division of Pearson Penguin Canada Inc.)
Penguin Books Ltd., 80 Strand, London WC2R 0RL, England
Penguin Ireland, 25 St. Stephen's Green, Dublin 2,
Ireland (a division of Penguin Books Ltd.)
Penguin Group (Australia), 250 Camberwell Road, Camberwell, Victoria 3124,
Australia (a division of Pearson Australia Group Pty. Ltd.)
Penguin Books India Pvt. Ltd., 11 Community Centre, Panchsheel Park,
New Delhi - 110 017, India
Penguin Group (NZ), 67 Apollo Drive, Rosedale, North Shore 0632,
New Zealand (a division of Pearson New Zealand Ltd.)
Penguin Books (South Africa) (Pty.) Ltd., 24 Sturdee Avenue,
Rosebank, Johannesburg 2196, South Africa

Penguin Books Ltd., Registered Offices: 80 Strand, London WC2R 0RL, England

Published by NAL Caliber, an imprint of New American Library, a division of Penguin Group (USA) Inc.
Previously published in an NAL Caliber hardcover edition.

First NAL Caliber Trade Paperback Printing, September 2008
19   20   18

NAL Caliber Trade Paperback ISBN: 978-0-451-22495-8

THE LIBRARY OF CONGRESS HAS CATALOGUED THE HARDCOVER EDITION OF THIS TITLE AS FOLLOWS:

Freeman, Gregory A.
The forgotten 500: the untold story of the men who risked all for the greatest rescue mission of World War II /
Gregory A. Freeman.
p. cm.
ISBN: 978-0-451-22212-1 (hardcover)
1. Operation Halyard, 1944.   2. World War, 1939–1945—Search and rescue operations—Yugoslavia.
3. World War, 1939–1945—Aerial operations, American.   4. Airmen—United States—
Biography.   5. Escapes—Yugoslavia.   I. Title.
D810.S45Y84 2007
940.54'21971—dc22                                     2007009950

Set in Electra
Designed by Ginger Legato

Printed in the United States of America

*For Nicholas*

# Contents

*A sense of duty pursues us ever. It is omnipresent, like the Deity. If we take to ourselves the wings of the morning, and dwell in the uttermost parts of the sea, duty performed or duty violated is still with us, for our happiness or our misery. If we say the darkness shall cover us, in the darkness as in the light our obligations are yet with us.*

—*Daniel Webster*
*Argument on the Murder of Captain White,*
April 6, 1830. Vol. vi., p. 105.

# Introduction

**One of the last untold stories of World War II is also one** of the greatest. It's a story of adventure, daring, danger, and heroics followed by a web of conspiracy, lies, and cover-up.

The story of Operation Halyard, the rescue of 512 Allied airmen trapped behind enemy lines, is one of the greatest rescue and escape stories ever, but almost no one has heard about it. And that is by design. The U.S., British, and Yugoslav governments hid details of this story for decades, purposefully denying credit to the heroic rescuers and the foreign ally who gave his life to help Allied airmen as they were hunted down by Nazis in the hills of Yugoslavia.

Operation Halyard was the largest rescue ever of downed American airmen and one of the largest such operations in the war or since. Hundreds of U.S. airmen were rescued, along with some from other countries, right under the noses of the Germans and mostly in broad daylight. The mission was a complete success, the kind that should have been trumpeted in newsreels and published on the front page of the newspapers. But it wasn't.

It is a little-known episode that started with one edge-of-your-seat rescue in August 1944, followed by a series of additional rescues over several months. American agents from the Office of Strategic Services (OSS), the precursor of the CIA, worked with a Serbian guerilla, General Draza Mihailovich, to carry out the huge, ultrasecret rescue mission.

These are the tales of young airmen shot down in the hills of Yugoslavia during bombing runs and the four secret agents who conducted their amazing rescue. These are the stories of young men—many of them first-generation Americans, the proud, patriotic sons of European immigrants—who were eager to join the war and fight the Germans, even finding excitement in the often deadly trips from Italy to bomb German oil fields in Romania, but who found themselves parachuting out of crippled planes and into the arms of strange, rough-looking villagers in a country they knew nothing about. They soon found that the local Serbs were willing to sacrifice their own lives to keep the downed airmen out of German hands, but they still wondered if anyone was coming for them or if they would spend the rest of the war hiding from German patrols and barely surviving on goats' milk and bread baked with hay to make it more filling.

When the OSS in Italy heard of the stranded airmen, the agents began to plan an elaborate and previously unheard-of rescue—the Americans would send in a fleet of C-47 cargo planes to land in the hills of Yugoslavia, behind enemy lines, to pluck out hundreds of airmen. It was audacious and risky beyond belief, but there was no other way to get those boys out of German territory. The list of challenges and potential problems seemed never ending: The airmen had to evade capture until the rescue could be organized; they had to build an airstrip large enough for C-47s without any tools and without the Germans finding out; then the planes had to make it in and out without being shot down.

**The setting for this dramatic** chapter in history is a region that, for modern-day Americans, has become synonymous with brutal civil war, sectarian violence, and atrocities carried out in the name of ethnic cleansing—an impression that, though it may ignore the region's rich cultural history, is not inaccurate. Serbia covers the central part of the Balkan Peninsula, also known as the Balkans, a region in southern Europe separated from Italy by the Adriatic Sea. Serbia borders Hungary to the north; Romania and Bulgaria to the east; Albania and the Republic of Macedonia to the south; and Montenegro, Croatia, and Bosnia and Herzegovina to the west.

Throughout history the area has been neighbor to great empires, a proximity that contributed to a rich mixture of ethnicities and cultures, but also to a long history dominated by wars and clashes between rival groups of the same country. The fractious nature of the region even led to the term "Balkanization" or "Balkanizing" as a shorthand for splintering into rival political entities, usually through violence. The word "Balkan" itself is commonly used to imply religious strife and civil war.

The former Yugoslavia is a region seemingly in a constant state of flux. During World War II, Serbia was part of the Kingdom of Yugoslavia, which then became the Socialist Federal Republic of Yugoslavia in 1945. In 1992 the country was renamed the Federal Republic of Yugoslavia, then the State Union of Serbia and Montenegro from 2003 to 2006. When Montenegro voted independence from the State Union, Serbia officially proclaimed its independence on June 5, 2006.

Serbian borders and regions are determined largely by natural formations, including the Carpathian Mountains and the Balkan Mountains, which create the mountainous region that formed a hurdle for crippled American bombers trying to return to their bases in Italy, but which also sheltered downed fliers from the German patrols hunting them.

From the 1914 assassination of Archduke Franz Ferdinand of Austria at Sarajevo, which set off World War I, to the Nazi occupation in World War II, the region was in the center of global conflicts while contending with its own internal strife. The former Yugoslavia is a mix of different ethnic and religious groups, including Serbs, Croats, Muslims, and Slovenes. Throughout history, ancient and recent, most of the fighting in the region has been a struggle among these groups for the control of territory. After World War II, the Bosnian Muslims were strong supporters of Communist leader Josip Broz Tito, partly because he was successful at keeping the ethnic groups peaceful—just as Italian dictator Benito Mussolini made the trains run on time. Serbs were the most populous ethnic group in the former Yugoslavia, with a national identity rooted in the Serbian Orthodox Church.

After World War I, the Serb monarchy dominated the new nation of Yugoslavia. During World War II, hundreds of thousands of Serbs, Jews, and Gypsies were killed by Croat Fascists, called Ustashe, and by Germans. Some Muslims fought for the Nazis, while many other Muslims and Croats fought for the Partisans led by Tito. Serbs supported the exiled royal government.

These age-old hatreds and ethnic disputes erupted in 1992 to cause the bloodiest fighting on European soil since World War II. More than two hundred thousand people, most of them civilians, were killed and millions more were left homeless. As the fighting raged and the world learned of atrocities committed against civilian populations simply for being of the wrong ethnic background, European nations responded with numerous peace proposals that produced no peace. Then the United States moderated peace talks at Wright-Patterson Air Force Base near Dayton, Ohio. The talks led to a November 21, 1995, peace accord that relied on sixty thousand NATO troops to stop the killing.

The Bosnian war of the 1990s was particularly vicious. While Serbs are generally considered the aggressors in the Bosnian conflict of the 1990s, there also are legitimate charges that Croats and Muslims operated prison camps and committed war crimes. Some critics accused former Bosnian president Alija Izetbegovic of looking the other way while his Muslim soldiers committed war crimes in retaliation against Serb attacks. Many Serbs acknowledge the well-documented atrocities committed by Bosnian Serb militia against Muslim and Croat civilians, but they also argue that Serb civilians were the victims of similar crimes and that the Western media coverage was skewed by a bias in favor of the Muslim and Croat sides.

The Dayton accord did not completely end the violence in the region. Between 1998 and 1999, continued clashes in Kosovo, a province in southern Serbia, between Serbian and Yugoslav security forces and the Kosovo Liberation Army prompted a NATO aerial bombardment that lasted for seventy-eight days. The peace among Serbs, Croats, and Muslims in the area of the former Yugoslavia still is a fragile one.

**American fliers who parachuted out** of their bombers over Yugoslavia in World War II had little idea of the complex, troubled history of the country in which they were about to land, or of the international disputes in which they were about to become entangled. They sought refuge and a way back home, and they were humbled by the outpouring of support from the poor Serb villagers who risked their own lives to help the Americans drifting down out of the sky.

As the world came to know only the modern-day violence of the Bosnian wars, there was a small band of men who knew that the people in that distant country had once done a great service to the American people and to many young men who were scared, tired, and hungry. They held on to that story and told everyone they knew, yet the story slowly died with the forgotten 500.

Only a handful of the rescued airmen and OSS agents are still alive to tell the stories, their health and memories fading fast. But they insist that the world know the truth of what happened in Yugoslavia in 1944, including the series of almost unbelievable coincidences and near misses—everything from an improbable meeting with a top Nazi officer's wife to a herd of cows that show up at just the right moment—that made their rescue possible.

They never forgot, and they refuse to let the story die with them.

# THE
# FORGOTTEN
# 500

# Chapter 1

## We'll Get Them Out

*Yugoslavia, August 1944*

**This village seemed just like every other village Clare Musgrove** had been through in the last four days, simple stone and thatch houses with minimal furnishings and even less food, occupied by people who welcomed him even though he had no idea who they were or what they intended to do with him. The smoke of a long-smoldering fireplace mixed with the earthy aroma of wet hay and livestock, the same pungent smells that permeated every one of these villages. Following the gesture of his armed escort, he entered the small house and looked nervously around, trying to assess what might happen. For all he knew, this was it; this was where they were bringing him. Was it some sort of safe house where he could hide from the Germans without running all the time? He had wondered that at every village where he and the other American airmen stopped in the past days, but each one turned out to be just a waypoint on a journey to . . . somewhere. Musgrove and the other bomber crewmen had no idea where they were being taken by these local escorts with guns. Hell, they weren't even sure they were being taken *anywhere.* As far as he could tell, they were just being passed around from one village to the next in search of a few bits of goat cheese and scraps of bread so stale that Musgrove thought he might be better off eating his shoes.

They had no idea what fate awaited them, but they were fairly confident that they wouldn't be turned over to the Germans. Though the Americans and the local Serb people couldn't communicate in anything but gestures and facial expressions, the airmen got the idea that these swarthy people were on their side. The women had nursed their wounds and fed them as best they could, and the men had provided protection from the Nazi patrols that were always on the lookout for Allied airmen whose planes crashed before they could get back to safe territory.

Though it seemed these locals were trustworthy, Musgrove still was apprehensive. The bomber crews had been warned that some of the Yugoslav people were Nazi sympathizers and might turn them over to the Germans who had occupied their country since 1941. In fact, they'd been warned that the people in this area would cut off the downed airmen's ears and then turn the men over to the Germans. But the burly men escorting the Americans seemed friendly enough. Then again, they were the ones with the rifles. Could they be taking Musgrove and the others somewhere else before handing them over? Possibly to a German unit that offered rewards for American airmen? It didn't seem likely, but Musgrove couldn't help worrying that this curious trip would not end well. He was at the mercy of people he couldn't understand, and they were moving him around from one place to another instead of just letting the Americans hide out. Musgrove also wondered if anyone was looking for them. He hoped he and the other downed airmen hadn't been forgotten, left for dead in Nazi territory.

Musgrove had been on this mysterious journey for four days, since bailing out of his B-24 bomber over northern Yugoslavia, behind enemy lines. His eighth mission—to bomb the oil fields of Ploesti, Romania, a critical source of fuel for the German war machine—turned out to be his last. All in all, Musgrove felt lucky to be alive and without serious injuries, unlike some of the Americans in his group. One of the men broke his leg badly on landing in his parachute, and every time he grimaced in pain during the all-day hikes Musgrove was grateful that all he could complain about was hunger, the occasional thirst, and being tired. Knowing how narrowly he had escaped his crippled bomber, Musgrove was happy to be walking around anywhere instead of dead in the wreckage. And with all the German patrols in this area, he was also glad that he could walk along without a German shoving the muzzle of his rifle in his back. Musgrove had gotten out of the bomber so late, just before it crashed into the mountains of Yugoslavia, that he had become separated from the other nine crew members, whose earlier exit put them down a few miles before him. He suspected they had made it to the ground okay, but he worried that they had been captured by Germans. It would be a long time before he found out his worries were justified and he was the only one of his crew not taken prisoner right away. Getting trapped in his ball turret and the agonizing minutes it took to extricate himself while everyone else bailed out of the rapidly descending bomber, as terrifying as that was, turned out to be the saving grace for Musgrove. He wasn't in the clear, of course, and he was joining the hundreds of other airmen who escaped their planes and capture by the Nazis only to find themselves in limbo, unsure of what would come next.

It was getting dark when Musgrove entered the home with three other Americans, the group having been split up among several houses in the village. A rather robust woman, obviously the wife and mother, gestured for them to sit at the rough-hewn and well-worn wooden table and then she started putting out some meager food rations for them—the same goat cheese, hard bread, and bits of rotting potatoes that they had seen in other villages. Though they were ravenous, the men tried not to rush as they ate. They knew already that it was a hardship for these people to feed them and that their meal probably meant the couple, maybe even some children, would not eat tonight. They tried to eat with some decorum out of respect for the family's generosity, smiling and nodding thanks to the woman as she sat and watched.

Just as Musgrove was choking down a last bit of dry bread, the door opened and a man entered, saying something to the woman, who responded and then stood up, leaving the room to the men. Musgrove and the other Americans nodded to the man as he entered and hung up his hat on a wooden peg, but they didn't say anything. They had gotten out of the habit of speaking to the locals in the past few days because no one could understand them. The man sat at the table with them and smiled in return as a couple of the Americans nodded and smiled a gesture of thanks for the food, lifting a piece of bread or a cup of milk.

"You are American?" he asked.

The Americans were stunned, and thrilled. They looked at one another and then back at the only Yugoslav they had met who could speak English.

"Yes, yes, we're American," all three of them said together.

The man introduced himself, but the name was a mash of consonants and vowels that the Americans could not catch. He asked if the men needed more food, but Musgrove and the other two men knew better than to say yes. Though they were still hungry, they could not ask this man to spare more of what little food he might have for his own family.

In all their excitement to find someone who spoke English, the Americans were momentarily dumbfounded about what to say. The man across the table spoke instead.

"I am principal of school," he said. "I study English."

"A principal, oh, okay," Musgrove said, nodding his head. After a pause, he continued. "Your English is very good." He spoke slowly in case the man's English actually wasn't so good. "Where are we?"

The man responded with something in Yugoslav that, like his name, sounded like a jumble of consonants and vowels to the men. Besides, they weren't really concerned with the name of the village. They wanted to know what would happen to them.

One of the other Americans spoke up. "Are we staying here? Did they bring us to you because you speak English?"

"No," the man said, "you go to other place. You go to place with more Americans. They help you."

Musgrove looked at the other Americans, puzzled. He turned back to the man.

"They're taking us to Allied territory? Across the border?" he asked. The Americans knew that was unlikely. How could a bunch of hungry, injured, unarmed airmen get across the border and out of enemy territory?

"No, no. You go to place where more Americans. Here, Yugoslavia."

Musgrove was still unsure what he meant. "You mean they're putting us all in one place? We're meeting up with more American airmen?"

"Yes, yes, more like you. You go there. More Americans. You go there."

Musgrove looked at the other two airmen and all three slowly cracked smiles. There was a point to all this hiking from one village to another, after all. But they still didn't know exactly where "there" was, how long it would take, or what would happen when they got there. All efforts to pry more information out of the principal resulted only in him smiling and shrugging his shoulders to indicate that was the extent of what he could convey in English. "You go there. More Americans" was the most he could explain.

Well, anything was better than just wandering like this, they thought. Let's hope there's a plan once we get there. Wherever there is.


**The villagers helping Musgrove and** the other Americans get to their destination were risking their lives. If caught helping the downed American airmen, they would be killed just as the Germans had already killed thousands for resisting the Nazi invasion. German troops had been vicious when they overtook the country in 1941, brutalizing anyone seen as resisting the invasion and bombing the country into submission virtually overnight.

In 1944 the country was firmly controlled by Germany. But as soon as the Nazi bombs had begun to fall three years earlier, those who had resisted the German invasion from the start had begun to fight back. The Germans may have rolled into Yugoslavia with little difficulty, but the Yugoslav people would not let them stay without a fight.

These poor people in the Yugoslavian countryside were resisting in every way possible, from acts of sabotage and the occasional Nazi soldier who never returned from a visit to the hills to aiding every American airman they could find.

**After another week of walking** through the Yugoslav countryside, sleeping in whatever village they could find or curled up in the bushes off the side of the road, Musgrove and the band of Americans were following their two armed escorts up yet another dirt road when they saw someone on horseback up ahead. They looked to the Yugoslav escorts for a reaction, ready to dive into the brush off the roadway and hide out until it was safe again, but the escorts were not concerned to see someone ahead and kept walking. The Americans assumed that the man on horseback was not German and might be someone the escorts knew, maybe an officer in their resistance. The group trudged along slowly. The fellow on horseback seemed to be waiting for them, and Musgrove grew more curious as they moved closer. *Maybe this guy can speak some English,* he thought. *Sure would be good to find out where we are and where we're going.*

As they came closer, Musgrove could see that the man on horseback seemed to be a local, a brawny guy with a bushy beard, similar to many of the other men they had encountered along the way. The Americans looked to their escorts expectantly, thinking they would say something to the man, but instead they just stopped when the group approached him. Then the man on horseback spoke and once again Musgrove was pleasantly surprised to hear English.

"Hi, boys," the man said in a deep voice, using perfect English. "Welcome to Pranjane." It sounded like *pran-yan-ay.*

The Americans didn't know what to make of this. The man looked Yugoslav but spoke clear English, and . . . was that a New York accent?

The rider was George Musulin, a special agent with the OSS—the elite group of spies and covert operatives that would later become the CIA—who had been dropped behind enemy lines to help the downed airmen. He and his team had been on the ground for a few weeks already, about as long as Musgrove, and they had news for the tired and hungry Americans.

"You made it. You're here," he said. He looked down at the Americans as if he expected them to be happy with that, but Musgrove and his companions still didn't know where "here" was.

"Where are we?" he asked. "What are we going to do here?"

It was then that Musulin realized the new arrivals hadn't been clued in yet. Some of the airmen arriving in Pranjane found out along the way about the plan, and others like this group showed up with no knowledge at all.

"We're going to get you out of here, boys," Musulin said, a smile showing through his bushy black beard. "There's going to be a rescue. There are already about two hundred Americans here. They've been assembling since January."

A rescue! Finally some good news. Musgrove and the other airmen rejoiced, finding the energy to raise their arms and shout, clapping their Yugoslav escorts on the back and hugging one another. They would be rescued! They could go home!

But how?

"C-47s," Musulin said, referring to the workhorse cargo planes that every airman knew well. "They're going to land in a field right over there." Musulin gestured off in the distance. "We've been working on a big plan that will get you boys out of here before long. Gotta build a landing strip, though."

And with that, Musulin turned his horse and trotted off.

Musgrove and the others stood there in the road, joyous but a little puzzled too. To be sure they understood, one of their Yugoslav escorts raised his flat hand and moved it along like an airplane, making a buzzing sound. Musgrove and the other two Americans nodded at him. They understood the plan.

But it sounded a little crazy to them. Build a landing strip? They certainly wanted to be rescued, but how could planes land in this mountainous region where they couldn't even walk down a country road without ducking into the bushes every time a vehicle passed, hoping they wouldn't be found by the Germans?

**The same questions were going** through the mind of George Vujnovich, the OSS control agent in Bari, Italy, with responsibility for sending secret agents on missions throughout much of Europe, including Yugoslavia. When Vujnovich heard that there were American fliers waiting for help in Yugoslavia, he knew they had to come up with a plan to get them out. He also knew right away that this would be no ordinary rescue.

Could they really pull this off? Could they go right into German territory and snatch these men out of harm's way? He had discussed the risks at length with Musulin before sending him behind enemy lines, but even with Musulin on the ground in Yugoslavia the questions remained.

It was more than his job duties that motivated Vujnovich. He was driven by his own memories of being trapped behind enemy lines in Yugoslavia a few years earlier; he felt a kindred spirit with the Americans stranded in the country where his parents had grown up. The Pittsburgh native was attending college in Yugoslavia when his studies—and his fledgling relationship with a beautiful local girl—were interrupted by the rapidly advancing German army. Two years of running from the Nazis, trying to find a way out of Yugoslavia and back to freedom, gave him a real appreciation for what these young airmen were going through. Vujnovich was determined to get them out of their limbo.

Could he make it happen? It hadn't been too difficult to send in Musulin and the rest of his team, but getting more than a hundred airmen out was a totally different matter. The plan, which the British were fighting vigorously, was to send in C-47 cargo planes to pick up the downed airmen and whisk them back to Italy. That was the plan: Just send in planes to pick them up. Allied planes flew over Yugoslavia all the time on the way to bomb targets in German territory, so it wasn't farfetched to think that one could drop down and pick up a few airmen. It sounded simple until Vujnovich started trying to work out the details. Already Musulin's team had radioed back that there were far more airmen to rescue than the one hundred and fifty that they'd expected when they para-chuted in to coordinate the pickup. Musulin's last message had informed Vujnovich that there were at least two hundred men there already, and more were coming in every day, sometimes a dozen or more at a time.

That meant the mission was growing exponentially harder every day, Vujnovich realized. It was not simply a matter of sending in a few planes to swoop down and snatch the men in a hurry; rescuing that many airmen would require a series of planes landing one after another. More planes meant more of a spectacle for the Germans to notice and much more time when the planes and the airmen would be easy targets for German fighters or ground troops. And the more he thought about it, the more Vujnovich worried that sending in any planes, even one, to this area was extremely risky. He knew the area was rugged and mountainous, with no airstrip nearby, and not even a clear field that could serve as a runway in a pinch. That was why all the bomber crews bailed out when their planes were dy-ing in this area; there was nowhere to even attempt a crash landing. The best they could hope for was to jump out and hang under a parachute as they watched the plane crash into a mountainside.

Now Vujnovich was trying to organize not just one but a whole series of cargo planes to land in that rugged countryside, right under the Germans' noses. It was an audacious plan, and some in the office weren't shy about telling Vujnovich that it was more than that, that it was just plain crazy. But Vujnovich kept thinking about all the young men trapped in Nazi ter-ritory, struggling to get through another day without being captured and hoping that someone was working on a way to get them out. He could identify with them. He could remember the cold terror that gripped his whole body as he held his breath and hoped a German patrol would pass by the young American and the girl he loved, the desperation of wanting to just get out of danger, to just get over the border, to get back home.

*We'll have to make it work. We'll get them out.*

# Chapter 2

## *Abandon Ship!*

**Clare Musgrove ended up in Yugoslavia in the same** way hundreds of other Allied airmen had in the few years before him and as many more would after him: He climbed into a bomber in Italy, flew into Nazi territory to bomb critical oil refineries and other targets, and never made it back to the safety of his home base. Every time a fleet of bombers went out, some were heavily damaged by German defenses and either went down immediately or limped back toward Italy, trying to make it as far as they could.

By 1944 downed American airmen were piling up quickly in Yugoslavia as bombing raids on Nazi targets, especially the oil refineries of Ploesti, Romania, resulted in many planes making it only that far on their return journey before the crews had to bail out and try to survive behind enemy lines. The quest to destroy Ploesti would leave hundreds of airmen stranded in the hills of Yugoslavia.

To get to Romania, the Allied bomber crews had to fly eastward, usually from bases in the recently liberated Italy, across the Adriatic Sea, then across Yugoslavia to their targets in Romania. Then they had to get back again, often limping home with planes and crew injured from the intense fighting at the target site. Romania was a top target because it represented one of the westward strongholds of the German military, and particularly because it was the major source of fuel for the German war machine. The country was smaller than the state of Oregon and had little chance of resisting the Germans, though it took a shot at staying neutral. Hitler, of course, saw pleas for neutrality as a sign of weakness and rolled into the country.

Romania was in an untenable situation, perched between German advances in Poland and Hungary and Soviet advances from the Ukraine. In June 1941 Romania officially joined the Axis, primarily in hopes of regaining some provinces that it had previously been forced to give up. Though Romania had fought Germany in the first World War, the country allied itself with the Nazis strictly as a desperate measure for self-preservation. Romania's pact with the devil would be costly, however. It was no surprise that once the country joined the German rampage across Europe, Britain declared war on Romania on December 5, 1941.

On June 5, 1942, the United States extended its declaration of war on Germany and Italy to include Romania, Hungary, and Bulgaria. Before long, the same resource that had made Romania so desirable to the German war machine—massive oil fields and high-capacity refineries—made it a prime target for the Allies. American bomber crews who had barely heard of Romania months before soon learned all about a Romanian city called Ploesti, an oil boom city in the plains below the Transylvanian Alps in northern Romania and thirty-five miles north of Bucharest, the national capital. Ploesti was a massive complex consisting of seven major refineries, storage tanks, and related structures covering nineteen square miles.

Oil refining had been big business in Ploesti since 1857, which means the city was one of the first to build riches on the resource that would dominate the world's economy within decades. By 1942 the refineries at Ploesti were producing nearly a million tons of oil a month, accounting for 40 percent of Romania's total exports. Most of that oil, as well as the highest-quality 90-octane aviation fuel in Europe, went to the Axis war effort. Ploesti, a prosperous but otherwise little-known city in a quiet country before the war, suddenly became a central component of the Nazi military, key to everything Hitler wanted to accomplish. The refineries of Ploesti provided nearly a third of the petroleum products that fueled Hitler's tanks, battleships, submarines, and aircraft.

The Allies had to put Ploesti out of the oil refining business and they were willing to risk as many lives as necessary to do it. The Germans were just as determined to protect this vital supply of oil, and they installed an astonishing array of antiaircraft guns all around the refineries for miles and miles. Some of the best German fighter pilots were stationed at airfields around Ploesti, with orders to protect the refineries from Allied bombers.

Ploesti was the first target in Europe bombed by American aircraft. Many more attacks would follow the first.

The honor of hitting Ploesti first went to Colonel Harry A. Halverson in May 1942. He led twenty-three factory-fresh B-24 bombers from Florida on a journey to bomb Tokyo in a follow-up to the Doolittle Raid, the daring assault on the Japanese homeland that was carried out as retribution for the attack on Pearl Harbor. But when the bombers reached Egypt, Halverson and his crews were informed that they had a new destination: Ploesti. The planes took off for their new target on the evening of June 11, arriving over the target at dawn the following day. The mission was a success: Ten of the bombers hit the Astra refinery at Ploesti, one B-24 attacked the port area of Constanta, and the remaining two B-24s struck unidentified targets. Damage to the planes was minimal.

The first bombing run caused substantial damage, but it was clear to the Allies that many more young men would have to risk their lives to keep the refineries off-line. Bombing runs continued, and then in August 1943 the Allies launched Operation Tidal Wave, intended as an all-out effort against Ploesti. Unlike previous attacks that had been made from thousands of feet in the air, Operation Tidal Wave called for striking the oil fields at very low levels—treetop level sometimes, so low that the exploding bombs and oil fires actually threatened the planes. And then, of course, there was the problem of a B-24 bomber making a very big, very easy target at that altitude.

The extreme risk required that the plan be approved all the way up the chain of command, with even President Franklin D. Roosevelt agonizing over whether the need to knock out Ploesti justified the extreme risk to the aircrews. He decided that it did, and the bomber crews were given terrifying orders.

The increased danger called for more than the usual mission preparation. The low-level raids on Ploesti were practiced on a full-scale replica of Ploesti built in the desert. The crews had to perfect their navigation skills and fly in strict radio silence if there was any hope of reaching their target without being shot down. Getting back home was even tougher, and more of an afterthought in the training.

One hundred and seventy-seven B-24s took off in Operation Tidal Wave on August 1, 1943, a huge wave of bombers that filled the sky but nevertheless intended to sneak into Ploesti. The extensive planning did not ensure success. Things went badly right from the start, as one B-24 crashed on takeoff. The strict radio silence caused the bomber groups to became separated on the long flight across the Adriatic, and then when the planes neared Corfu, Greece, the lead aircraft—the one carrying the route navigator that was to lead the whole group into Ploesti—suddenly dove into the water for no apparent reason. Another plane, this one carrying the backup route navigator, circled down to check for survivors but lost so much time doing so that it couldn't catch up with the formation. So it turned back to base, leaving the lead bomber group with no expert navigators to lead it on this extremely dangerous low-level approach to Ploesti.

The planes continued on anyway, the importance of their mission having been drilled into them. They met thick cloud cover as they approached the mountains around Ploesti, and the various bomber groups making up the overall attack chose different paths through the clouds. The two lead bomber groups carefully made their way through or under the clouds, while the three other groups climbed over them. The high-flying bombers took a while to get back down and by then they were half an hour behind the others. The carefully choreographed mission was falling apart.

As they approached Ploesti, the crews were looking for waypoints to mark their path, especially other towns they could recognize from the air. One of the bomber groups confused the town of Târgovişte for Floreşti, an error that went undiscovered until it led them to the outskirts of Bucharest, way off target. At that point, the crews realized there was little hope of carrying out the attack they had practiced for so long. They broke radio silence and turned north to attack the complex of refineries in Ploesti as best they could. *Hit anything you can*, they told one another. *Just find a target and drop your bombs.*

German fighters attacked the bombers, which did their best to pick out high-value targets and bomb them at very low altitude, as planned. The fighters pursued the bombers as they left Ploesti, shooting down fifty-four planes, each with a crew of ten or twelve men. Another fifty-three planes were heavily damaged. Though reconnaissance flights confirmed that the damage to Ploesti was significant, it was a costly victory. Allied bombers would continue hitting Ploesti over and over again until August 19, 1944.

**Every bomber that left from** an Allied base to bomb Ploesti carried up to a dozen young men like Clare Musgrove. Some of them would die before they ever reached their target, many would die as they reached the target and met withering antiaircraft fire and attacks from German fighter planes, and others would make it through the worst of the fighting only to find themselves in a crippled, rapidly dying airplane that would not make it back to base. The bombing runs were always harrowing and violent, with every successful return seeming like a triumph over fate.

Musgrove was typical of the bomber crews that flew these critical missions, wondering each time he climbed into the plane if he would make it back alive. Growing up in Hersey, Michigan, a small community north of Grand Rapids, Musgrove never imagined he would be flying missions that were so important to the Allied war effort and that could kill him every time. One of four children, Musgrove had spent much of his childhood helping his grandparents on their small, twenty-five-cow dairy farm and graduated from high school in 1937. He then went to a local community college and spent four years teaching in rural schools, which he enjoyed but knew he would not make his life's work. Instead, Musgrove looked to the military for a better career, one that might offer more adventure than he saw in central Michigan. When the Japanese attacked Pearl Harbor, Musgrove knew his path was clear.

America had been at war in Europe for about six months in 1942 when, at age twenty-two, Musgrove volunteered for the air force because he wanted to fly. Most of his former classmates and most of his friends were volunteering also. Everyone wanted to fly because it was the glamorous way to serve in the military. The recruiting posters showed handsome young men in flight suits and leather caps, heading off for grand escapades that outshone anything in a schoolteacher's life, so that was the choice for Musgrove. Unfortunately, Musgrove ran into the same roadblock that stymied many young men's aspirations for flight. He couldn't pass the eye test. Musgrove's less-than-perfect depth perception meant the government wasn't going to put him in the pilot's seat, but hey, there are plenty of other seats on those big bombers, the air force pointed out.

Musgrove could still fly if he found another position, so he considered navigator, radio operator, and engineer. But the one that sounded best was aerial gunner. The air force obliged and transferred him from Shepherd Field, near Wichita Falls, Texas, where he had undergone basic training, to Laredo, Texas, on Rio Grande River at the border with Mexico. This was the site of the air force's first aerial gunner school, and Musgrove excelled at his work so much that he was tapped to stay on as an instructor in how to use the ball turret gun on a B-24 bomber. Having already gotten his fill of teaching before joining the service, Musgrove taught for a year before becoming restless as he watched other, less experienced men, go off to war. He lobbied for an assignment to active duty and the air force relented, sending him overseas to the Fifteenth Air Force stationed in Italy.

Musgrove still didn't leave his teaching role, however. The air force assigned him to be the instructor for ball turret gunners with the Fifteenth Air Force, reinforcing what the newly arriving crew members had been taught Stateside and helping them hone their skills for life-or-death missions over Europe. And there were always plenty of new recruits to bring up to speed. Every time a plane went off on a bombing mission and came back loaded with dead and dying crewmen who lost their fight with a storm of shrapnel, or when a plane never returned at all, that meant more young men had to be brought in as replacements. Musgrove stayed busy teaching the new ball turret gunners how to protect their bombers and how to stay alive. Neither was an easy task for someone hanging in a Plexiglas sphere from the belly of a bomber.

Nobody really wanted to be in a ball turret. This Plexiglas ball hanging from the bottom of the bomber was one of America's latest innovations in warfare. An ingenious piece of machinery built by the Sperry Corporation, the ball turret was a heavily armed bubble just big enough to hold a grown man—but only one on the small side. It had room for the gunner and its two fifty-caliber machine guns—and little else. The extremely cramped quarters meant that the gunner was the only crew member on a bomber who did not wear a parachute during the mission. His was left sitting up in the main part of the plane, where he would have to go get it and put it on before escaping with the rest of the crew. Musgrove always told his students: "Stow your chute where you can find it in a hurry. You won't have much time."

The ball turret was not a place for the claustrophobic. It was a tiny space, though it had a great view of the scenery below—or the fighter planes coming up to kill you. The entire unit rotated around in a circle and also up and down, so that the gunner could fire on planes coming from any direction. Being suspended underneath the plane gave the gunner a sensation of flying free, and that often meant that the attacking fighters seemed to be going after him personally rather than trying to shoot down the bomber itself. Everyone on the plane was riding an adrenaline surge during a fighter attack, but none more so than the ball turret gunner who was furiously firing his fifty-caliber machine guns at the German plane trying to kill him in his little glass bubble.

The ball turret gunner sat curled up in a fetal position, swiveling the entire turret as he aimed the two guns. As he moved the turret quickly to find attacking planes and then follow them with his guns, the gunner could be in any position from lying on his back to standing on his feet. The gunner sat between the guns, his feet in stirrups positioned on either side of a thirteen-inch-diameter window in front, his knees up around his ears and very little room for moving anything but his hands. His flight suit provided the only padding for comfort.

An optical gunsight hung in front of his face, and a pedal under his left foot adjusted a reticule on the gunsight glass. When the target was framed in the sight, the gunner knew the range was correct and he let fly with the machine guns, pushing down on the two firing buttons located on the wooden handles that also controlled the movement of the ball. Shell casings were ejected through a port just below the gun barrel, pouring out as fast as the beads of sweat on the gunner's face.

The plane carried two hundred fifty rounds of ammunition per gun for the ball turret, fed down from boxes mounted on either side of the hoist. The ball turret in the B-24, which Musgrove flew, was electrically raised and lowered, unlike those in the B-17 bombers, which had to be manually cranked up into the fuselage. Musgrove thought this was a great improvement over the B-17 design, because no one wanted to be trapped in a ball turret. There was no way to exit the turret without raising it into the fuselage of the plane, so a turret that could not be retracted was a deathtrap for the gunner. Any system that made it faster and easier to retract the turret was welcomed by the gunners. They had all heard the stories of ball turret gunners who were trapped in their glass bubbles when battle damage prevented them being retracted into the fuselage. Not only was the gunner left out there with no protection, probably with his guns empty or inoperable, but he also faced the prospect of the big plane landing with him hanging from the belly.

It was every ball turret gunner's nightmare, and it became a horrifying reality for some. If the gunner was already dead in the turret and it could not be retracted into the plane, the crew sometimes would jettison the whole apparatus because the plane was not designed to land with the ball turret hanging underneath. But if the gunner was alive, they would have to tell him that they had no choice but to put the plane down eventually. The ball turret gunner had a long time to contemplate his fate, maybe to say good-bye on the intercom to his crewmates, as the damaged plane limped back to base or looked for a field in which to crash. All he could do was sit in the glass bubble like a helpless fetus in the womb, watching the ground come up closer and closer.

When the plane landed, the ball turret was scraped off the belly, taking the gunner with it.

**Musgrove knew the risks, and** he had heard all the terrible stories about how ball turret gunners died. But he wanted to fly missions, not just teach others how to risk their own lives. His superiors agreed to let him fly missions as long as his main priority remained teaching the new crew members who were streaming in all the time. That meant Musgrove couldn't be teamed up with one flight crew that always went out on missions together, as most of the crew members did. Instead, he would rotate through the different flight crews to fill in for ball turret gunners who were out of action that day or whose replacements had not yet been assigned.

Musgrove never knew when he was going to fly and when he was going to stay at the base and watch the planes leave on their bombing missions. Less than two weeks shy of his twenty-fifth birthday, he had been on eight missions already—bombing power plants and railroad junctions and participating in the invasion of southern France—and he had seen a fair share of heavy-duty combat from his position in the ball turret. He was sleeping soundly when, on the morning of July 28, 1944, an officer came to his bunk and woke him up much earlier than he had planned.

"Get ready to fly. Be at the briefing by 0430," the officer said, pausing only briefly to make sure Musgrove was awake and then turning to leave. When Musgrove made his way to the briefing with a dozen other bleary-eyed men, he found out that he was flying on a mission to Ploesti. The briefing officer explained that a number of bombers would be flying directly over the main production areas of the Ploesti oil fields.

"It's a very hot target area, well protected by the Germans," the officer explained. "This target's been hit almost daily for about ten days, and we're trying to eliminate this last energy source for the Germans. They're desperate to protect it, so you can expect a lot of resistance. But you're the best damn bomber crews in the air force, so they've got a real fight coming!"

Despite the somber warning about how tough the mission would be, the young airmen left the briefing feeling elated and eager to get underway. At dawn, Musgrove climbed into a B-24 with nine other men and found a position near the tail gunner for takeoff. In addition to Musgrove, the B-24 carried a pilot, copilot, navigator, and a bombardier—all officers. The crew also included an airplane mechanic, who operated the top turret located above the cockpit, and a radio operator, who manned the nose turret when he wasn't on the radio. Two wing gunners manned the big fifty-caliber machine guns on either side of the fuselage, and the tail gunner protected the rear of the plane. Because the ball turret gunner didn't lower the ball until after takeoff, he was the only crew member who was away from his assigned position when the plane sped down the runway. And because Musgrove was a floater who flew with whatever crew needed him, he was the only member of this crew that had not flown with the others on previous missions. He was welcomed and the rest of the crew were glad to have a talented gunner onboard, but Musgrove knew he was not part of this plane's tight-knit brotherhood, a bond that forms naturally when men fly into danger together over and over. This crew had been in Italy for only a short time, and they were going out on their third mission. But Musgrove knew they had trained and flown together, so they were a family, and he was a stranger to them.

"All right boys, let's go show 'em what we got!" the pilot called out over the intercom as the plane taxied for takeoff. Musgrove and the other crew responded with a hearty yell.

Thirty-six B-24 bombers from bases all over Italy formed up for this mission to Ploesti. Musgrove and the other crew members were mostly lost in their own thoughts as they flew four hours to the oil refineries in Ploesti, the unmuffled noise of the plane combining with the rushing wind to make conversation difficult without using the intercom. They each sat at their stations, going through checklists and confirming operational details with one another, sharing a bit of dark humor here and there about their prospects of returning from the mission. They all knew that each mission could be their last. But despite the looming threat of death, the men were not overtly scared or apprehensive. They were excited, eager to do the job they were trained for, to accomplish the task they knew was so important for the Allied war effort. Like the rest of the young men on the B-24, Musgrove wanted to get the job done, return, and celebrate a successful mission.

Musgrove was trying to stay warm as the plane climbed higher and higher, soon putting on a flight suit over his summer khakis when the air became colder and colder. By the time the plane reached twenty-two thousand feet, Musgrove had already plugged his flight suit into an electrical port that allowed the garment to heat up like an electric blanket. After a few minutes, the suit was warm enough that he could forget the bone-chilling cold wind rushing through the plane.

As they crossed over into enemy territory, Musgrove heard the pilot call out to him on the intercom. "Ball turret gunner, take your position." That was his signal that it was time to leave the interior of the plane and drop down underneath it. He unplugged his flight suit from the port in the plane and stuffed himself into the ball turret so that his knees were almost up around his ears. Then he used the electro-hydraulic controls to lower it into position beneath the plane. Once he was in position, Musgrove gripped the handles to maneuver the turret fully through its rotations and test the movement of the guns, ensuring that the turret was ready for action as soon as German planes showed up. Once he was satisfied that everything was in order, Musgrove plugged his suit back into the warming port and settled in. There was nothing for him to do but sit and wait for the inevitable leg cramps and the itch you couldn't reach.

He rode another couple of hours toward Ploesti, scanning the skies all around the bomber for any sign of German fighters as the formation descended down to ten thousand feet. The planes made it nearly all the way to the target without being intercepted, but then Musgrove could see that the Germans were well aware of their arrival. The sky ahead of the bomber was already filled with the inky black bursts of antiaircraft fire.

\* \* \*

**The flak over the target** rattled Musgrove like a piñata, the explosive concussions shaking the plane hard and bouncing him around in the tight confines of the turret bubble. With every booming blast, Musgrove waited for the one piece of red-hot shrapnel that could come flying through the Plexiglas and kill him like so many other ball turret gunners. That piece of shell casing never came, and the plane flew on through the inky black clouds left by the explosions. After what seemed an eternity, as any flight did when flak was exploding all around you, Musgrove saw the bombs fall and felt the lightened plane rise higher in the air.

Musgrove began to breathe a bit easier after the bombs were away and the plane pulled away from the target, but once the immediate danger died down a bit, Musgrove could hear the telltale sounds of a sputtering B-24 engine. The plane had been hit by the flak, and Musgrove could tell right away that the damage was serious. He heard what he thought was first one, and then two of the plane's four engines coughing and sputtering, sounds that were disturbingly different from the incessant drone that the crew listened to for hours on end when flying. The open intercom line allowed the entire crew to hear the pilot and copilot talking, so Musgrove followed the play-by-play as they dealt with the damaged engines.

"Engine two! Losing power!" the copilot shouted. "Engine three's going. We got hit bad!"

And then he heard the two troubled engines shut down. First engine two stopped struggling, and then engine three. Both inside engines were dead. The sudden end to the noise was even more troubling than the rough engine sounds. Musgrove listened as the pilots throttled up the other two engines to compensate and try to keep the plane aloft. The plane stayed in the air, but on only two engines it was too slow to keep up with the formation as all the surviving planes turned away from Ploesti and started their journeys home.

From his position in the ball turret, Musgrove could see that his B-24 was dropping out of formation. Then he watched as the dozens of other B-24s flew on toward Italy, leaving Musgrove's plane to limp along behind. The plane could make it back on just two engines, Musgrove knew. He'd seen plenty of planes come struggling back to the base on two engines; they just showed up a lot later than everyone else.

The real danger came from being alone in the sky. With dozens of bombers flying in formation, each of them loaded with fifty-caliber machine guns, there was safety in numbers. Fighter planes attacking the formation had to get through not just one plane's defenses, but several. Now Musgrove and the rest of his crew were on their own. If a German fighter found the lame duck, defending the bomber would be much more difficult. Musgrove was sweating in his flight suit now and unplugged the heating port. He moved the ball turret around in all directions again, making sure it was ready if a fighter appeared. He had not yet fired a single shot that day because German fighters never came up to greet them.

Musgrove listened in as the B-24 pilot called on the radio for a fighter escort to help them make it back without being torn to shreds by a German attack, and then it was only about ten minutes before two P-51 Mustangs came alongside to offer protection, diving down from where they and other Mustangs had been providing cover for the entire formation during the bombing run. The other fighters remained with the faster-moving pack of bombers in formation. Musgrove was glad to see the sleek fighters and gave the pilots a wave as they took up positions on either side of the slow, lumbering bomber. He kept his hands on the ball turret controls, ready if a German fighter thought the slow plane made a good target.

After a short while, Musgrove could see that the plane was steadily losing altitude. He could hear the pilots talking about losing power and trying different strategies to keep the plane up, but it was clear to him that the plane was not going to make it back to Italy. Then the pilot made an announcement to the crew.

"Hey, guys, I don't think we're going to make it back to our base," the pilot said calmly. "We just don't have the energy to get back over the mountains." He didn't say anything else, but the crew knew what he meant: Get ready to bail out. It won't be long.

A few minutes later the navigator came on the intercom and told the crew that the plane was approaching the Bulgarian/Yugoslavian border. *Thanks for the information,* Musgrove thought, *but it doesn't help me much. Where on the border? Where are we going down?*

It was about eleven a.m. when the pilot came on again.

"We're going to have to get ready to abandon ship because we're just not going to make it," he said, sounding more tense than before. Musgrove's stomach came up into his mouth as he heard the words "abandon ship." Like the rest of the crew, he had been trained in the procedures but hoped he would never have to jump out of a B-24. The very idea sickened him, the thought of jumping into the unknown when you thought you would be sleeping in your own bunk again that night.

"Okay, we've gone as far as we can go. We better bail out," the pilot said, hitting the switch for the bailout bell, an alarm no flier wanted to hear. The words seemed to pound in Musgrove's ears through the intercom headset. "Everybody bail out. Bail out!"

The bailout bell rang incessantly as the rest of the crew started double-checking their parachute harnesses and then making their way to a side door in the fuselage and throwing themselves out. Musgrove first had to get out of the ball turret, so he hit the switch to raise it up into the plane and climb out. Nothing happened. He hit the switch again. Nothing. He hit the damn thing over and over, harder and harder, and still the turret didn't move. He was trapped.

Musgrove called out on the intercom, "I've got no power! No power! I can't get up!" There was no reply. The rest of the crew were bailing out already, and besides, Musgrove knew there was nothing the crew could do for him anyway. He was on his own.

Musgrove realized he had to use the backup method for raising the turret—a hand crank that relied on pure muscle and a few gears to lift the heavy mechanism up into the fuselage. He had taught his students this lesson a thousand times and now it was his turn to put it to use. Musgrove wasted no time grabbing the crank and furiously winding, winding, and winding. He could feel the turret moving, but he was sure the ground was coming up faster. Musgrove's adrenaline surged and sweat poured off his face as he cranked as hard and as fast as he could in the cramped bubble, his heart pounding so vigorously he felt it throbbing in his eardrums.

*I've got to get out! I've got to get out before I'm too low for my chute to work!*

Musgrove cranked the handle for almost ten minutes, his wide eyes focused intently on the landscape below, trying to gauge how low the plane was getting. Finally, with his arms searing from the work, the turret was up in the fuselage far enough for Musgrove to get out. He furiously undid the latches and scrambled out of the hatch, crawling out backwards. He stood up quickly and looked around, but he was all alone. There was no one else on the bomber with Musgrove. In the ten minutes it took him to get back up into the plane, they had all successfully abandoned ship, even the pilots who customarily were the last out. They knew it would take Musgrove a while and they couldn't do anything to help, so they wisely left without him. Musgrove was eager to follow them, so he went to the spot where he had stowed his parachute at the beginning of the flight, in a corner of the fuselage framing just behind the ball turret.

It wasn't there.

The rough flight and flak concussions over Ploesti had bounced the plane around so much that Musgrove's parachute wasn't where he left it. It took a panic-filled moment to look around and find it; then Musgrove quickly attached it to the parachute harness he already wore. With the parachute in place, Musgrove went to a side door and looked out. The plane was getting lower all the time, but he thought it was still high enough for his chute to work. He got down on his knees, as he had been trained, and rolled out into the rushing wind.

After waiting as long as he could stand, to ensure he was clear of the plane, Musgrove pulled the rip cord on his parachute and braced for the sharp jerk on his harness. He had already winced in anticipation when he realized nothing was happening. He looked down to make sure he had really pulled the rip cord and, sure enough, there was the thing clenched tightly in his hand. His chute wasn't opening.

Furiously, as fast as he could while in a free fall from about ten thousand feet high, Musgrove reached into the parachute pack and dug out the cloth with his own hands. He grabbed the soft silk and pulled over and over, until a pocket of the cloth caught the air and the rest exploded out above him.

## Chapter 3

# Counting Parachutes

**The young men parachuting into the hills of Yugoslavia** had no idea what awaited them. They knew only that this was their last chance to live when their bomber was on fire or the engines went out or they had lost too much fuel from shrapnel on their bombing runs over Romania. Some, like Musgrove, made several death-defying missions before they were forced to get out of their crashing planes, while others like twenty-one-year-old Tony Orsini had to bail out of his bomber on his first mission.

Orsini had been in Italy for only a week when he was assigned to his first bombing mission over Ploesti. A navigator, Orsini had guided a B-24 from Lincoln, Nebraska, across the Atlantic Ocean and up the coast of Africa. The crew of greenhorns reported to an air force base in southern Italy named Grottaglie as part of the 716th Squadron of the 449th Bomb Group. Orsini had been there for only a few days, waiting for more orientation and local maps, when he was awakened at four a.m. on July 21, 1944, by someone shouting, "Briefing at 0600!" At the briefing, Orsini learned he had been assigned to fly a mission with a more experienced crew. They would be bombing the Ploesti oil refineries.

In addition to all the usual information about the target, the bomb loads, the route, and what resistance to expect, the officer briefing the crew gave them a curious warning, one they had never heard before.

"You're going to be flying over Yugoslavia. If you have to bail out, avoid the Chetniks. They're the followers of General Mihailovich," the officer said sternly. "Seek out the Partisans. They're the followers of General Tito."

The advice was completely wrong, but the officer believed it and was trying to be helpful. It would be years before the source of the misinformation became clear. But at the moment, Orsini didn't give it much thought anyway. Orsini had heard only the sketchiest information about the ongoing civil war in Yugoslavia and the two factions that were fighting for control of the country while simultaneously fending off the Germans who occupied their land. He took note of the warning, but gave it much lower priority than everything else he had heard that morning. This was Orsini's very first mission, and the rest of the crew would be depending on him to navigate their B-24 skillfully. He didn't want to miss anything.

Orsini was scared to death as the plane neared its target in Romania. He tried to focus on the maps on his small desk in the plane, checking and double-checking everything he could think of, but he was terrified by the thought of the air defenses around Ploesti. When his map coordinates showed that they were nearing the oil fields, Orsini looked out a window and saw his fears take form. The sky was filled with exploding shells, the shrapnel tearing through anything in its path—aluminum, steel, or flesh. German fighter planes were zooming through the bomber formation, strafing planes as they held their course and attempted to drop their loads on the target. Orsini was waiting to hear the bombardier call out, "Bombs away!" over the intercom, because that would mean their work was done and the pilots could hightail it out of that god-awful mess. After what seemed an eternity, with explosions booming all around and buffeting the plane back and forth, Orsini heard the bombardier's call.

And almost immediately after, he felt the plane shudder violently, a sensation he hadn't felt before. He knew right away that the bomber had taken a direct hit from the antiaircraft fire. The explosion knocked the

B-24 out of formation and the pilots struggled to maintain level flight as two of the four engines died. Just as with Musgrove's crippled bomber, the crew of Orsini's plane worried that a German fighter would find them separated from the protection of the pack, flying slow and low. Every so often the pilot would ask Orsini, who had been carefully plotting the plane's progress, for an update on whether they could make it back to Italy at this speed and fuel consumption. Each time, Orsini replied that it would be close, but they could probably make it. A couple of hours went by that way, the plane slowly losing altitude and the crew deathly silent as they prayed for a good outcome and watched the skies intently for German planes. The quiet was broken when the tail gunner's voice came on the intercom.

"Fighters at six o'clock!" he screamed, indicating the sky behind the plane. "Fighters at six o'clock!"

The gunners all tensed and prepared to fight off the attack, but then the tail gunner came back on the intercom about thirty seconds later and said, "They're P-38s. It's okay." P-38s were American fighters, and these had spotted the B-24 limping home. They flew in alongside and escorted the B-24 as it continued descending, eventually reaching ten thousand feet, far lower than the twenty-one thousand feet where it had dropped its bombs. At that point, the pilot turned back to Orsini and asked him for a final assessment of whether they were going to make it back if they continued descending at that rate.

"No sir," Orsini answered. "There's no way." The continuing rate of descent had removed any optimism.

The pilot was prepared for that answer and immediately called out on the intercom, "Abandon ship! Abandon ship! I repeat, abandon ship!" Orsini wasn't surprised because he had contemplated that possibility for the past hour, and he knew the pilot was making the right decision. Better to bail out now instead of waiting until they were over the Adriatic Sea. The bailout bell was almost a welcome sound by then.

The only problem was that Orsini didn't know exactly where they were. He could tell from his calculations that they wouldn't make it back, but he was missing several key maps that would have told him what region they were about to jump into. When he realized at the morning briefing that he was missing the designated maps, he had asked an officer for them. But the officer dismissed him, telling him not to worry because his plane would be number four in the formation and he only had to play follow the leader. Now Orsini was frustrated that he couldn't give the crew any idea what they were jumping into. He had some idea that they were over Serbia, but he didn't know they were in a very mountainous region called Ravna Gora.

As Orsini prepared to jump out of the ailing plane, he suddenly wished he had taken better care of his parachute. Since it was issued to him nearly six months earlier, he had tossed it around nonchalantly, using it for a pillow and a football on more than one occasion. Now his life would depend on that chute opening.

He had been trained to count one-thousand-one, one-thousand-two, one-thousand-three before pulling the rip cord, but Orsini was so anxious about whether the abused parachute would work that he couldn't wait. He yanked the rip cord immediately and was relieved to see the canopy snap to attention over his head. After the brutal yank of the chute on his harness, everything became surreal.

The sky was so quiet, with just a soft whisper of wind passing his ears. Orsini had been in the loud plane for hours, the constant rumble of the engines overshadowed only by the deafening booms of the antiaircraft fire. The sudden silence was unsettling.

Orsini felt like he was suspended in space, as if he were not descending at all but just swaying back and forth, back and forth, back and forth. The sensation, along with all the fear and dread that gripped him for hours already, caused him to vomit on the way down.

**A navigator like Orsini,** Robert Wilson knew it was practically inevitable that he would be shot down eventually. He was a navigator on B-17 bombers, similar to B-24s, and he was specially trained in a new type of radar that enabled the Allies to bomb the Ploesti oil fields even when there was heavy cloud cover or smoke. Normally the bombing runs had to be delayed or cancelled when the cloud cover or smoke was too heavy or else the bombardiers would just be taking a wild guess at where they were dumping all that firepower. The Allies did not indiscriminately drop bombs, so the planes would divert to another target that they could see. The Germans knew this and installed giant smoke pots all around Ploesti, creating black clouds that effectively obscured the target on some days.

But with the system Wilson used, the planes could still find their targets no matter how obscured they were. Wilson had grown up in Peoria, Illinois, and had completed one semester of college when, at age nineteen, he signed up for the air corps, attracted by the glamour of flying like so many others. And like many others, he was cut from pilot training. He went to navigation school instead and completed his training in December 1943. B-17 crews trained as a unit, but when Wilson's crew graduated they didn't immediately go to active duty like their classmates. Instead they were sent for secret training on the new equipment that required Wilson to be looking for the target on his equipment at the same the time the bombardier was looking for the target visually with the Norden bombsight. If the bombardier couldn't see the target, Wilson released the bombs based on his readings.

The radar system improved the effectiveness of the Ploesti bombing runs. However, the air force didn't have many of these new units. There was only one in the region around Italy where Wilson was based, so it was used as much as possible. The other problem was that the one B-17 with that radar unit—and Wilson operating it—had to be at the front of the pack of bombers every time it flew. Normally, the many flight crews took turns as the lead plane because that was considered the most dangerous spot in the formation, and the pilots had to work much harder to manage the formation and get the bombers to the target. With enough crews rotating, nobody had to put themselves at the head of the pack too often. But when the mission depended on the radar unit finding the target, Wilson's plane had to be at the front so it could drop its bombs first. Seeing the bombs away on Wilson's plane was the signal for all the other bombers to drop theirs.

When they got to their base in Italy to begin active duty, the rest of the crew that Wilson had trained with was assigned to another B-17 and they rotated through the front position like everyone else. But not Wilson. He was permanently attached to the one plane that housed the radar unit, and a different crew was slotted to fly that plane at the lead on every mission. For the other nine crew members onboard, it was just their unlucky day to be in the most dangerous position. For Wilson, it was every mission.

In July 1944, with twenty missions under his belt already, Wilson was one of the more experienced fliers in his unit. But he knew that every time he climbed into the B-17 again, he was pressing his luck. How many times could he fly into danger, at the head of the formation, and make it back to the base? He found out on his twenty-first mission.

It was July 15, 1944, and Wilson was making his third trip to Ploesti. As he had twenty times before, Wilson braced himself for the long, uncomfortable ride to the target—bundling up as the plane climbed into the high-altitude chill, donning his oxygen mask at twelve thousand feet and then a steel helmet and bulky, chafing flak vest as the plane neared the target. It was standard on these flights for each crew member to be extremely uncomfortable for as long as nine hours—cold, sweaty, with gear rubbing the wrong way, the griping in your head momentarily taking your mind off the fact that you might die very shortly.

When the B-17 approached the target at Ploesti, the pilot put the plane on a form of automatic pilot that shifted control to the bombardier, and in this case, to Wilson also. They would fly the plane, making minor course adjustments to get the plane on target and then release the bombs. As the outskirts of Ploesti came into view, Wilson could see that the refinery they were hitting that day, Romana Americana, was covered by smoke. He knew he would be dropping the bombs on this mission.

As soon as Wilson called, "Bombs away!" he felt a direct hit on the left wing, and then the two engines on that side sputtered to a stop. About the same time, Wilson heard someone calling over the intercom.

"Larry's hit!" someone yelled urgently, referring to Lawrence Norton, the engineer. "He got it in the head!"

Wilson ran forward from his station to see about Norton and found the young man dazed, with blood streaking down his face. Norton was leaning against a support frame in the plane as Wilson took a look at his injury, trying not to react too strongly as he saw the large piece of jagged shrapnel sticking out of the man's head, right on top. The still-hot piece of an exploding antiaircraft shell had come through the fuselage of the plane, penetrated Norton's steel helmet, and embedded itself deeply in his head. The wound was not bleeding profusely, but it left Norton semi-conscious. Wilson and another crew member applied a dressing to the wound and helped Norton sit down. Then they gave him a dose of morphine from one of their escape kits, opening his warm flight suit to press the syringe into his upper arm, but there was little time to fret about their injured crewmate.

There was more trouble. The antiaircraft fire had severed the fuel tank in that wing also, and Wilson looked up from his radar station to see gasoline pouring into the fuselage from the broken lines. The fumes from the fuel started filling the fuselage, burning Wilson's eyes, and in moments the crew members were standing in two inches of gasoline.

Wilson, and every other man onboard, was terrified. The gasoline had them thinking that the next bit of red-hot flak, a spark from the damaged wiring, anything, might turn them into a flying fireball. There was nothing they could do to stop the fuel rushing into the fuselage and no way to get the gas out, so they sloshed around in it as they continued looking for German fighters that might want an easy target. Meanwhile, the pilot was struggling to keep the plane aloft with just two engines on one side of the plane. The plane was descending quickly, even with the remaining engines pushed to their limits.

"We gotta lighten the load! Get rid of everything! Everything!" the pilot called out on the intercom. "The guns, ammunition, anything you can throw out!"

The crew reacted quickly, heaving out anything they could pick up: chairs, spare equipment, ammunition boxes, and finally the big fifty-caliber machine guns. They hated to fly without the big guns, their only defense against a fighter attack, but they were desperate to get lighter and stay aloft. All the while as they were heaving the gear over, Wilson and the other crew thought the gasoline might explode at any moment. By now, they were all soaked in it. They could feel the caustic liquid burning their skin as they worked; the fumes stung their eyes and burned in their noses. They knew that if the fuel ignited, they had no hope of survival. This was the worst, Wilson thought, sweat pouring off his face even in the frigid air. *Not only am I going to die on this mission, but I'm going to burn to death.*

The lighter load enabled the plane to hold its altitude enough to get over the first chain of mountains on the way back to Italy, and once he was finished throwing out anything not essential to flying the plane, Wilson saw something that surprised him. The rest of the squadron had stayed with them. His B-17 was crippled, flying low and slow, but the rest of the formation had stayed with it instead of continuing on. Wilson was surprised and elated. At least they weren't alone.

The safety of numbers proved its value before long when German fighters showed up and immediately zeroed in on Wilson's B-17 as the weak point of the formation. His crew couldn't do anything since their machine guns had been thrown overboard, and they knew that just one lucky shot by a German pilot would send the B-17 up like a Roman candle. All they could do was crouch and try to avoid any stray gunfire as the other bombers in the formation fired on the German planes swooping in and out of the formation. Wilson scarcely breathed for several long minutes, and then the fighters turned, leaving the bomber formation on its own again.

With the situation calm again, but far from resolved, Wilson and several other crew members turned their attention back to Norton, the engineer with the serious head wound. They knew they might have to bail out of the dying plane before long, and they worried that Norton might not be in any shape to parachute out and land safely. They debated what to do.

"We could just pull his chute and throw him out. It should open okay," one man offered.

"He'd land like a bag of bricks. He's barely awake," another countered.

"That thing in his head has him all messed up. Besides, if he lands hard and hits his head, he might just jam that thing in deeper. It would kill him right away."

Wilson agreed and offered the only solution he could think of. He didn't like the idea, but he said it anyway.

"We need to pull that shrapnel out," Wilson said. They all looked over to Norton, who was still too groggy to know what they were talking about. Nobody wanted to do it, but Wilson volunteered. "I need some pliers."

It took a while because the toolboxes had been thrown overboard, but Wilson came up with a set of pliers and went over to Norton, followed by three other crew members. One held Norton's shoulders firmly and another tried to steady his head as Wilson went in with the pliers. He wanted to do it quickly and firmly. He couldn't stand the thought of wrenching and twisting on something that might be deep in Norton's brain.

One good yank pulled the jagged metal out of Norton's head and Wilson threw it down in disgust. Over the next half hour, the injured man recovered his senses somewhat and the crew felt more confident that he would be able to bail out if that time came.

That time came in short order. The two engines on the undamaged side of the plane had been pushed beyond their limits and, as expected, they started to overheat and churn out thick black smoke. The pilot, William J. Kilpatrick, gave the order that everyone knew was coming sooner or later: "Abandon ship! Bail out now!"

The crew members were ready for the order and, after making sure Norton made it out, they started tumbling out of the side door one after another. Wilson jumped out and braced for the jerk of the chute on his harness, welcoming it even as he cringed with pain. He had made it out of that flying bomb alive, and assuming he could make it to the ground without running into any ignition sources, he wouldn't burst into flames the way he had been fearing for hours.

But even as Wilson realized his worst fear would not come to pass, he saw more tragedy unfold. This terrible day was not even close to finished. Wilson hung under his parachute, gently gliding to whatever fate awaited him on the ground and watched his B-17 continue on without him.

He looked around and could see several other chutes in the air and he thought he saw seven others, plus his. That was eight chutes in the air.

*Good. That means we're all out except for the pilot and copilot.*

Wilson knew that when bomber crews bailed out, it was customary for the pilot and copilot to be the last out because they remained at their post as long as possible, holding the plane steady to facilitate everyone else's bailout. Wilson kept his eyes on the B-17, waiting for the other two chutes to appear.

He could see that another bomber had dropped out of the formation to fly alongside the crippled bomber, its crew watching intently as the young men bailed out one by one. The crew of the other plane was especially interested in the outcome of this drama because Kilpatrick, the pilot on the ailing plane, was the pilot that usually led most of the crew on the other, undamaged B-17. The crew rotations had split them up that day, and Kilpatrick's regular crew members wanted to make sure he made it out of the damaged plane safely. Several of them were at the hatch on that side of their bomber, watching the damaged plane.

Kilpatrick's buddies in the other bomber flew alongside, counting the parachutes as Wilson and his fellow crew bailed out. Then they watched intently to see Kilpatrick and the copilot bail. The entire crew on the other plane was watching out the windows and hatches, wanting to count ten chutes and be certain their crew leader had made it.

Wilson watched too, praying that everyone would make it out safely. Then the two B-17s flew into a cloud, obscuring the moment when the pilot and copilot bailed out. Wilson saw their chutes emerge a moment later from underneath the cloud. He was relieved, realizing his entire crew had made it out safely, but then he felt a horrific knot in his stomach as he saw the two bombers emerge from the cloud, still side by side. The undamaged B-17 was not breaking away even though all of Wilson's crew had made it out. And they were rapidly approaching a mountainside.

*Oh my God. They didn't see the pilots get out. They're still waiting.*

Wilson understood that Kilpatrick's regular crew mates had not seen him bail out because they were in a cloud, and now it looked like they were so focused on waiting for two more chutes that they didn't realize they were following the crippled plane down. All he could do was hang there under his chute and watch.

*They're out! Pull up!*

He watched helplessly as both planes crashed into the mountainside. Everyone had made it out of Wilson's damaged B-17. All ten crew on the other plane died as the bombers exploded and fell in heaps on the mountain.

Wilson floated there in eerie silence, gently moving through the sky wherever the breeze sent him. All he could do was turn his head to the side and close his eyes tightly. He couldn't stand to look anymore.

# Chapter 4

## *Americanski?*

**As terrifying as a B-24 bomber could be when the en-**emy was lobbing antiaircraft shells, fighters were zooming to strafe you with large-caliber machine guns, and the plane was dying a slow but steady death, Clare Musgrove found it even more frightening to be hanging in the calm air over a land he knew nothing about, with no idea what awaited him on the ground.

Descending from thousands of feet, Musgrove had time to pray.

*Dear God, I ask you to watch over me and protect me in this place. Please guide me, Lord, and direct me to someone who can help me. Please watch over me, God.*

Having survived the terror of being trapped in his ball turret and having to dig his parachute out with his bare hands, Clare Musgrove did find relative peace in the near silence, hanging under his canopy and looking out over the rugged countryside below as he prayed. He couldn't see any of the crew of his B-24 because they had bailed out of the plane much earlier, meaning they were probably miles behind Musgrove. The immediate danger seemed to be over, but he knew that his time in the air would be only a brief respite. It would take only moments to land, and then he had no idea what would happen to him. He had only a vague sense of where he was—somewhere in Yugoslavia—and all he could remember from his briefings was that there were some people in this area who would help you, and some who would kill you, or worse.

As the parachute drifted lower, Musgrove spotted a small flock of sheep grazing on a hillside, oblivious to the American airman descending nearby. He knew that he had to find help once he hit the ground, because a lone airman would never survive in rugged, enemy-occupied territory.

*If I ever get on the ground, I'm going to head toward those sheep. I might as well find out who's around here.*

The parachutes worn by the bomber crews afforded very little ability to steer, so Musgrove was nearly helpless as he drifted into a stand of trees and hit the limbs hard. His parachute lines tangled in the tree, the chute draped over the top, leaving Musgrove dangling about fifteen feet off the ground. With some difficulty, he managed to get out of his parachute harness and scurry across a large limb, climbing down to others until he was low enough to jump down to the ground. Following his training, Musgrove snagged a dangling line from this parachute and worked hard to pull the rest of the chute down to the ground, bundling it up as small as he could and shoving it under some bushes to conceal the evidence of his landing. The exertion left him sweating in his heavy flight suit, which reminded him that the temperature on the ground was much warmer than it had been at several thousand feet. He peeled off the flight suit and hid it also.

Despite the rough landing in the tree, Musgrove was unhurt other than a few cuts and scratches. With his heart pounding from the exertion and the adrenaline coursing through his body, Musgrove scanned the area for any threats, or anyone who might help him. He saw no one. He had a general sense of the direction in which he had seen the flock of sheep, so he headed that way, planning to approach cautiously until he knew who was in this area.

Once he crossed a small ridge, he saw the sheep again. And then he saw people. From at least a half mile away, he thought he could make out two women and two young boys. They were staring back at him but didn't seem to be making any movement toward him or away from him. Musgrove was relieved to see the seemingly harmless group, though he also suspected that they could summon men with weapons if they were so inclined. He almost would have rather seen men there instead, he thought, because they probably would be more helpful. The women and boys continued to watch Musgrove as he began walking toward them, with no specific plan other than going closer to see what they would do.

As he got within a few hundred yards of them, Musgrove slowed his pace and then sat down on the ground for a minute, primarily to rest but also to let the others know that he was not approaching in an aggressive way. He sat there for a few minutes, trying to think clearly about the situation. Was he doing the right thing? Should he just walk up and say hello?

*Dear God, please help me through this. I don't know what these people will do with me, but please look over me and protect me.*

He rose again and walked slowly up the hill toward the group still watching him. He didn't know what he would do or say when he got there, because he didn't speak any local language. Musgrove kept going closer and closer, seeing no movement from the women and boys. As he got within a few yards, he stopped, his heart pounding, every sense heightened. They all stared at one another for a moment, and Musgrove could tell the others were apprehensive too.

Musgrove wanted to tell them he was American, one of the good guys. So he pointed to the unit patch on his uniform shirt and said, "U.S. . . . Air Force . . . American." The sturdy, gray-haired woman nodded and seemed relieved, understanding Musgrove. The women nodded their heads and pointed to themselves, saying, "Yugoslavian." The tension eased, but Musgrove still had no way to communicate with these people. Then he thought of the hard candy he had stashed in a pocket of his uniform. He reached in and brought out several pieces, then offered one to each of his new acquaintances. This broke the ice more, and the women said things that Musgrove assumed were thank-yous. The young boys smiled at him and seemed to be hoping for more to come from his pockets.

After that, Musgrove was out of ideas. The women seemed fine with him being there, but they didn't offer anything or even try to talk to him, realizing the effort would be futile. They talked among themselves and continued tending the sheep, while Musgrove just sat nearby and watched. Apparently they were uninterested in changing their routine just because a sweaty airman dropped out of the sky and gave them candy, so all Musgrove could do was sit and wait while the afternoon passed and the sheep grazed. He knew they would go back to their village before dark, but he had no idea if they would take him along. He desperately wanted them to. The idea of staying out in this countryside on his own scared him to death. If he could have communicated with them, he would have been pleading with them to take him along. But he could only sit and wait to see what would happen.

The hours passed slowly and Musgrove watched the sun begin to dip lower. He followed the women's movements intently, waiting for any sign that they were about to leave. Then they nonchalantly picked up their few belongings and started herding the sheep down a path. They had gone a few yards, with Musgrove watching and his heart racing, before one of them turned around and motioned for him to follow. She did it as if she was surprised he wasn't already on their heels.

Musgrove was grateful. He sprinted to catch up with them and then walked in silence for more than an hour. As they approached a little village, no more than a dozen stone and thatch cottages, a burly man with a beard came out to greet them. Musgrove thought he must be the husband of one of the women from the way they spoke with each other, and he was pleased to see the big man walk right up and stick out his hand. Musgrove grabbed the man's hand and shook it hard and tight, assured now that he was in friendly hands. He didn't know yet that the man was a Chetnik, a follower of Yugoslavian General Draza Mihailovich, who was fiercely loyal to the Americans, but the warm handshake was a welcome sign for Musgrove. *These people are going to help me, whoever they are.*

The man spoke more to the women and the group went inside the modest home. Musgrove sat on a small wooden chair outside the front door, feeling uneasy about walking into the house without an explicit invitation. He watched as a few people came and went in the village, each one looking at Musgrove with a strong curiosity, especially the children. But everyone kept their distance. Musgrove sat for a long while, wondering if these people were going to help him find a way out of Yugoslavia or if they saw him more like a stray dog. His thoughts were interrupted when one of the women stepped outside and motioned for him to come in, then directed him to the wooden table near the fireplace. Musgrove could see that dinner was set on the table and he realized he was being invited to a dinner of mutton, potatoes, and bread. He was too upset and anxious to have much of an appetite, but he nodded a thank-you to the woman and sat down next to the man of the house, who nodded toward Musgrove and began eating. The rest of the family, two sons and a daughter, sat at the table but seemed more interested in staring at Musgrove than eating. The American was poking at a bit of tough mutton and eating a bit of potato when suddenly there was a hard rapping on the wooden door. Everyone looked at one another expectantly, and then the Serb man stood up and went to the door, opening it to find another bearded villager there. The two exchanged words that Musgrove could not understand, but he could tell that they were arguing about something and the frequent gestures and glances toward him made Musgrove think he must be the topic. His best guess was that the other villager was saying the American had to go or the Germans would come looking for him, and Musgrove's host was saying he could stay. The two men argued harshly, with vigorous gesticulation and raised voices, but finally Musgrove's host told the other man to leave and slammed the door in his face. Then he came back toward the table, muttering something to the women, who seemed alarmed by the argument. Musgrove didn't quite know what to think. He was grateful that the man had defended him, but he was more worried than ever that the Germans were coming for him. When the man did not sit down at the table to finish his meal, Musgrove knew he was right. The big villager grabbed Musgrove by an arm and pulled him from the table, walking to a small bedroom in the back of the house and motioning for him to get under the bed. Musgrove didn't know exactly what was happening, but he figured he had no choice but to follow the man's instructions. He got down on the floor and slipped under the heavy wooden bed, his heart racing as he lay there waiting for something else to occur. He could see the man walk back into the main room and sit down at the table, resuming his meal and talking to his wife. Musgrove lay quietly, trying to slow his breathing, just waiting. From his vantage point under the bed, he could see only the floor in the bedroom and into the other room, nothing higher than knee level. Musgrove lay there for about two hours, alert and anxious, waiting for whatever was going to happen, and finally there was another hard knock at the door, more like a pounding.

Before the man of the house could get to the door, it was flung open so that it banged against the wall and caused the women to gasp with fright. There was a lengthy conversation between the visitor and the man of the house, but this time the visitor spoke with a German accent and clearly had the upper hand. Then the conversation stopped and the only sound was a pair of boots walking across the wooden floor. Musgrove was sweating and his heart was pounding so hard in his chest that he was sure it must be heard throughout the house now, and his eyes were frozen on the swath of floor that he could see from under the bed. He scooted back against the far wall another half inch, trying to hide himself as best he could.

His whole body tensed as he saw the big black boots, shined so bright that they stood out against everything in this drab village. They walked around the farmhouse, the heels clicking on the floor, and Musgrove was not surprised when they started walking right toward his hiding place. He knew without seeing anything more than the boots that this was a German officer looking for the downed airman. *This is it. They've got me. God, please just don't let them kill this family for helping me.*

The boots walked right into the small bedroom and stopped, no more than a couple feet from Musgrove's face. He couldn't take his eyes off the shiny black leather. They remained motionless for a moment, the house totally quiet, Musgrove praying that he could remain perfectly still, perfectly silent. All the German officer had to do was bend down and look under the bed, where Musgrove had little room to hide himself from view, and the airman would be captured. But he didn't.

After a long, long time, the boots turned and walked out of the room briskly, stomping through the main room and out the door. Musgrove breathed again.

**The officer was looking for** Musgrove because he was the only crewman missing from his bomber. The other nine had been captured already and were on their way to a prisoner-of-war camp.

Musgrove's experience was typical of the airmen drifting down in Yugoslavia. On the ground, the local villagers were counting parachutes too. They wanted to send help to every American who made it out, before the Germans could find them, but the airmen didn't know what to expect as they drifted down into the hills of Yugoslavia. They had been given only scant briefings about the conditions in this Nazi-occupied territory that they flew over on every bombing run, and all they really understood was that there were plenty of people to stay away from. There were Germans everywhere, and the local people were split into two warring groups—those who followed Mihailovich and wanted him to run the country after kicking out the Germans, and those who followed a man named Josip Broz Tito. Some of the airmen were told to seek out Tito's forces if they went down in Yugoslavia and not to trust the Mihailovich army.

But it turned out that the airmen didn't have much opportunity to seek out one side or the other. Wherever you landed, the locals found you quickly. Most of the airmen landing in the hills of northern Yugoslavia, like Musgrove, Orsini, and Wilson, were lucky to land in the hands of Mihailovich's forces and the villagers who supported him.

Though most of the Americans didn't know for a while if they were in good hands or bad, before long, a big, rough-looking, bearded man with a rifle—one of Mihailovich's forces—would show up and say, *"Americanski?"* When the airman said yes, the scary fellow would embrace the flier in a bear hug and let him know that he was safe.

The airmen had time for the fear to build as they drifted down, sometimes taking as long as twenty minutes to reach the ground. As Tony Orsini was drifting down to an unknown fate, he saw a heavyset woman in a long dress racing toward him. He didn't know what to think of this, other than to be glad that she was not a German soldier carrying a rifle. He kept his eyes on her as he drifted down and didn't realize until the last moment that he was flying right into a tree. With little time to brace, Orsini hit the tree hard and broke his clavicle, falling hard to the ground and passing out.

When he awoke, his face was in the ample bosom of the woman he had seen racing toward him. She was cradling his head and wiping his face, wrapping her arms around to hug him and saying soothing things in a voice that was foreign to him yet still remarkably comforting. The pain from his shoulder was sharp and unyielding, but he immediately knew he had come down in the right place. After waiting for him to regain his strength a bit, the woman helped Orsini to his feet and then guided him down a rugged path toward her village. As he approached, Orsini could see that the bombardier from his crew also had been found and had arrived in the village only moments earlier. The residents of the village were pouring out of their homes to greet the two Americans, everyone excited and chattering among themselves as Orsini and the other man tried to take in this incredible scene. Only a short time earlier, they'd had no idea what they would find on the ground and here they were being greeted like heroes. One family even brought out a piece of red carpet for the Americans to sit on as the other villagers brought them water, goats' milk, and bread.

After a few hours of socializing and eating, Orsini and the bombardier were sent off with several men, the rest of the village waving good-bye and kissing them on the cheeks as if they were sons going off to war. The Americans had no idea where they were going, since they still had not met anyone who spoke English, but they felt assured by this point that the local people were looking out for them. After a hike of an hour or two, the Americans arrived at an encampment of Mihailovich's guerilla fighters in a mountainous area. Unlike in the village, these were all tough-looking men, looking older than their years because of their bushy Old Testament beards and weather-worn faces. Their clothing varied somewhat, the officers wearing more complete uniforms, the lower ranks outfitted in bits and pieces of uniforms plus whatever else they could find. The better-dressed officers wore woolen jackets with leather belts, woolen breeches with leggings that wrapped from the ankle to the knee, and round caps with no bill and a crest on the front. The luckier guerillas had sturdy military boots, but many had to make do with simple felt slippers.

They were a formidable sight to leery fliers, but they greeted Orsini and the other Americans in the same way, with bear hugs and hearty claps on the back, accompanied by shouts of, *"Americanski!"*

There was still not much communication, other than a few simple words of English from some of the Yugoslav guerillas, but Orsini knew he was safe for the moment. He still didn't know how he would get home, but he could trust these fierce-looking soldiers to protect him in the meantime.

As he lay down to sleep that night, Orsini found that one of Mihailovich's soldiers had taken a particular liking to the good-looking young Italian-American boy. Drifting off to sleep after a long day, Orsini suddenly awoke when he felt the man sleeping next to him fumbling with the zipper on his uniform pants. Orsini pushed the man's hands away, explaining that he wasn't interested, but the man was insistent. The American had to keep fending off the brawny, hairy man's advances for several minutes, finally pointing to his injured shoulder and explaining that it hurt too much. This seemed to convince the amorous Yugoslav, who nodded and smiled at Orsini before going back to his own blanket.

Orsini was relieved. After such an eventful day, the man's advances were just one more unexpected problem that he had overcome. He was too tired to think much about it and soon went to sleep. The next morning, however, the same man approached Orsini with a smile and handed him a picture of himself. The Yugoslav knew Orsini would be moving on soon, and he wanted the American to remember him. On the back of the picture, he had written, "Remember your days in Ravna Gora."

Orsini thanked the man and shook his hand. No hard feelings. He put the picture in his pocket and would end up keeping it for many years.

**Still reeling from watching the** tragic crash of the bomber flying alongside the one he had just bailed out of, Wilson had his eyes closed tight when he heard dogs barking. The sound caused him to open his eyes and look at the countryside he was dropping into. It was rugged terrain, but he could see that parts of it were farmland also, and the dogs seemed to be with a flock of sheep nearby. Though these dogs weren't making a move toward Wilson, many of the airmen dropping into northern Yugoslavia had to contend immediately with angry dogs that the local shepherds used not just to herd the flock but also to keep the wolves away. The aggressive dogs looked even scarier with the large, spiked iron collars that many wore to help protect them in fights with wolves. Fortunately for most of the airmen, the barking of the dogs attracted the shepherds before any serious damage was done.

Wilson could see local people in the fields and realized immediately that he would not be able to hide after landing. Everyone saw him coming down, and he was sure they would be on him soon, friendly or not. He landed well and undid his parachute harness quickly, leaving the canopy snagged in a tree because there was no use trying to hide it. He walked out of the small clearing where he came down and saw a burly man in heavy woolen clothes walking toward him. In the July heat, Wilson thought it was a strange sight. The man's appearance made Wilson feel like he had landed in the Middle Ages.

The man was walking toward Wilson briskly and when he got within earshot, Wilson could hear him yelling, *"Americanski or Englaise?"* Not knowing yet whether the man would help or hurt him, Wilson felt like he had no choice but to answer. "American!" he yelled back. "I'm American!"

That caused the man to break into a jog and then embrace Wilson in a tight bear hug, almost lifting the bewildered American off his feet. Wilson didn't quite know how to respond as the man kissed him on both cheeks, his beard scratching the airman's face. The Yugoslav was all smiles as he shook Wilson's hand and slapped him on the back, saying, *"Americanski!"* over and over. Wilson could only manage a weak smile because he was exhausted from the ordeal on the plane, plus he didn't really know what was going on. But when he saw the man gesture to a girl nearby who was carrying a wooden cask, he perked up at the sight. He was desperately thirsty and wanted nothing more at that moment than a drink of water.

The girl ran over and handed him the cask as the big man smiled and gestured for him to drink. Wilson pulled out the wooden plug and turned the cask up, drinking deep before he realized it wasn't water but what the locals called *rakija*, a strong plum brandy. Wilson choked and coughed as the man laughed and the girl smiled at him.

The brandy helped quench Wilson's thirst somewhat, and the resulting buzz took the edge off the rest of his discomfort for a while. He wasn't at all sure what these people were going to do with him, but they did seem happy to help him so Wilson began to relax a bit after the terrible ordeal he'd been through. He sat and rested while the others talked excitedly, looking toward him often and gesturing in a way that made it clear they were discussing him. Before long, the burly man who had hugged him gestured toward a nearby path and helped Wilson stand up, saying something that Wilson understood to mean they were leaving. He walked with a small group of men for a short while, coming upon a building that Wilson took to be some sort of military site, east of a fairly large town called Jagodina and southeast of Belgrade, the national capital. There were several men with rifles standing guard, and Wilson could see boxes of ammunition and other supplies.

The group rested for a long time, the Yugoslavs talking but Wilson not understanding anything. Then he noticed another group approaching the building, and as they came closer he could see that one of the group was not like the others. He was wearing a flight suit. It didn't take long for Wilson to recognize one of his crewmates from the B-17 and he rushed out to greet him. Over the next eight hours, several more groups straggled in with an airmen or two in tow, until eight of the B-17's crew were gathered together again. Only the pilot and copilot were still missing, and Wilson suspected that was because they had bailed out much later and farther away than the other crew.

The plane's radio operator, Norman Brooks, had broken his ankle on landing, but otherwise the crew were in pretty good shape considering the ordeal they had been through.

**The same scenes were repeated** all over northern Yugoslavia throughout much of 1944. Mike McKool, a Texas native, was a machine gunner on a B-17 when he bailed out over Yugoslavia on July 4, 1944. His story was similar to those of the other fliers: His bomber was on a mission from Manduria in southern Italy to the oil fields of Ploesti when two engines went out on the return flight over Yugoslavia. Two German fighters had been waiting in the area for damaged bombers and attacked, destroying a third engine and prompting the crew to bail out near Lapovo, about eighty miles south of Belgrade. On landing, McKool immediately found a hole to hide in but watched with trepidation as fifteen to twenty people came running toward him with pitchforks and sickles. McKool worried that he was about to be hacked to death by angry villagers, but they threw down their farming tools when they got to McKool and hugged him tightly, fighting one another for the chance to kiss him on the cheek. McKool was still bewildered by the warm welcome when two men with rifles came running up, shouting to the crowd urgently. Whatever he was saying, McKool understood that Germans were coming. They must have seen his parachute.

The two soldiers, members of Mihailovich's forces, pushed the other locals away and one grabbed McKool's parachute, quickly bundling it into a ball and carrying it away. The other one grabbed him by the arm and urged him to come along. For the next six hours, McKool was on the run with his escorts through thick woods and up steep hillsides. They kept moving because they could hear German soldiers chasing them, along with the occasional gunshot.

Thomas Oliver's flight on May 6, 1944, started out badly because he was flying a borrowed plane. A B-24 pilot, he normally flew the *Flying Mudcat*, but the plane was being repaired that day so he and his crew had to take another. Oliver was a superstitious man and didn't like it.

He had another little superstition for each flight. During the briefing for each mission, he would estimate his return time and write it on the briefing sheet, then stuff it in a pocket of his flight suit. The estimate didn't serve any real purpose, but Oliver liked to have some written proof that he intended to come back. Having the time written down gave him some sense of confidence that he was going to make it back, and he never flew without the piece of paper on him. On May 6, he was taxiing the plane across the runway in preparation for takeoff when he reached for something in his pocket and the paper with his estimated return time flew out the open cockpit window. *Not a good sign*, he thought.

Hours later, Oliver's B-24 was in the middle of a hell fight over Ploesti, flak rocking the plane and German fighters attacking with a vengeance. Soon after the call of "bombs away," the number three engine was hit and started losing oil pressure. It wasn't long before the engine seized up, followed soon by number four. The crew jettisoned anything that could be heaved overboard, but the plane could maintain only eight thousand feet of altitude, barely enough to clear the Dalmatian Alps near the Adriatic Sea. Maybe they could make it back to Italy. Maybe.

The navigator, John Thibadeau, was trying to keep the plane on a course that would avoid any antiaircraft batteries, but it turned out that one German battery near the Yugoslavian town of Bor was not on his maps. A direct hit of antiaircraft fire took out their number two engine and set the plane on fire. Oliver hit the bailout bell and told his crew over the intercom to abandon ship. He was the last to bail out, watching the bomber dive nose first into the ground and explode in a massive fireball as he hung under his parachute.

Oliver was alarmed at how slowly he was descending, figuring there would be plenty of time for a German patrol to spot him and meet him on the ground. As it turned out, he drifted directly down on top of a family of Yugoslavs who were having lunch at a wooden table outside their small farmhouse. Oliver immediately noticed from his high vantage point that there was an entire sheep's head sitting on the table, staring up at him. The family looked up in time to see an American crashing down on them and were able to jump up and grab Oliver as he came closer. Like the other airmen, Oliver was greeted warmly with hugs and kisses and words he couldn't understand. Though uninvited, he felt like an honored guest at their picnic, which was confirmed when they offered him the eyeballs right out of the sheep's head. Oliver politely declined, but he eagerly accepted a glass of wine.

Oliver had been at the table for only ten minutes when two men approached with rifles over their shoulders, leading a horse. They talked briefly to the family and to Oliver, and he thought he heard them mention Draza Mihailovich. One of the men motioned for him to mount the horse, and after more bear hugs and kisses from the family, Oliver was off.

Another pilot blamed Dinah Shore when he found himself in trouble over Yugoslavia. In 1942 the New York native was full of patriotic fervor and envisioning a glorious military career as a pilot, and hearing the wholesome blond beauty sing "He Wears a Pair of Silver Wings" was all it took to push Richard Felman over the edge. Humming the song the whole way, he immediately went out and volunteered for the air force. He soon found himself piloting a B-24 from a base in Lecce, Italy, leading a crew of ten men who had trained together and bonded like family.

In just over two months, the crew of the "Never a Dull Moment" had flown twenty-three missions and counted up 212 hits all over the plane. Yet not one of the crew had suffered even the slightest injury. But then came a mission in July 1944. At three a.m., the duty officer woke Felman and his crew and told them to report for a mission briefing. They found out they were flying that day to bomb Ostro Romano, the most well-defended oil refinery in Ploesti. After the usual briefings about the target, the bomb load, expected resistance and so forth, the crew was given one more bit of advice, with the now-common warning to protect their ears: "If you go down over Yugoslavia, look for the Partisan fighters, the supporters of Tito. They wear caps with a red star. Stay away from the Chetniks, the local peasants who support Mihailovich. They'll cut your ears off and hand you over to the Germans."

Felman thought that sounded odd. He didn't know much about the warring factions in Yugoslavia, but he knew that Mihailovich had been on the cover of *Time* magazine not too much earlier, profiled as a heroic American ally. *Now he's going to cut off my ears?*

The warning was curious but overshadowed by all the other dangers of the mission. At 5:13 a.m., Felman's B-24 took flight and joined a wave of two hundred and fifty bombers headed to Ploesti. Felman and his crew had seen rough times over Romania before, but on this mission they saw hell open up before them when they were ten minutes away from their target. The antiaircraft fire was intense; Felman watched bombers explode in front of him and drop out of the air. He and his crew were scared and wanted so badly to just turn the plane around and run, but they knew they had to get to their target and drop their bombs. After what seemed an eternity, Felman finally heard the bombardier call, "Bombs away." The plane jumped up abruptly as the five-thousand-pound payload was released, and Felman took the controls to turn the plane back toward home.

After escaping the target area, the crew was relieved to see that, once again, they had made it through Ploesti without any injuries, and the plane was still flying just fine. Then Felman heard one of the gunners call out, "Hey, look at that P-51 over there. What a beauty." A P-51 was an American fighter plane, and bomber crews always welcomed the sight of one coming alongside to provide protection. The problem was that this gunner, known to the crew as Sergeant Carl, actually was a quartermaster sergeant the crew met in Italy who had never been trained to fly. The crew unofficially adopted him as a sometimes member because he had grown bored of his ground duties in Italy and wanted some air experience that might hasten his rotation out of the unit. They taught him how to man the fifty-caliber machine guns and were satisfied with his performance. Unfortunately, Sergeant Carl had never been trained to recognize enemy planes from the air, so the P-51 he thought he saw was actually a German

Messerschmitt, a German fighter that could pounce on a bomber with little warning. And it wasn't the only one eyeing them.

Within minutes, the Messerschmitts tore the bomber to bits from nose to tail. Fuel was pumping into the fuselage from broken lines and Felman could tell right away that the flight was doomed. It all happened so fast that there was no time for discussion, no time to warn anyone. Felman issued the command to abandon ship, hit the bailout button, and he was flying out the side hatch before he had time to think about how scared he should be. He waited as long as he could stand it before pulling the rip cord on his chute, not wanting to hang in the air and make himself a good target any longer than necessary. When he landed hard, he first thought he might have broken his leg. It took a moment to realize he had been shot in the leg. Until now, he'd been too focused on other matters to notice. He tried to stand but couldn't.

Suddenly it seemed that villagers were coming out of every bush and from behind every tree. He looked all around him in shock, and with great trepidation, as at least twenty people came running toward him from all directions—men, women, and children. Before he could decide whether it was worth trying to defend himself, they were on him, hugging and kissing him fervently, smiling from ear to ear. More women and children stood at a distance, watching eagerly and trying to get a look at the American.

Felman realized immediately that these people were Chetniks, the locals he was supposed to avoid. But they weren't making any moves to cut off his ears. In fact, they were actually lining up so they could each take a turn at hugging and kissing him.

After everyone was satisfied that they had greeted the airman sufficiently, several of the bigger men picked Felman up and carried him on their shoulders for about half a mile to a grouping of three small cottages, the rest of the group following and chattering excitedly. As they arrived, another thirty villagers started streaming in from the countryside, having heard that an American dropped out of the sky. With each new villager, Felman was greeted like a celebrity and accepted more hugs and kisses. He couldn't understand exactly why they were treating him like royalty, but he wasn't complaining.

The Chetniks were in a festive mood and brought out fruits, flowers, and a bottle of *rajika*, the plum brandy that could be found in most villages. Someone started playing music and children danced. After offering Felman a toast of *rajika*, a burly Chetnik man quickly poured the rest of his cup over Felman's leg wound without warning. The American winced as the alcohol seared his open flesh, but the man offered another drink of brandy and Felman soon forgot the pain. When he next looked down at his leg, there was a clean bandage covering the wound.

The party continued for some time, and later Felman was resting in one of the cottages when an older villager approached him cautiously. The old man seemed as if he didn't want to intrude on Felman, but he pointed outside the cottage, gesturing as if he were asking Felman to go with him. Felman wasn't sure what he meant, and he was too tired to go outside for more festivities, so he only smiled in return. Then the meek man put his hands together as if praying and nodded toward the door. Felman understood and nodded yes.

The old man gave Felman a stick to use as a crutch and then helped him hobble over to the village's small church. Felman knelt with the man and prayed, each of them speaking to the same God in a language the other could not understand. The American could not tell what the Chetnik was thanking God for, but he was thanking the Lord for delivering him into the hands of the very people he had been told to avoid.

Later that afternoon, Felman was introduced to Colonel Dragisâ Vasić, a senior officer under Mihailovich who had come to meet the downed American. Felman was immediately struck by Vasić's appearance. Unlike the burly, rough-looking soldiers and villagers he had met so far, Vasić had a more refined, almost courtly air about him. He was in his mid-seventies, with snow-white hair and a neatly trimmed mustache and goatee. Vasić was dressed in a clean, handsome uniform. His wife accompanied him, and Felman was relieved when she introduced herself and Vasić in English. She was the first English-speaking person he had met in Yugoslavia.

The three of them sat under a large tree, with soldiers standing guard nearby and the villagers watching with interest from a polite distance. With his wife acting as interpreter, Vasić explained that he had been a prominent writer before the Nazi invasion but had left his home in the city to join Mihailovich's forces in the mountains. He was serving as a political counselor to Mihailovich himself.

Vasić was warm and cordial, explaining to Felman that Mihailovich would do everything in his power to protect the downed airmen. Felman expressed his gratitude and related that the villagers had been very kind to him already. The local people felt honored in his presence, Vasić explained, because they considered American airmen to be brave warriors who were risking their lives to help them beat back the German invaders. And for most of them, Felman was the first of these heroic fliers they had ever seen.

The colonel went on to explain how he and others had retreated into the mountains after Yugoslavia fell to the Germans in 1941, following Mihailovich, who had been minister of defense under King Peter the Second. Though the guerilla forces were poorly armed, they were determined to fight the Nazis with whatever they had. Felman was inspired by Vasić's demeanor, the look of determination in his eyes when he spoke of beating back the German occupiers. As they wound up their discussion, Vasić's wife explained that there was one more thing the colonel needed to tell Felman.

"Our soldiers found ten parachutes," she said, translating Vasić's quietly spoken words. Felman knew he was talking about the crash of his own plane, and that there had been eleven crew members onboard that day—the usual ten plus a photographer on a special assignment. "The Germans reached the plane first and the other man was dead. We do not know his name because the Germans took his identification tile. The Germans took everything valuable in the plane and then started looking for you and your friends."

Vasić explained that Mihailovich's orders were to protect the Americans at all costs, which Felman understood to have real meaning when the cost might include retaliation against the local villagers. He then called over a young soldier who had been standing nearby and introduced him as Miodrag Stefanovic.

"He will be your bodyguard," Vasić's wife explained. "He is one of the best fighters. He will protect you."

From that day forward, Stefanovic stayed by Felman's side day and night, never leaving him unguarded for a moment. The next morning, after a sound sleep on a straw mattress, Felman awoke to a hard pounding rain. When he looked outside the door of the little cottage where he had been put up, he saw Stefanovic huddled with nine other soldiers out under a nearby tree, shivering in the downpour. Felman called his guard over and asked, through hand gestures since Stefanovic understood no English, why the soldiers had not come inside. Stefanovic mimed the answer: They had been afraid of waking their special guest.

Later that morning, the rest of Felman's crew started arriving in the village, brought in by soldiers a few at a time, and in one case, by two boys who led a couple of horses on which the flight engineer Leonard "Tex" Pritchett and radio operator Israel "Bronx" Mayer rode with flowers in their hair and stuck in their uniforms by the villagers they had met earlier. Another crew member abandoned his hideout in the woods, where he was following his training by laying low and waiting for rescue. Unable to stand the cold and hunger any longer, he just walked down to the nearest village and was shocked to see Felman and the rest of his crew there, being treated like royalty.

Eventually all of the surviving members of Felman's crew made it to the village. After an initial celebration that included rolling around on the ground, wrestling one another, and laughing wildly with each new arrival, the crew soon came to realize who was missing. It was Tom P. Lovett, a nose gunner from Roxbury, Massachusetts. Once they saw he wasn't among them, they remembered that he had delayed bailing out of the plane, staying at his position while the others bailed out, yelling that he wanted to stay just a moment longer to kill another Nazi fighter. Apparently he never left his post and went down with the plane.

The local villagers recovered Lovett's body and held a formal funeral, attended by three hundred people, including Felman and his crewmates. The Serbs made a small headstone inscribed with Lovett's name, military number, and hometown. Later they gave Felman some photographs of the grave and the funeral ceremony to take back to Lovett's family.

**Meanwhile, news of the airmen's** plight was reaching their relatives back home. All over the country, families were facing the moment that they feared as soon as a loved one left to join the service. They answered a doorbell in the midst of cooking a pie, or they crawled out from under a car they were working on when someone called from the driveway, or they went to the window to see what the dogs were barking at. Their hearts skipped and their throats grew dry in an instant as they saw the Western Union delivery boy standing there with a telegram in his hand.

Tony Orsini's mother, Angiolina Orsini, was in the kitchen on August 3, 1944, when she heard the knock at the door. Unaccustomed to receiving visitors with no notice, she immediately tensed and wondered if anything was amiss. But it couldn't be Tony, she thought. She had talked with him on the phone only two weeks earlier when he was in Manchester, New Hampshire, preparing to go overseas. And she knew he had been in Europe for only about a week. She worried about him constantly, but she had not yet started dreading every knock at the door.

Looking every bit the part of the Italian immigrant mother in the kitchen, Mrs. Orsini wiped her hands on her apron before heading to the front door. As she opened the door, she saw a young boy in a Western Union hat standing there. He couldn't have been more than fifteen years old. She saw his bike leaning against the front steps. The boy stared down at the floor and mumbled, "Telegram for you, ma'am," never making eye contact. He had done this many times before, and he wanted to just hand over the telegram and leave.

*"Per me? Che cosa è esso?"* she asked, not knowing what the telegram was or why he was handing it to her.

The boy thrust the envelope at her and she instinctively took it from him, freeing the boy to turn quickly and jump on his bike. He pedaled hard and raced away, leaving Orsini's mother standing there with an envelope that said "Western Union Telegram" and "Mrs. Angiolina Orsini=28 Beacon St, Jersey City, NJ." She looked down at it and suddenly realized what it was. She gasped and put a hand to her mouth, then tore the envelope open. She fumbled with the paper folded inside but quickly saw that it was in English. She could not read a word of it, but she knew it was about her dear Anthony.

She began to cry as she stared at the telegram, fearing the worst. Then she looked next door and bolted down the front steps toward a neighbor who was an Italian immigrant like herself but who could read and write English. She went to the side door and pounded hard. When the woman appeared, she saw Orsini's mother standing there in a panic, tears running down her face and clutching the telegram tightly in both hands.

"*Colto esso a me! Prego colto esso a me!*" she cried to the neighbor. *Please read it to me!*

Startled, the woman had no idea what the distraught woman was talking about. Then she saw that it was a telegram Angiolina Orsini was holding. She knew immediately that this would be terrible news. She didn't want to read the telegram.

"*No, no, non posso,*" she replied, shaking her head, full of sympathy but not wanting to be the one to give this poor woman such bad news. *No, I can't.*

"*Per favore! Prego, dovete!*" Orsini's mother cried. "*È circa il mio Anthony!*" *Please, you must. It's about my Anthony.*

The neighbor couldn't resist the anguished woman's pleas. She took the telegram and slowly read it aloud in Italian as Orsini's mother began to sob into her apron.

"*La Segretaria della Guerra lo vuole per esprimere il suo rincrescimento profondo che il vostro tenente Anthony J. Orsini del figlio in Secondo Luogo è stato segnalato I missing nell'azione . . .*" she read. "*The*

*Secretary of War desires me to express his deep regret that your son Second Lieutenant Anthony J. Orsini has been reported missing in action . . ."*

Her Anthony had been away such a short time and already he was gone. She prayed that he was still alive, but she knew that this telegram was often followed by another.

# Chapter 5

# *Long Journey to Somewhere*

**Once they were on the ground, the airmen's only goal** was to survive. Survive right now, survive for another hour, for today, then for another day. They had no way to communicate with their home bases, and there was next to nothing in the countryside that would help them, other than the generous local people who took them in. The rough terrain made any travel difficult, and besides, the airmen didn't have any idea which way to go. Moving down the mountains into more populated areas might offer more opportunity for escape or signaling for help, but that would mean walking right into areas that were heavily patrolled by Germans. Better to stay hidden in the mountainside even if they didn't know what they would do next.

Escaping from this Nazi-held territory seemed like an impossibility to most of them. They were airmen used to flying over dangerous country, not special agents trained to infiltrate and make their way through enemy territory on the ground.

After meeting up with his fellow crew members at the military outpost of Mihailovich's guerillas, Wilson realized that his best bet for survival was to stick with these armed men for as long as they would have him. For the next two months, the

Serbian fighters harbored Wilson and his crewmates, feeding them as well as they could manage and taking them along when the group moved from one village to the next by narrow, sometimes overgrown trails—another group of ragtag Americans moving through Yugoslavia, like the groups that included Musgrove and Orsini. Each group had their own adventures and difficulties along the way, and one of the worst parts was not knowing what other Americans were out there and whether they would ever join up.

Occasionally the Chetnik soldiers would hide Wilson and the other Americans in the bushes until a German patrol passed or until they could be certain that a village was safe. Wilson got used to trudging through the mountainous countryside and looked forward to each new village, where the fliers would be greeted as heroes and offered whatever rations could be found. Though the villagers always welcomed them, the soldiers escorting them would allow the group to stay only a day or so before moving on. They knew that the generous villagers would give every scrap of food to the Americans if they stayed too long.

The mood of the Americans changed when they met a man named Bogdan, who greeted them in English as they entered another village. He embraced the fliers and welcomed them, causing the Americans to break into broad grins as they realized that finally they were meeting a Chetnik who spoke English. Maybe they'd find out where they were going and what would happen to them.

They quickly found out that Bogdan had learned English while working in the steel mills of Gary, Indiana. He had returned to Yugoslavia to retire and found himself directly in the path of Hitler's army. They spoke eagerly with Bogdan, pumping him for any information, but he had little to pass on. All he could tell them was that the soldiers were protecting them until they could figure out somewhere to take them.

"Right now, they will take you from one place to next," he said. "They will protect you. But I don't know where you are going."

Bogdan joined them on their journey, serving as their interpreter, helping the Americans understand what little there was to discuss along the way. If nothing else, he could help the Americans understand how far the next village was, how long it might be before they found some food. As they moved on, the Americans would watch for anything edible along the way, stopping to gather berries or any fruit that looked remotely like something they recognized. Whenever they came across a stream with small minnowlike fish, the airmen used their shirts to weave a seine that would catch the little fish by the dozens. They didn't seem like much of a meal, but the Americans would take the fish to the next village and ask a local woman to fry them, offering some of the fish in appreciation for the cooking and any butter, goat cheese, or bread she might spare.

When they came to a bigger river, the men sometimes took advantage of the chance to get out of the July heat and cool off. One day the men were drawn to the sound of rushing water, which promised relief from the incessant heat of the day and they couldn't wait to jump in when they saw the river up ahead. With the blessing of their Chetnik escorts the Americans stripped down and jumped in the cool water, forgetting for a moment that they were in enemy territory and in constant danger. One of the guerillas indicated that he was going off in the direction of the local village to see if they should stop there or keep moving on, disappearing back through the woods and leaving the Americans with a few other Chetniks who sat down in the shade and indicated that it was okay if Wilson and his friends wanted to swim. The young men jumped in immediately, and it didn't take them long to let their guard down. They were just young men taking a swim, shoving one another underwater and splashing with abandon. Wilson was enjoying himself, immersing himself over and over again to cool down, while trying to scrub off some of the grime that was ground into every inch of his skin. He was scrubbing when he looked downstream and noticed someone else in the water, maybe half a mile away.

Wilson couldn't see him clearly, but he pointed the man out to the other Americans and wondered aloud who it might be. Everyone calmed down for a moment to take a look, but then the group decided the man must just be a local villager. The man appeared to be naked, like them, and he was standing there staring back at them. Several of the men waved at the other fellow, but he just stood there. One of the Americans got the attention of a Chetnik soldier on the shore and pointed down-river to the other man. The soldier took a look and, seeing nothing to suggest the man was anything other than a local villager, shook his head as if to say there was no problem, then went back to resting under a tree. Wilson and his crewmates shrugged their shoulders and returned to enjoying the cool water.

Suddenly they could hear the Chetnik guerrilla who had gone to the village crashing through the woods, hurriedly returning to the riverbank. He started shouting to the other Chetniks excitedly, yelling something that caused the men with rifles to spring to their feet. They started waving furiously at the Americans in the water. Wilson and his crewmates stopped their horsing around and looked up at the anxious men on the bank, not knowing what was wrong but getting the message that something was. They were starting to slowly make their way out of the water when Bogdan ran over and shouted to them.

"Germans! There are Germans here! You must go! Go now!"

The Americans churned the water as they ran to shore quickly, as fast as they could, grabbing their clothes on the way out and sprinting into the woods on the heels of the Chetniks. They ran for a long time, naked and half naked, struggling to put on some clothes along the way, until finally the guerillas decided they had run far enough. They all sat down in the woods, panting from the exertion, the Americans still soaking wet.

"Where are the Germans?" one of the Americans asked Bogdan.

Their interpreter could hardly speak as he tried to catch his breath. "The village . . . Germans are in the village. Taking pigs, other food," he said.

Several of the Americans looked puzzled. The village wasn't all that close to where they were swimming, so why were they running for their lives like that?

Bogdan was breathing better now and could explain more. "That man you saw in the river, he was the commandant of that unit, the Germans," he said. "He went to the river to bathe while his men went to the village."

Suddenly the picture became clear to the Americans. They were whooping and hollering like schoolboys just upstream from a German officer who could have had them all arrested or killed on the spot. They had even waved at him. The only reason they were still alive and free, they figured, was that the German officer was by himself and didn't know how well armed the American group might be.

But surely he had reported the Americans, and he might even be mobilizing his own unit to chase them down. They had to keep moving.

**As they marched on and on,** nearly every day, the Americans wondered where they were going. Before long, the wondering became just an idle thought in the back of their minds, not the all-consuming question it had been at first. It was only days before Wilson stopped obsessing about how he was going to get out of Yugoslavia and back to his base in Italy. With each passing day, the question seemed more futile and soon he put it out of his mind. He just kept walking through Yugoslavia. Wilson and his crewmates talked among themselves about everything under the sun because they had plenty of time to pass. Baseball gave way to cars, and then to favorite foods, which led to starlets and pinup girls, which segued into girlfriends, wives, and mothers. No matter how jocular the conversation started, it seemed to always lead to morose longing for those back home. And that led to silence as the men marched on.

All over northern Yugoslavia, American airmen were trudging along, hoping the next turn of the trail would offer more hope. Mike McKool had spent several days at a military camp with Chetnik escorts, waiting while the other members of his crew were brought in from the surrounding countryside. Fortunately for McKool and his fellow crew members, the commander of the Mihailovich army post, known as Captain Milankovic, spoke English. Though he could reassure the Americans that they would be protected, he also explained how serious their situation was.

A couple of days after they landed in Yugoslavia, Captain Milankovic explained to McKool that the Germans were looking for them. And worse, they had taken twenty villagers prisoner, threatening to kill them if they did not reveal the whereabouts of the Americans. McKool and his crewmates were horrified at the idea and wondered aloud if they should give themselves up.

"It will not help," the Chetnik officer explained. "The Germans will kill who they wish. You cannot stop them."

Nevertheless, the villagers weighed heavily on the minds of the Americans as they rested in the secret military camp, eating and drinking plum brandy. After several days, they left the camp and started walking toward General Mihailovich's headquarters, eighty miles away. They moved mainly at night and stayed away from roads, until they met up with a brigade of Mihailovich's fighters numbering eight hundred. When the commander of the brigade was introduced to the Americans and found out that McKool was from Texas, he nicknamed him "Tom Mix," after the movie cowboy popular at the time, and gave him a horse to ride.

With the protection of the brigade, the group's travel was safer but no faster. It took three weeks to reach their destination, during which there were several skirmishes with German patrols. But even more than the moments of danger, the Americans were impressed by the way the Serbian people greeted them along the way. They were offered the best food in the village and learned not to eat all they were offered, lest the family be left with nothing. Villagers offered their homes and beds for rest, and when the brigade moved out again, the Americans were singled out for special good-byes and bits of bread and goat cheese wrapped in a small cloth. As the group marched on, the column more than half a mile long, local Serbs would line the path or road to see the soldiers and especially the Americans they had only heard about, never seen. More often than not, they would step forward as the Americans passed by, offering a kiss on the cheek or a cup of goats' milk.

Sometimes the American airmen didn't even realize immediately how generous the local people were, not until it was too late to be gracious. Some of the airmen, when first on the ground with the local villagers, eagerly scarfed down all the food put in front of them because the amount was small, they were hungry, and they thought it was all intended for them. Their bellies were full by the time they realized the peasant couple and their child had intended to share the food and were only waiting for them to eat first. One airman was sheltered in a villager's home on his first night in Yugoslavia and made a snide comment the next morning about the uncomfortable wooden bed. Another airman, who had been there longer and knew how far the villagers' hospitality extended, took the first airman around to the small stone barn behind the house and showed him that the mother and her two children had slept with the animals so the American could have their bed.

One day McKool was overcome by the outpouring of emotion from an elderly woman in a long dress and the traditional head covering who rushed forward and grabbed his hand as he passed by on horseback, kissing it fervently and speaking words he could not understand. He could tell, however, that there was great emotion behind the words. She sobbed and held on to his hand as long as she could. As they passed and the woman fell back, McKool asked the Serbian officer he was riding alongside why the woman responded that way to him.

"Many of these people have lost sons to this war. Some of them have sons in German prisoner camps," he explained, looking ahead as his horse walked on. "They see you as their own children, Americans especially, because you come here to help us fight. That woman was kissing her son when she kissed you."

**Thomas Oliver's brief stay with** the family who found him was followed by an afternoon on horseback, accompanied by three soldiers. He understood almost nothing they said to him along the way, other than their mention of the name Draza Mihailovich. Oliver didn't know a lot about Mihailovich but figured that the men were taking him to the general.

The group moved at a steady pace through the hills, stopping late in the afternoon to talk with a Yugoslavian doctor who had been educated in France. He didn't speak any English, but Oliver was able to use his rudimentary French to communicate, noting that talking with a Yugoslavian who spoke French was much easier than any of his previous attempts to speak French with a Frenchman. The doctor understood that Oliver could not speak French well but understood the language when he heard it. So the doctor translated in French what the soldiers told him, and Oliver had only to answer, *"Oui,"* or ask, *"Ou?"* The doctor conveyed that the rest of Oliver's crewmates had been found, and one was slightly wounded.

With an *"Au revoir!"* to the doctor, Oliver got back on his horse and kept moving through the countryside, stopping in the evening at a farmhouse where the woman offered him a cup of hot goats' milk. Oliver was ravenously hungry by then and took the cup eagerly, but he hesitated when he looked at the cup. The milk had some kind of scum all over the top, and whatever it was, it didn't look appetizing. But Oliver thought to himself that he had to eat something, and whatever this was, apparently the locals did fine with it. So he brought the cup to his lips and tossed the scummy milk back in one big gulp, hoping not to taste it on the way down. It turned out not to be as bad as he'd expected.

After that meager supper, Oliver was put to bed on a pile of straw, where he slept soundly for a few hours until the soldiers woke him up. He saw that three other soldiers had arrived in the night, and the group of seven all rode off into the night, Oliver in his flight suit and the Chetniks in their tight-fitting jackets and Cossack-style fur hats. As they moved along quietly, the only sound the jangling of the horse bridles and the scuffing of hooves on the trail, Oliver felt like he was in a Grade B cowboy movie.

When the sun rose, the group traveled through a series of larger villages and continued their journey at a more leisurely pace. As the day wore on, Oliver started to think that the goal was to stop at every café in every village, or at least any establishment that could sell them a round of drinks. The Chetniks were generous in buying brandy and whatever other libations might be available for Oliver, which helped take his mind off not knowing where he was going. With the brandy flowing, the Chetniks escorting Oliver loosened up and started laughing, telling jokes he couldn't understand but nevertheless including him in the revelry. At one point, one of the soldiers noticed that Oliver carried two knives, one on his belt and one strapped to his leg.

The Chetnik motioned to Oliver as if to ask why he had two knives instead of just one. Oliver was trying to figure out how to explain that he liked having a backup when another of the soldiers interjected. He pointed to the knife on Oliver's belt and said, "Ahhh . . . Hitler!" and made a gesture as if cutting his throat, followed by a dramatic death. Then he pointed to the knife on Oliver's leg and said, "Mussolini!" followed by the same gesture and overacting. Oliver joined the other Chetniks in hysterical laughter.

**After a night of revelry** with his escorts, Oliver experienced a more somber morning. The soldiers and the local Serbs took Oliver to a religious ceremony at the graves of two American airmen who had been shot down earlier but hadn't made it safely into the arms of the local people. Oliver watched silently as a Serbian Orthodox priest conducted a service for the dead, passing a cup of wine around for all to sip. Then he poured a small amount from the cup onto each grave. Oliver was moved by the solemnity of the moment, the way these local people conducted the service as if the Americans were their own brothers.

He thought about it for the rest of the day as he waited in the small village, not knowing how long they were staying before moving on again. As night fell and he was given a bed to sleep in, Oliver figured the group would head out after daybreak the next morning. But in the darkest early hours, Oliver awoke to screams of "Heidi! Heidi!" or at least that was what it sounded like to him. The Serbs were yelling "Hurry!" in their language, the terror in their voices conveying quickly to Oliver that Germans were coming. Several men rushed into the cottage and grabbed Oliver, practically dragging him outside and deep into the woods, where he hid for hours until the danger had passed.

Later that day, as he lounged around the village waiting for any signal that he was moving on, the rest of his bomber crew straggled in, led by a few more Chetnik soldiers. They were accompanied by an old man who was acting as their interpreter, having spent several years living in Wisconsin and working in the logging business. Because he had worked mostly with Swedish immigrants, the Serb spoke English with a Swedish accent that always made Oliver chuckle. With the help of the old man's English, Oliver was introduced to the local Chetnik commander, known as Kent. He was young and handsome, charismatic and a natural leader, Oliver thought. It was no wonder that he was leading all these soldiers. Kent explained to Oliver that he and the other Americans in the village, totaling twenty-four now that several groups had been brought to the same place, were not going anywhere anytime soon. They would stay in this small village close to the Danube River on the eastern border of Yugoslavia while Kent tried to arrange an evacuation with the Allies. Kent hoped to get supplies or other aid from the Allies in return for his help.

So Oliver and the other Americans waited and waited. A month passed with almost nothing happening. Kent kept saying he was waiting on the Allies to agree to an evacuation plan, but the men saw no evidence of any forward progress. They had little to do but lie around the village, helping the locals with their chores and scrounging for food as they grew thinner and thinner. Oliver and the other Americans started pressuring Kent to do something with them, anything. They couldn't stand the thought of staying in this little village for much longer, with the food shortage getting more desperate every day. Finally they convinced him to send them west to an area closer to General Mihailovich's headquarters. Maybe something more could be done for them there, they thought.

Kent arranged to have the Americans taken west, appointing Captain Ivan Milac as the leader of their escorts. The Americans were pleased, as Milac was one of their favorites in the village, a former officer in the Yugoslav Regular Army who had learned English mostly from listening to radio broadcasts. Milac issued rifles to the Americans and warned them that their journey would be dangerous. The village they were in was relatively safe because it was remote and offered nothing that would attract the Germans. But traveling to the west would mean heading into more heavily occupied territory. The Americans had to be ready to defend themselves.

Their journey started on a mountain railroad, where they followed the tracks until they approached a large town that was sure to have German units patrolling. From there the group hiked through the woods, through fields, in the sun and the rain, just constantly marching westward and trying to avoid Germans. They traveled in the brush and sometimes at night to avoid the German patrols that they knew would either take them prisoner or just kill them. They knew that the shorthanded German occupiers had little time to corral and care for dozens of downed airmen, so the more expedient solution would be to open fire with a machine gun.

They would sleep in haystacks, on the wooden floors of whatever buildings they came across, anywhere they happened to be when night fell. Days blended into weeks, and Oliver could scarcely tell when one day ended and the next began. They were all filled with the same hunger, the longing for home, and fears about what might be around the next bend.

Only once on the journey did Oliver forget his aching feet and his desire to be anywhere but Yugoslavia. It was the middle of the day when the group of Americans and their Chetnik escorts came to a village where the locals greeted them warmly, as always, and offered them bits of food and drink. But Oliver and a couple of his crewmates were singled out by three girls who stood out from the rest. They were young, probably in their late teens, and the Americans immediately locked onto them as the most beautiful girls they had seen since landing in this country. While all the villagers were as hospitable as anyone could desire, the Americans had noticed that the girls in the mountains tended to the robust and hardy, with babushka-type kerchiefs on their heads that reminded them more of grandmothers than pinups. These girls, however, were different. They were more slender, they wore nicer dresses, though still simple, and their hair was uncovered. Oliver and his crewmates surmised that they must be city girls who somehow landed in this country village, possibly fleeing the Germans in town.

The American boys were smiling from to ear to ear and doing their best to charm the girls, who seemed equally interested in the Yanks. The girls gestured for the three Americans to come into their cottage and have lunch, and they didn't have to ask twice. Oliver and his friends eagerly took seats at the rough-hewn wooden table and smiled at the girls, who shot flirtatious looks every time they brought a plate with bread and cheese to the table. The six of them sat there smiling at one another, the men eating and commenting among themselves about how nice it was to see a pretty girl again. The girls were chatting among themselves too, quietly, and giggling every so often as they looked at the three men.

Then one of the girls started talking to the men and gesturing toward the back room, which had two simple beds. At first the men didn't know what they meant, but with more gestures and simple words, they got the idea. The girls were telling them that they could stay with them for the night. When it dawned on them, the Americans could hardly contain their excitement. They looked at one another and grinned; then they turned back to the girls and all three men said yes at once. They nodded in the affirmative, said yes several more times, and nodded some more to make sure the girls understood.

And just at that point, they heard the Chetnik soldiers come running by outside. "Heidi! Heidi!" they yelled. The Germans were coming. The Americans had to run. They truly hated to leave these beautiful girls, stuffing down more bread and cheese before taking a moment for just the briefest of kisses on the girls' cheeks as they raced out the door and into the woods.

Richard Felman, accompanied by his doggedly loyal bodyguard, was growing more and more fond of the Serbian people as he continued his own march through the Yugoslavian countryside. Though he and his crewmates were in constant danger, he came to appreciate the interaction with local people and wanted to learn more about this country. His bodyguard Stefanovic managed to find an old Serbian-English dictionary somewhere along the way, and Felman eagerly took to learning the local language. At each village where they stopped to rest and eat, Felman tried to speak a few words of Serbian, which invariably thrilled the locals. Stefanovic beamed with pride, as if showing off his pupil. Once they became comfortable communicating with short phrases and pantomime, the villagers usually got around to asking Felman about his home, this wondrous place they had only heard of. "How much does a worker earn?" was a common question. Knowing that dollars would have little meaning to these people who were always hungry, Felman instead told them of how much bread or how many dozens of eggs could be earned in one day by a typical worker in America. The answer always astounded them, and many said they wanted to go to America after the war.

Only once did Felman encounter a Serbian villager who was not happy to see the American. As was their custom when entering a village to stay for the night, the soldiers divided the Americans up among the various homes and expected the local people to play host. Stefanovic had taken Felman to a house where the married couple welcomed him as usual, but it didn't take long for the mother-in-law to make it clear that she didn't appreciate some strange American barging in and eating their scarce food. The old lady was railing about Felman's presence, while the married couple tried to calm her down, when Felman tried to smooth things over. He picked up a cup of plum brandy and raised it high.

"Long live King Peter!" he shouted, looking expectantly at the old woman. He motioned to her with the cup, and she could not refuse the toast. She begrudgingly took a sip, followed by Felman.

"Long live Draza Mihailovich!" Felman shouted. The woman muttered something and took another sip of brandy. Felman followed with enthusiastic toasts to President Franklin Roosevelt and British Prime Minister Winston Churchill. The woman stopped complaining about Felman and soon became warmer, eventually laughing with him and offering him more food. When Felman left with the soldiers the next morning, the old woman clutched him tightly and sobbed, kissing his hands and waving her kerchief as he pulled away.

**After weeks more of marching** and scrounging for food, but no more pretty girls, Oliver and his cohorts finally arrived near General Mihailovich's headquarters. Milac explained that they were going to stay there, the men dispersed throughout the peasant farmhouses in the area, until Mihailovich could determine how to get them home. Oliver looked around and didn't see anything that would explain why they had walked for weeks to get here.

"Why here?" Oliver asked Milac. "Where are we?"

"Pranjane," he replied. "This is where you will wait. There will be more."

And soon there were. Mike McKool, Richard Felman, Tony Orsini, Clare Musgrove, and Robert Wilson also converged on Pranjane over the course of several months, along with hundreds of other airmen. They all had been shot down over Yugoslavia, bailing out of their bombers and landing in the arms of the local Chetniks. Each was greeted like a long-lost brother and then assigned to a group, the hundreds of airmen divided informally to facilitate housing assignments in the local village and the assignment of some small tasks. They all had similar stories to tell when they straggled into the remote mountain village and were assigned to stay with different farm families. Tony Orsini regaled the Americans with the story of how he received three marriage proposals along the way, including one from the daughter of a local brewery owner who was very insistent that the young Italian-American take his daughter back to the United States with him. Noting that the girl would have made a better linebacker than a wife, Orsini politely declined.

Once they arrived in Pranjane, the Americans had plenty of time on their hands. There was little to do except stay out of sight of any Germans that might pass by, but thanks to the remote mountainous location and the nearly ten thousand Mihailovich soldiers surrounding Pranjane, German units rarely ventured into this territory. Still, the Americans were always ready to sprint into the woods or bury themselves in a haystack if someone shouted that Germans were coming, or if a German plane flew overhead. The Americans were keenly aware that their presence put all the local villagers in danger, so they didn't want to be spotted and invite a brutal German retaliation on these locals who were being so generous. Most of the Americans spent their days idly in the villages, whittling corncob pipes and smoking whatever locally grown tobacco they could find. They all rued the fact that the normal source of tobacco in Yugoslavia, a city to the south called Nis, had been bombed. The airmen watched the locals go about their humble daily routines, learning how to bake bread by putting the dough on a plate in the fireplace, covering it with an overturned bowl and then heaping hot ashes on top. They also pitched in with the local villagers as they worked the fields, sometimes joining in what the locals called "mass work," in which many residents would work on one farmer's fields at the same time to get the season's work done. Then they would move on to the next farmer's fields, each grateful landowner thanking them with a celebratory meal—or the closest that could be provided under the circumstances—when the work was complete. Even on the best days, the food was always simple: whole-grain bread, cheese, milk, maybe some butter, and mixed root vegetables. Any sort of meat was a rarity, but it would always be offered first to the Americans. The one thing that could always be counted on was plum brandy. Plum trees covered this part of the country, growing wild and heavy with fruit, so even the poorest household had its own still for making plum brandy and plenty of casks to get them through to the next spring when the trees would be full again. The villagers and the airmen might have been hungry most of the time, but their cups were always full.

Occasionally as they worked in the fields or lay around waiting for something to happen, the airmen would see squadrons of bombers flying overhead, more planes from the Fifteenth Air Force in Italy, their own home bases. First they would hear the rumble in the distance and then the sound would get louder and louder as the big planes flew over, prompting the airmen and the villagers to whoop and holler, cheering the Allied planes on. But each flight of bombers made the airmen grow wistful as well, the planes so close but so out of reach and then disappearing into the distance without them. They also knew that every time they saw another dozen planes on their way to Ploesti, a few of those crews would soon be joining them in Pranjane.

**While most of the airmen** stayed in Pranjane and grew more and more bored, others, like Felman, wanted to get back in the fight. Felman, who quickly emerged as a de facto leader of the downed airmen gathering in Pranjane, made more contacts with the Chetnik fighters in the area and convinced them that he could be an asset to their work against the Nazis.

Relying on his growing familiarity with the local language, Felman joined Mihailovich's forces in conducting sabotage against the Germans. Felman had been moved by Colonel Vasić's description of the Chetniks' determination to fight against overwhelming odds, and his encounters with the local people motivated him to help in any way. He could not sit idly by while these people risked their lives for him and his fellow airmen.

Sabotage, especially the very careful use of certain types that were hard to trace, was a key element in the Chetniks' fight against the Germans occupying their homeland. Though they were not overly sentimental about losing their lives in defense of their country, the Serbs had learned early on in the Nazi occupation that skirmishes with German patrols and open defiance resulted only in a disproportionate response from their enemy. Shooting a few German soldiers who wandered into Mihailovich's territory might prompt a bloody raid on an entire village, and sneaking into a rail yard to blow up a Nazi supply train might lead to dozens of innocent Serbs being hung from the light poles as a warning against further uprising. The Chetniks were not discouraged from fighting, however. They just had to fight smarter, and they taught Felman what they had learned.

Felman and Stefanovic joined six other guerillas on a dark night, working their way quietly through the woods to a railway station farther down the mountainside. A railway worker had risked his life by informing Mihailovich's forces that a train loaded with food was leaving the next morning for German units stationed in Romania. The eight men carefully made their way to the station, stopping at the edge of the woods and scanning the area for German guards. Few were out at that hour, but all of the men were armed and ready to fight if necessary. They lay low and watched for a while, making sure the train yard was quiet before carrying out their objective. Once the Chetnik soldiers were confident that a German guard would not surprise them, the youngest of them—a fifteen-year-old boy with more experience in sabotage than Felman would ever know—scurried out of the wood line and to the train parked on a siding. As Felman and the others watched from the distance, the boy hid among the big engine's wheels for a moment, making sure he had not been seen, and then he clambered up onto the coal tender directly behind the engine. He quickly pushed aside the top layer of coal, digging down as far as his arms could reach, and then he pulled a small black package out of his coat. He shoved this parcel down into the hole and raked the coal back over it, covering it completely. Taking a quick look around before jumping off the tender, the young man raced back to the wood line, where the men greeted him with whispered congratulations for a job well done. The saboteur was covered in coal dust, his smile showing clearly against his black skin.

The group turned to leave, and Felman at first thought they were only going back into the woods a short distance for more safety, since the Germans would be on high alert after the train blew up. But as they kept moving, Felman asked his friend Stefanovic why they were not waiting to make sure the train blew up.

"No, not now," Stefanovic whispered, using a few words of English that Felman had taught him. Then he said something in Serbian that Felman couldn't understand and motioned with his hands to show the train leaving and then—*boom!*—blowing up. It was then that Felman understood. This was delayed sabotage. The bomb the boy hid in the coal tender wasn't intended to blow up now, while the train was still in the station, because then the Germans would know it was the local Serbs who did it and they would exact revenge. The explosive was hidden deep in the coal tender so that later, long after the train had left Pranjane, the train's fireman would unknowingly shovel it directly into the boiler of the engine. The fire would set off the explosive, the train would be destroyed, and it would not be obvious to the Germans how it happened or who did it.

Ingenious, Felman thought. As he went out on more sabotage runs with the Chetniks, he learned other ways to sabotage the Germans without inviting a bloodbath. One favorite method was to discreetly pour sand into the engines of German vehicles. The damage would be delayed but crippling to the machinery.

Felman's work helped him blend in seamlessly with the local people, and after months on the ground, he started to look like one too. His clothes were in tatters and constantly filthy, and he wore pieces of gear that his Chetnik friends had offered him along the way. He fit in so well that the Chetniks were comfortable taking him along when they went into nearby towns without weapons or anything else that would identify them as Mihailovich's soldiers. They weren't looking to engage any Germans they might encounter, so they assumed the role of local villagers instead of soldiers. Felman was with a group of Chetnik fighters one day when they decided to go into a nearby town for a drink, taking off their rifles and knives before marching down to the tavern for some rest and recreation. (Felman always carried his military insignia patch inside his shirt, however. If he were caught by the Germans, that patch might count as him being "in uniform" and deserving of protection under the Geneva convention as a prisoner of war. Otherwise, he could be considered an enemy combatant in civilian clothes, classified as a spy and shot dead on the spot. It was all theoretical, of course, because the Nazis weren't sticklers for following the rules.) They'd had a few drinks already when they heard a car pull up outside. The sound of a vehicle was alarming in itself, because few locals had a car. That sound usually meant Germans were coming. As the group peered outside, they could see a German staff car stopped and a young officer about to come inside. The driver stayed with the car.

Felman and his friends were worried, the American most of all. The other Chetniks could pass easily if they didn't want to cause a ruckus with this Nazi officer, but Felman suddenly doubted his camouflage. *Do I look like a Serb? Or do I look like a Jew from New York?*

He found out soon enough when the young officer, who appeared to want nothing more than a brandy, said hello to the men sitting at the tables. They all nodded in reply, wary but not wanting to provoke the German's suspicions. Realizing that the officer suspected nothing, and feeling a bit cheeky about his deception, Felman gestured for the lieutenant to join them and pushed a chair out for him. He glanced over at his friends, whose eyes showed that they thought he was mad. Stefanovic, in particular, looked like he was about to leap out of his chair, and Felman wasn't sure who would be throttled first—Felman or the Nazi. The German accepted the offer and sat down for a drink, not saying a lot because of the language barrier, but enjoying his brandy. He insisted on buying another round for the table, even though the Chetniks tried to decline because they wanted him to leave as soon as possible. Felman, however, was enjoying the moment, relishing this face-to-face deception. He smiled congenially at the Nazi, who seemed at the moment like a pleasant drinking companion. But Felman was seething inside.

*Here you have a Jew you can't throw into the gas chamber,* he thought. After a long, uncomfortable interlude, the lieutenant finished his drink and left, saying something that sounded friendly to Felman and the others. When he had left, the men all let out heavy sighs and rolled their eyes at one another, amazed that they had just shared brandy with a German officer.

Felman had not been fooled by the German lieutenant's apparent good nature. Despite the Chetniks' efforts to avoid needless acts of retribution from the Germans, Nazi brutality invaded their lives regularly. One incident in particular reinforced for Felman how much the local villagers were risking by harboring so many American airmen—now more than a hundred—around Pranjane.

Colonel Vasić, the debonair officer that Felman had met soon after landing in Yugoslavia, came to him one day and explained a difficult situation to him. As the leader of the downed airmen in Pranjane, he said, Felman should know that the Germans had delivered an ultimatum to Mihailovich. Hand over the American airmen you are hiding, they said, or we will raid a Serb village and kill all two hundred men, women, and children.

Felman was appalled. How could they even consider letting those people die? He started telling Vasić that he and the other men would surrender and take their chances in a German prison camp—even though it was entirely possible that the Germans would simply kill them on the spot—but Vasić quickly cut him off. Speaking through an interpreter, he explained that he was not asking Felman to decide but merely informing him about the situation. Mihailovich would not give up the Americans; it was not their choice to make.

"But we can't let those people die in our place," Felman protested.

"Understand that the Germans will not stop killing because they capture you," Vasić explained. "In our history, the Serb people have fought for our freedom and dignity against many enemies. We have learned that it is better to live with one leg than to spend your life on your knees. It is more important that we protect you, the people who have helped us fight our common enemy."

Felman protested further, but Vasić would not be swayed. The next day, Felman insisted that Stefanovic take him to the village that had been threatened. As they approached, he could smell the burning wood before he saw the remains of the village. The Nazis had burned it to the ground and killed everyone. Felman could only stand on the hillside and weep.

## Chapter 6

# *Escaping Yugoslavia*

**The airmen spent days, weeks, months waiting for help,** hoping they wouldn't be found by the Germans and trying to figure out a way to escape from enemy territory. They concluded that there just weren't many options, and so they became steadily more depressed about their situation.

General Mihailovich, who came to Pranjane to meet with the American airmen more than once, was well aware of the men's festering depression and the reality that there appeared to be no effort by the Allies to rescue them. In addition to protecting them during their stay in Yugoslavia, Mihailovich was doing all he could to get the men home. He was sending information to the United States through indirect channels, making sure the U.S. government knew these men were here, that he was helping them, and that he would assist with any proposed rescue attempt. While Mihailovich truly cared about the airmen and their welfare, he also saw the potential for more aid from the Allies in his effort to fight the Nazis and Communist Josip Broz Tito, his opponent in the simultaneous civil war that threatened to tear the country apart. Mihailovich knew that helping the Allied airmen get home could lead to more support for his men, who were barely surviving on minimal food rations, old and insufficient arms, and ragged clothes. Many of his men, fierce fighters, had to make do in the cold mountainside with only felt slippers or boots so worn that their bare feet touched the ground more than what was left of the soles of the boots.

In the months that he had been harboring the downed airmen, Mihailovich had been diligently sending information about each one by shortwave radio so that the Allies would know they were in safe hands. He even got messages to some of the airmen's families, assuring them that their loved ones were safe for the moment. Part of Mihailovich's concern was that the families of the airmen not be informed that they were simply "missing in action," because he knew that would only inspire worry. It was reasonable to assume that a loved one reported as missing in action was dead, or at least captured, so Mihailovich thought he was doing a favor by letting the Allies know that these men were relatively safe in the hills of Yugoslavia. Mihailovich had his men send shortwave radio messages on a regular basis, reporting the name, rank, and military identification number of each airman his men had collected. The messages went first to the Yugoslav government, which was operating in exile in Cairo, Egypt, and from there they were sent to Konstantin Fotić, the ambassador of Yugoslavia stationed in Washington, DC. In one message, Mihailovich said:

> Please advise the American Air Ministry that there are more than one hundred American aviators in our midst. We notified the English Supreme Command for the Mediterranean a long time ago. The English replied that they would send an officer to take care of the evacuation. Meanwhile, to date this has not been done. It would be better still if the Americans, and not the British, take part in the evacuation.

Fotić delivered the information to the War Department, with assurances that Mihailovich was protecting the men for the moment, but also requesting that something be done to rescue them; the situation was grave, and there was no telling how long the airmen could last before the Germans found out where they were gathered. The information was dutifully received and recorded, but little else was done. No rescue was planned. Most of the airmen's relatives were not notified that the airmen were alive and in good hands. They received the standard "missing in action" telegram like everyone else whose husband or son went down over enemy territory, the same one that Orsini's mother received.

**With the War Department sitting** on the information and making no effort to organize a rescue, the lives of the airmen fell into the hands of a sophisticated, learned, beautiful blond woman in Washington, DC. If only the airmen had known that such a brainy beauty back home knew of their plight and was worried for them. That simple knowledge would have made another day pass more easily.

The woman was Mirjana Vujnovich, a lady in the Eastern European tradition—gracious, proper, and conservative, but at the same time warm, generous, and funny. While she was outspoken with family and close friends, she was reserved in public. Slender, with fine features and lively deep blue eyes, her blond hair worn in a modest shoulder-length style, Mirjana always caught the attention of young men who soon found there was much more to this gentle woman than her good looks. Mirjana was a great listener, skilled at drawing people out by listening intently, asking the right questions, and offering support. Her great passions, after her family, were literature and the arts.

Mirjana was married to George Vujnovich, the control agent with the OSS in Bari, Italy. George was a tall, ruggedly handsome man, an all-American son of immigrants who seemed custom-built to look good in a uniform. The OSS was, in essence, home of the spies and secret operatives that got things done behind enemy lines. They did whatever was necessary, using trickery, subterfuge, exotic weapons, and nerves of steel to slip in among the enemy and accomplish things that might be impossible for an entire battalion of soldiers to do. From the post in Bari, in the recently liberated Italy, Vujnovich was responsible for operations in several nearby countries, including Yugoslavia. Mirjana knew what her husband did for the military, even though most OSS officers kept their job description close to the vest. Mirjana was more than just an adoring wife waiting back home for her husband serving overseas, though she was that too. A native of Yugoslavia herself, she had been through plenty with George and knew some of what he and the men serving under him were going through in Europe.

In May 1944, however, Mirjana was safely ensconced in Washington, DC. Eight and a half months pregnant with their first child, Mirjana had little contact with her husband other than the occasional letter and spent her days with friends, including the other Yugoslav nationals who had immigrated to the United States. With a job at the Yugoslavian embassy, Mirjana was able to adjust well to a more comfortable, safe life in the United States, while still maintaining contact with the people and the culture of her homeland. It was through those contacts that she heard about the plight of the downed airmen halfway around the world. The community of Yugoslav expatriates was a tight one, and news from back home spread through the group quickly. When the embassy received reports from General Mihailovich about the hundreds of downed airmen hidden in the countryside, the news raced through the hallways. As it became clear that the War Department was not responding quickly to the notice, the plight of the American airmen became fodder for gossip every time a few Yugoslav immigrants got together for coffee in the morning or a drink in the evening. *I hear Mihailovich is helping some airmen in the hills, a lot of them.* Word of the airmen's situation, sketchy as the information was by the time it was filtered down from officials in the embassy, spread quickly among anyone with a connection to Yugoslavia. *All those boys are waiting for help. Mihailovich is protecting them. But the War Department isn't doing anything.*

Mirjana's friends knew that her husband was serving with a military group in Italy that was more than just a typical unit, so they wasted no time in getting the news to her. She was intrigued, just like everyone else who heard the story, and wondered why no one was doing anything to help the downed airmen. The next time she wrote George in Bari, she asked about the rumor she had heard, more as idle chitchat from back home than any sort of urgent request.

*There is plenty of talk here about the men whose planes were shot down in Yugoslavia, and how Draza Mihailovich is helping them until they can be rescued. I hear that there are perhaps a hundred gathered in one place. Are you involved in trying to get them out?*

Mirjana didn't really expect an answer from George. She knew that he couldn't and wouldn't write back with any information about OSS operations, but she was making conversation with her husband as best she could. And she was genuinely curious nonetheless, so she asked just to get it off her mind.

When George Vujnovich received the letter from Mirjana, his first concern was her pregnancy and whether there was anything new to report in that regard. He was pleased to hear that all was fine with his first child and he would soon be a father, though it pained him that he would not be there for the birth of his daughter, to be named Xenia. Among all the other news from home in Mirjana's letter, her offhand comment about the men in Yugoslavia was the one that stayed with him as he put the letter away and went about the rest of his day. He kept thinking about that question. He hadn't even heard about this particular group of downed airmen awaiting rescue, and he was in a position to know more about such matters than most people in the military. It was no surprise to him that there were downed airmen in Yugoslavia, of course; it was common knowledge that plenty of fliers had gone down in that region while on Ploesti bomb runs, and the OSS knew that some had survived and were evading capture.

*But a hundred airmen all in one place, waiting for rescue? Could Mirjana's information be right?*

Reports from OSS agents in the field had made it clear that any airman stranded in Yugoslavia was in dire straits. One agent reported finding a half-starved B-24 tail gunner who had been shot down in the first raid on Ploesti. He was discovered rooting around in a farmer's pigsty, fighting the animals for bits of rancid food. Another agent reported that two fighter pilots had been hidden in a convent, only to be discovered by Germans when their army-issued boots protruded from underneath the long black habits supplied by the nuns. Other agents reported finding injured American airmen hidden and tended by peasants in the hillside.

A year earlier, General Nathan Twining, commander of the Fifteenth Air Force, organized a joint rescue effort for the airmen known to be in Yugoslavia, using the resources of the air force and the OSS agents already at work behind enemy lines in the occupied country. The OSS agents delivered escape maps to the downed airmen that would point them toward friendly areas where they could be picked up and with safe houses marked along the route. Agents also provided the Yugoslav villagers, almost all of them illiterate, with posters showing how to recognize Allied planes and the insignia of the friendly forces. With OSS agents providing covert organization on the ground and air force planes making taxi runs, about a hundred fliers had been rescued in 1943. The effort was aided by both Mihailovich's Chetnik forces and Tito's Partisans, in the last year before those two sides erupted into an all-out civil war. Vujnovich knew any such rescue would be even more difficult now, with those two sides fighting each other as bitterly as either fought the Germans.

The OSS and the air force had both performed admirably in the 1943 rescues, but if there were a hundred fliers waiting for rescue this year, why hadn't he heard about it? If they were being protected by Mihailovich, could they be organized enough to effect a real rescue? Vujnovich was intrigued by this curious question from home, and he had to find out if there was a job here for his OSS team.

*If there are a hundred men in Yugoslavia waiting for us to do something, we've got to get going. I've got to see if Mirjana is right.*

**Vujnovich was driven by more** than just professionalism or a dedication to duty. Vujnovich instantly felt a bond with the Americans stuck behind enemy lines in Yugoslavia because he had been there himself only a few years earlier. Vujnovich had never flown a plane or served behind enemy lines, but he had spent plenty of time in Nazi territory, and he sympathized with the airmen in a way that no one else in the OSS could.

A Pittsburgh native of Yugoslav descent, Vujnovich had been visiting

Yugoslavia as a student when the war broke out, leaving him trapped behind German lines. He spent the next two years trying to get out of occupied territory and to safety, and if Mirjana's rumor was true, he knew the danger these Americans were in. He also was proud to know that the local villagers, the people of his family's homeland, were safeguarding these men until he could get them out.

Vujnovich had grown up as an all-American boy in Pittsburgh, but in the same Serbian-American community that now embraced his wife, Mirjana. Vujnovich's parents had emigrated to the United States from Yugoslavia years earlier, and like many others from there who spoke no English, they settled in a labor-intensive part of the country—in their case Pittsburgh, with its steel mills. His father had arrived in 1912, immigrating to the United States from his village near Ogalen, close to Zagreb. Used to a hardscrabble life in the countryside, he was being pressured by authorities to join the Austrian army, and chose a new life in America instead. Two years later Vujnovich's mother joined him. Vujnovich estimated that about half of the south side of Pittsburgh—where they lived—was of Serbian descent, and his father worked in the steel mill with men who had grown up in the same village in Yugoslavia. The neighborhood stores had signs in Cyrillic Serbian and it was as common to hear the Serbian language in the streets as it was to hear English. Vujnovich grew up speaking both languages with his parents and his brother, Peter, and sister, Mary.

When Vujnovich graduated from high school in 1934, he had no notion of even joining the military, much less becoming a top officer in the country's premier spy agency. His parents wanted him to become a doctor, and though Vujnovich originally wanted to become an engineer, he had to admit that his math skills were not up to par. The binomial theorem was too much for him. So the thought of becoming a doctor started to sound more appealing. There was still a big problem, though. The son of a steel mill worker in Pittsburgh would find it difficult to pay for medical school in the United States, so Vujnovich considered another opportunity that his parents suggested: Go to study in Yugoslavia. Go back to our homeland. See the country where your family comes from.

Get to know the country that we left so we could give you a better life in the United States.

The more Vujnovich looked into the idea, the more he liked it. In the Yugoslav system, he would start studying medicine right away instead of first getting an undergraduate degree. And as he talked about the idea with his friends, he learned that there was a scholarship that could make it all possible. The Serbian National Federation, a group organized by immigrants like his own parents, offered scholarships for young Serbian Americans to go back to Yugoslavia to study. The Federation wanted to keep these young American-born Serbs connected to the homeland of their parents, fearing that without a special effort to show them the culture of Yugoslavia the connection would be lost in two generations. In the same year that Vujnovich decided this was a great opportunity, so did eight others from around the country. The Serbian National Federation provided full scholarships for study in Belgrade, transportation across the Atlantic, and a stipend of twenty-five dollars per month. Vujnovich's parents explained to him that this was an extreme blessing for him, one that he could not possibly appreciate as an American-born young man who had never known hunger.

"Twenty-five dollars a month, George," his father said to him in Serbian, shaking his head as if he just could not believe his son was so fortunate. "That is so much. That is enough to keep a family of five in Yugoslavia. You can get a dinner, a very good dinner, for five dinars. The exchange rate is *fifty dinars* to the dollar, George. *Fifty.*"

The son of a Pittsburgh steel-mill worker was going back to his parents' home country to study and live a life they could have only dreamed of when they set sail for America. The Vujnovich family saw George's departure as fulfillment of the American dream, the proof that if a poor Yugoslav couple came to this country and worked hard, their children could reap unimaginable benefits. His parents were thrilled to think of him boarding the *Majestic*, at the time the largest ship in the world, part of the White Star line that had sailed the *Titanic* only a few years earlier. Like its ill-fated predecessor, the fifty-six-thousand-ton *Majestic* was a magnificent sight with her three tall funnels and long black hull, the interior filled with stately dining rooms, lounges, and libraries milled of expensive wood and fine fabrics.

His parents relished the thought that Vujnovich was traveling in comfort, going to a promising future, not as one of hundreds of immigrants packed in steerage, fleeing poverty, war, and hunger.

**The *Majestic* docked in Cherbourg,** France, where the American boys boarded a train to Paris and then on to Belgrade, arriving in mid-September 1934. They found a city that, much like any other European capital, was steeped in a rich and colorful history that included war, occupation by other countries, and myriad hardships. But by the time the Americans arrived, Belgrade was on the upswing, gaining recognition as a cultural cornucopia and a center of higher education. After the occupation by Austro-Hungarian and German troops from 1915 to 1918 during World War I, Belgrade experienced faster growth and significant modernization as the capital of the new Kingdom of Yugoslavia during the 1920s and 1930s, growing in population to 239,000 by 1931. Located at the confluence of the Sava and Danube rivers, Belgrade is one of the oldest cities in Europe and since ancient times it has been an important traffic focal point, an intersection of the roads of Eastern and Western Europe.

Vujnovich and his companions were amazed by what they found in Belgrade. Their parents had talked a lot about the old country, but most of them knew the tiny villages of Yugoslavia more than they knew the metropolitan centers like Belgrade. The Americans found themselves in an exotic big city and they couldn't wait to explore. They enrolled in the University of Belgrade as planned and then they immediately set out to confirm every image that Europeans had of wild, ill-mannered Americans. Flush with cash and with very few worries, they ran wild in Belgrade, a cosmopolitan European city that offered plenty in the way of bars, restaurants, and cafés where the young men could spend their money and wile away the evening. A typical night found them drinking wine and singing at a *kafana,* an establishment common in the Balkans that served primarily alcohol and coffee, often with a live band. Not quite a restaurant but not exactly a bar, the *kafana* was a perfect place for the boys to drink and flirt with the singers in the band. The Americans would invite a few Serbian friends to join them, and the dozen or so would inevitably create a scene when they went out, even appearing in the newspaper occasionally, such as the time when one of the group stole a hansom cab pulled by two horses. The chase went on until the horses were too tired to keep running from the furious cab driver. Vujnovich enjoyed the good times as much as anyone else, but he was the self-described teetotaler in the bunch, preferring to watch his friends get drunk and foolish while he counted up how many bottles of wine the group had gone through that night.

The rowdy group of Americans was hard to miss in Belgrade, especially for the other students at the university. They were well liked, though also seen as the bad boys on campus sometimes. The fact that they were from America, not to mention that they had plenty of money to throw around, made them interesting to the other students, and so they had no problem socializing as much as they wanted. Much of their time was spent at the Anglo-American Club on campus, a hangout for American and British students and the locals who found them appealing. The club was located across the street from the old Yugoslav palace, and its comfortable lounges, full of rich wood and luxurious furniture, made a fine place for the Americans to make the acquaintance of any Yugoslavs who might find them interesting. It was there on a November night in 1935, not too long after he arrived in Yugoslavia, that George Vujnovich met Mirjana Lazic for the first time. It was a Thanksgiving celebration and the room was crowded.

The Americans had invited Mirjana and several of her friends to their club that evening, ostensibly so the two groups could improve their language skills. Mirjana wanted to improve her English and the Americans wanted to improve their Serbian. They had realized that the Serbian they learned around the dinner table back home was a little rough when used daily in Yugoslavia. But both groups knew that there was more at issue than language skills.

When he first saw Mirjana across the room, Vujnovich had the same reaction as every other young man who met her. She was beautiful.

He had another reaction, too. He knew from that first moment that she was the woman he wanted to marry. Vujnovich couldn't settle on exactly what drew him in so quickly. It might have been her blue eyes, her lovely voice, or her quiet, dignified demeanor. He even liked the way she stood. And her dress. And the way she wore her hair.

*That's the girl for me. I have to get to know this girl.*

Vujnovich fell for Mirjana hard, like nothing he had ever experienced before. He had no idea that, like many of the people in Yugoslavia, Mirjana had already been through a lot in her young life. Her father had been interned by the Austrians in connection with the assassination of Archduke Ferdinand of Austria in 1914, which had set the wheels in motion for World War I. Though he was not actively involved in the assassination, he was in Sarajevo, Yugoslavia, at the time of the assassination and was an unabashed supporter of Young Bosnia, the political group responsible for the killing. Her father returned to their home in Novi Sad, a Serbian village on the Danube River, after the war ended and then moved his family to Belgrade for a better job. The family did well in Belgrade and Mirjana entered the university at the same time as Vujnovich. A learned woman already, Mirjana spoke Serbian, English, German, and French, and she taught languages in addition to her own studies.

Vujnovich immediately struck up a conversation with Mirjana. She found him handsome and interesting, but she thought he had some wild friends. She gave the Pittsburgh boy a chance, drawn by his playful, engaging demeanor. But then he went too far with his American-style familiarity. He offered to take her home that evening and she told him, in English that was crystal clear in both pronunciation and meaning, that such a suggestion was out of line, an insult to a young woman he had only just met.

"I'm a professor at a high school for girls, and if anyone saw me walking in the evening with a strange man, there would be talk," she explained. "I don't want people to talk about me."

Vujnovich understood that he had been too eager, falling back on his American sensibilities and forgetting where he was. He was disappointed that he had blown his chance with this beautiful woman and could only watch her march off.

He would not see Mirjana again for four years. In the intervening years, Mirjana's mother died and she received a scholarship to study in Cambridge, England, for six months. After returning to Yugoslavia, she settled again in Belgrade.

By 1939 Vujnovich and his friends had settled down somewhat, becoming more serious students and less the rowdy Americans. So when he saw Mirjana again one night at the Anglo-American Club, he thought he might have a chance to make things right. This time he would proceed very slowly. He spoke to her gently, politely, and briefly, making no effort to monopolize her time at the club. But he watched carefully and, when she showed an interest in ping-pong, so did Vujnovich. When she wanted to play bridge, so did he. They slowly became well acquainted and after two months Vujnovich very carefully suggested one evening that he might walk her home. He braced for the same retort as before, but this time Mirjana said yes.

As they walked slowly for three miles along the Milosavelikog, a large boulevard leading to her home, Vujnovich made small talk until he thought the moment was right to say what he'd been thinking for a while.

"I remember when I saw you the first time, years ago. It was 1935," he said.

She looked at him as if he were crazy. Just as he had suspected for the past two months, she had no memory of their first meeting. "What? I never saw you before in my life, not before a couple months ago."

"I saw you in 1935," he said. "At the club." He then proceeded to describe exactly what Mirjana looked like that first night—the color of her dress, her brown shoes, how she wore her hair, the way she stood. He said it as if it had been running through his mind for four years, and it had. Mirjana was touched that he remembered. She was moved by how he described this vision, standing there on the boulevard with her. Vujnovich had already fallen in love with this beautiful local girl, and now she was falling in love with the tall, handsome American. They dated through

1939 and 1940, a happy time when there was little to concern them except their studies and each other. Then everything changed in 1941.


**Prior to 1941 it was** easy for George Vujnovich and Mirjana Lazic to ignore the gathering cloud of Nazism even though it was just over the horizon from Belgrade. They were young university students and they were in love. For Vujnovich especially, it was hard to imagine that war could intrude on this wonderful time in his life because he came from the American mind-set in which tanks rolling through the streets and armies invading your home were something that happened "over there." The problem was that Vujnovich was over there. He was in Belgrade, in the path of the advancing German armies, and all signs pointed to trouble ahead for Yugoslavia. Vujnovich was aware of what was happening in the rest of Europe, but he was not involved in politics and found it hard to believe this beautiful city could be overrun. Others around him were more worried. Some of his American and British friends were making plans to leave before things got worse. The assistant professor of anatomy at the university, however, was German and tried to convince Vujnovich that if Germany invaded Yugoslavia, the Serb people should not resist. His name was Mueller. "Go among your friends and tell them," he urged Vujnovich. "Tell them that the Germans will not be oppressive if they do not resist."

Vujnovich did not believe the instructor, and his entreaties made him only more concerned, not less. In the early months of 1941 the dominoes fell quickly, and suddenly German troops were in Bulgaria, Romania, and Austria. Yugoslavia was next in line. As many knew would be inevitable, Yugoslavia went from peace to horror in just a few quick steps. Politicians in the country tried to keep Yugoslavia neutral as they saw Hitler advancing across Europe, but the task became more challenging with each of Hitler's victories. Unable to compete militarily with Hitler's forces, Yugoslavia faced two possibilities: Either bow before Hitler, or resist him, relying upon support from Western powers. The decision rested with Yugoslavia's Prince Paul, who had taken leadership of the country in 1934, after King Alexander's assassination in Marseille. Prince Paul was a forty-one-year-old cousin of the king and called on to rule the country because King Alexander's son, Peter II, was only eleven years old. Prince Paul was pressured by his advisers to make a deal with Hitler in hopes of favorable treatment, and he eventually acquiesced, signing the Tripartite Pact with the World War II Axis Powers in Vienna on March 25, 1941. By signing the pact, Yugoslavia officially became part of the Axis along with Germany, Japan, and Italy. But the prince never intended to join the Axis aggression in Europe. Rather he was only trying to spare his country the barbarism he knew the Nazis would bring if the Yugoslavian people resisted.

The people of his country did not agree with the prince's effort, preferring to face down the German invaders than join them, even in name only. Prince Paul's decision prompted massive demonstrations in Belgrade and other cities. When the Axis Pact was revealed to the people, they protested in the streets, chanting, *"Belje rat; nego pakt!"* which meant "War instead of a pact; death instead of slavery." Vujnovich and Lazic could see people marching in the streets around the university, shouting condemnations of the prince and showering flowers on the Serbian troops who had been sent to maintain order. The protesters made their intentions clear, that they supported the country's army but not its appeasing prince.

Vujnovich watched as his bucolic student life was turned upside down. German-owned shops were destroyed, windows broken in the homes of German residents. Anyone with a German name was afraid to go out on the street. Vujnovich couldn't believe what he was witnessing. He considered just leaving, heading home to Pittsburgh. He and his American friends thought it was fascinating to see these events unfolding in front of their eyes, but they didn't feel it concerned them. They were Americans; this wasn't their war. They just happened to be there witnessing the world change, and they could leave when they wanted.

But what about Mirjana? He had fallen madly in love with this local girl, and she would not be able to leave the country with her Yugoslav passport. Vujnovich's American passport was a free ticket home, but he couldn't bear to leave behind the blond beauty who had captured his heart from across the room at a party and occupied his thoughts for almost four years until he saw her again. So he stayed longer than he should have. Vujnovich was thinking about this at the club that evening when he again ran into Mueller, the assistant anatomy professor who had assured him the German invaders would be benevolent. The warning was more stern this time: "You can't do that," the man said, looking out on the broken shop fronts. "You people are going to suffer."

Things kept moving so quickly that it was hard for Vujnovich to keep up with each day's progress. Only two days after the pact was signed, on March 27, 1941, Peter II, now seventeen years old, was proclaimed of age and took the throne as King of Yugoslavia. He immediately supported a group of pro-English officers and middle-class politicians in executing a coup d'état on the same day, and Air Force General Dušan Simović became prime minister. Yugoslavia backed out of the Axis in all but name.

The new rulers opposed Germany, but like Prince Paul, they acknowledged the overwhelming power of the enemy. They feared that if Hitler attacked Yugoslavia, the United Kingdom, their strongest ally, was not in any real position to help. For the safety of the country, they declared that Yugoslavia would adhere to the Tripartite Pact.

Westerners praised Yugoslavia as an exception among the neighboring nations who had capitulated and accepted Hitler's terms, congratulating the country's people on standing up to resist the German hordes. But the West could offer little other than words of encouragement. The people of Yugoslavia were buoyed by the success of their uprising, but the joy would not last long. On the evening of April 5 Vujnovich was at the Anglo-American Club and ran into Mueller again. The German instructor's mood was grim, as were the moods of most in the room despite the copious flow of alcohol.

"Something's going to happen," Mueller told Vujnovich. "Something bad. Please tell people not to do these things. Don't provoke Germany."

Vujnovich didn't pay any attention to Mueller, chalking up the comments to the wine and a dour personality. He went home and went to bed, expecting to go to class the next day. Instead he woke up at six a.m. to his apartment building shaking and the sound of bombs falling. He raced to the window and threw back the curtains, squinting in the morning sun. He was stunned to see planes directly over the city, dropping bombs by the hundreds.

This American from the south side of Pittsburgh was watching Hitler's response to the previous weeks' events. When Hitler first heard of the coup d'état and the country's attempt to withdraw from the Axis, he thought it was a joke. When he realized the people of Yugoslavia had defied his will, Hitler became infuriated at the country's resistance and decided to destroy Yugoslavia, ordering his staff to carry out his orders "with unmerciful harshness." The German *Luftwaffe* started by raining hell down on an unarmed, defenseless city. British Prime Minister Winston Churchill described what happened next:

> On the morning of April 6 German bombers appeared over Belgrade. Flying in relays from occupied airfields in Romania, they delivered a methodical attack lasting three days upon the Yugoslav capital. From rooftop height, without fear of resistance, they blasted the city without mercy. This was called "Operation Punishment." When silence came at last on April 8, over seventeen thousand citizens of Belgrade lay dead in the streets or under debris. Out of the nightmare of smoke and fire came the maddened animals released from their shattered cages in zoological gardens. A stricken stork hobbled past the main hotel, which was a mass of flames. A bear, dazed and uncomprehending, shuffled through the inferno with slow and awkward gait down towards the Danube. He was not the only bear who did not understand.

The royal family escaped abroad. King Peter II went with his government to Greece, then to Jerusalem, the British Mandate of Palestine, and Cairo, Egypt, eventually landing in England in June 1941. There he joined numerous other governments in exile from Nazi-occupied Europe. The king completed his education at Cambridge University and joined the Royal Air Force. For the remainder of the war, Prince Paul and his family remained under house arrest by the British in South Africa.

**When he could pull himself** away from the incredible sight at the window, Vujnovich raced down to the basement of the building in his pajamas, joining dozens of men, women, and children there. Everyone screamed and cried, the wails increasing with each bomb blast that shook the building. But in the chaos, there were elderly Serbian men who were calmly smoking their pipes and comforting the others, reassuring them, saying over and over, "Your time has not come. This will be over in a few minutes." Their soothing manner calmed the crowd and Vujnovich realized these men probably had lived through several wars in their lifetimes. He was impressed by their demeanor, and used it to overcome his own terror. Once he was calmer, he decided he had to find his beloved Mirjana.

Vujnovich raced back up to his apartment, glad to see that the building had not yet taken a direct hit. Bombs continued falling all around the city, terrible explosions thundering and debris flying like rain in a summer storm. He put on some clothes and grabbed a few essentials; then he ran to Mirjana's house about three miles away, praying the whole way that he would not find it a pile of rubble. Vujnovich ran as fast as he could, through crowds of panic-stricken people, no one seeming to know where to go or what to do. His heart was pumping wildly, his senses nearly overwhelmed by the sounds of bombs and people screaming, the smell of burning buildings and the sight of those who had been caught in the explosions. As he ran down a street and tried to stay close to the buildings for cover, Vujnovich witnessed a scene that would be burned into his memory for the rest of his life. As he ran, his eyes fell on a streetcar packed full of people, its driver moving as fast as he could and not stopping, presumably trying to get his passengers out of the city and to a safer place. Vujnovich's eyes were on the streetcar when it took a direct hit from a falling bomb. The streetcar and the dozens of people inside exploded in a bloody mess of body parts and metal, limbs flying through the air and landing all around Vujnovich. He was momentarily stunned, not just by the explosion but by the terrible sight before him. As he regained himself, there was nothing he could do but to keep running.

About two hours after the bombing started, the planes disappeared and the explosions ceased. Vujnovich hoped the bombing was over, but this actually was just the lull between German bombing runs. Just as he got to Mirjanas's house and was elated to see that her home was still standing, the bombs began to fall again. Vujnovich ran through the front door, shouting Mirjana's name and looking quickly through the home. Then he went to the basement, where he hoped she would be hiding. He found Mirjana and her brother, Mirko, there, embraced them both and then huddled in a corner with them, all three terrified that a German bomb might end their lives at any moment. The home's location on the outskirts of Belgrade, near the German embassy, kept the bombs from falling too closely, but they were still close enough.

When the bombing stopped again, the trio ran out of Mirjana's house carrying several suitcases and headed down to the railroad station, hoping to get a train out of the city. Obviously Belgrade was paying for its resistance to Hitler, and they hoped they might be safer in the country. The group walked for a while and then caught a ride on an army truck, which Vujnovich instantly regretted as soon as he saw a German fighter plane come over the horizon. The planes were attacking anything on the road, particularly anything that looked military in nature, so it quickly swooped down on the truck and opened fire. Vujnovich, Mirjana, and Mirko were perched on the top of the truck, with nowhere to hide, so Vujnovich did his best to cover Mirjana with his own body as the plane strafed them. Through nothing but sheer luck, the large-caliber bullets passed them by, popping all around them and hitting the car behind the truck. Then the plane pulled away and went off in search of bigger targets.

After a few more miles, they were able to get on a train that had stopped in a small town. They rode that train for two days until they reached Herzeg Novi, a small village on the Adriatic Sea coast, located at the entrance to the Bay of Kotor and at the foot of Mount Orjen. They stayed there for fourteen days as the Germans continued their invasion.

As Belgrade was being bombed, German troops invaded Yugoslavia in the early morning of April 6, 1941, from several directions. The Yugoslav army tried to resist but was no match for the Nazi steamroller. On April 13, German troops entered Belgrade.

The little village of Herzeg Novi was filling up fast with refugees from Belgrade, all of them fleeing the bombing like George and Mirjana, and few of them with any plans for where to go. Mirjana ran into some of her friends from the university, and George met up with several other Americans. There was also a big contingent of British citizens, nearly seventy, many of them arriving in Rolls-Royces as they joined the evacuees fleeing as far west as they could get. The Rolls-Royces parked alongside all the beautiful Packards and other big sedans driven by the Americans, giving the village the look of a luxury resort for the wealthy. In reality, the town was overwhelmed, with refugees sleeping ten to a room and very little food to share. Everyone talked of their next move, how they would get out, how long they had before the Germans made their way into the countryside. For a few days there was talk of a British Navy cruiser that would come to the coastal village and take anyone who wanted to evacuate to Greece. There was still the question of how to get to the cruiser, however. It would be unable to dock in the coastal town, so boats would have to ferry the refugees out to it. Already people were fighting for the few fishing boats in the village, squabbling and arguing over who could pay the most. Vujnovich knew that if that cruiser appeared on the horizon, there would be a mad dash for those boats and people would die. He didn't want to put Mirjana in that chaos.

Instead, he heard about a large sailboat in the town of Risan, which was about twelve miles farther inland. The boat could carry about thirty people out to the cruiser, so Vujnovich and a few of his friends quietly made their way to Risan when they heard the cruiser was coming. He paid for Mirjana and her brother to sail on the boat, knowing that his American passport would bring him opportunities later. They rode to Risan with nearly all of the British refugees, who were eager to be rescued by Her Majesty's navy. As they boarded the sailboat for the first of several trips to the cruiser, the British citizens gave their car keys to Vujnovich, the only refugee in Risan who wasn't planning to leave on the sailboat. He ended up holding keys for about thirty cars, including several Rolls-Royces and a number of Packards, and he could have done anything he wanted with them. No one was coming back for their cars. But ironically, Vujnovich didn't know how to drive. He couldn't get even one of the cars back to Herzeg Novi, and even if he did, there was nothing to do with it. So he turned to one of local villagers in Risan and gave him all the car keys before walking back to the coastal town.

# Chapter 7

# *Passports, Please*

**It was hard to kiss Mirjana good-bye, but he knew it was** for the best and he had every intention of seeing her again. He just hoped the war wouldn't keep them apart for too long. But when he returned to the coastal village, his dear Mirjana was waiting for him there. Vujnovich was shocked to see her and feared she had somehow missed her opportunity with the sailboat. Then Mirjana explained that she and Mirko had taken the boat as planned, sailing out to the open sea to meet the British cruiser. Once they got within sight of the ship that could take them to safety, Italian fighter planes appeared and attacked the ship. It was badly damaged and turned away, unable to take on Mirjana and the other refugees. The British citizens who had made it onboard on earlier trips by the sailboat, were arrested by the Italians and interned in Italy. The sailboat had no choice but to deposit Mirjana and her brother back in Herzeg Novi. Vujnovich was at once elated to see her again, relieved that she hadn't made it to the cruiser any sooner, and disappointed that she was still trapped with him.

They had no immediate alternative, so they just waited in the little village again. As the day wore on, Vujnovich decided to talk with Mirjana about something that had been going through his mind on the long walk back from Risan. He took Mirjana on a walk in the monastery garden.

"We've been together about three or four years, and I love you, Mirjana," he said. "We could get married right away. We don't know what's going to happen." He paused for her reaction.

She was taken off guard by the comment, though she had been wondering about the same thing. "Yes, I suppose we could."

"But . . . with the Italians in control of the sea here, there's not going to be any more evacuation from here. We don't know if we can find another way out."

"Yes, I understand," she said. "It would be easier for you by yourself."

George knew what she was getting to, but he wasn't eager to discuss that possibility. He wanted to be pragmatic, but he couldn't bear the thought of just walking away from Mirjana. Instead he tried to back into the topic of splitting up.

"Well . . . if we get married, don't expect me to be faithful for five or ten or fifteen years. I wouldn't last that long," he said, unable to look her in the eye as he spoke. "I may find someone else. You may find someone else. Who knows? It's human nature."

In truth, it wasn't the fidelity that worried him. He just couldn't stand the idea of being without Mirjana again. It was easier to talk practically about what the future might bring rather than tell her how deeply it would hurt him to lose her again, less painful to feign a lack of confidence in his fidelity than to admit that he would be heartbroken.

Vujnovich was troubled by what he was suggesting. Mirjana understood, and she spared him the pain of having to say it himself.

"Yes, well, you can get out, George. Maybe that's for the best," she said, her voice stronger than she felt inside. "I'll find a way and then we can be together again."

Vujnovich was disturbed to even be discussing this. He didn't want to leave Mirjana behind. But the situation was dire. This wasn't a time for blind romance.

Mirjana felt the same way. She didn't want to be separated from George, but she didn't want him to stay in danger when he was free to leave. She didn't say anything for a long moment and George spoke again.

"Without a passport, you'll never get out through any regular route. I'd have to leave without you and come back sometime, whenever I could." The unspoken follow-up was "And hope you're still alive." They both knew what could happen if Mirjana stayed behind. She was scared but couldn't bear to ask him to stay with her. He couldn't bear the thought of leaving her.

They held each other for a long time, neither one wanting to say what had to be said, but both knowing. Finally George spoke up and said it out loud.

"I'm going to have to leave, Mirjana," he said. "I'll come back for you sometime in the future. You know I will."

"Yes, I know you will," she said. She couldn't help crying even though she was trying hard to be strong.

"As soon as I can, Mirjana. I promise. After the war, we'll be together again."

**Vujnovich knew that Herzeg Novi** no longer offered any possibility of escape, so he agreed with other Americans in the village, including several reporters, that it was time to move on. After a difficult and tearful farewell with Mirjana, he piled into a car and joined about fifty Americans in a caravan headed to Dubrovnik, then on to Sarajevo. They had to get out of the country while their American passports still meant something in Yugoslavia. No one knew how long that might be.

It was late evening when the Americans reached Sarajevo, located in a valley in eastern Yugoslavia, surrounded by the Dinaric Alps and situated around the Miljacka River, and the group split up to find places to stay. Vujnovich went to a small hotel and asked the desk clerk if a room was available, and much to his surprise, the answer was yes. Noting Vujnovich's American accent, the clerk asked for his passport. Vujnovich reached into his coat pocket and fumbled for the all-important document. It wasn't there. He couldn't believe it.

"I . . . uh . . . it's not here," he stammered, bewildered as to how he could have lost it.

An armed guard sitting near the clerk's desk suddenly became interested. The man was one of the Ustashe, the rebels who had taken control of Croatia and Bosnia under the German occupation. They were known for being cruel and unpredictable, sort of like auxiliary versions of the Nazis themselves. The guard stood up and looked sternly at Vujnovich, who was still fumbling in his pockets, frantically looking for the document.

"Show me your passport!" the guard yelled. Vujnovich explained again that he had one but couldn't find it at the moment. He was growing more and more distressed as each pocket came up empty.

"Maybe he is a spy," the Ustashe said to the clerk. "Spies can be shot. It's better than arresting them."

Vujnovich didn't know what to do, so he kept looking through the pockets he already knew were empty. At the mention of shooting him, several other Americans spoke up and tried to vouch for Vujnovich, waving their own American passports and insisting that he was just another American trying to get home. Among those trying to defend Vujnovich were a U.S. consul official and Ray Brock, a reporter for the *New York Times*. They were arguing vociferously with the Ustashe guard, and he withered under the American onslaught. After a moment he relented and agreed to let Vujnovich stay in the hotel that night.

"You can find your passport," he said to Vujnovich. "But if you do not have it tomorrow, you will be arrested."

Vujnovich was only partly relieved. He still had no idea where his passport was and he knew the Ustashe would not be deterred the next morning. He spent a frantic night searching through his belongings and trying to think back to where he had seen the passport last. He slept hardly at all as he pondered what would happen in the morning. He thought about trying to run off during the night, but he was sure the Ustashe guard or his cohorts would spot him. That would guarantee a bad outcome.

And then at six thirty a.m. there was a knock on the door. Vujnovich jumped at the sound and his heart went to his throat. *It must be the Ustashe coming for my passport,* he thought. *He was annoyed by last night's confrontation and wants to arrest me right away.* Vujnovich slowly went to the door and opened it, surprised to see the chauffeur of the car he had ridden in standing there. Apparently the man had no idea what trouble Vujnovich was in and was simply running an errand.

"You dropped this in the car," he said, and handed the critical passport to Vujnovich. He turned around and left, with no idea that he had just saved the American's life. Vujnovich realized that he must have missed his inside breast pocket when he tried to put his passport away in the car. The document had lain in the car all night long. Vujnovich wasted no time in showing the passport to the Ustashe and soon the Americans continued on their trip, driving on to Belgrade. They had no firm plans for how to get out of Yugoslavia, but they all thought their chances better in the big city, where they had contacts and more resources than in the countryside. They found a city completely unlike the one they had left. The city was beaten and bowed, the occupying Germans tightening the noose every day. There was a six-p.m.-to-six-a.m. curfew, after which anyone on the street would be shot without warning. Any resistance was met with exaggerated retribution: The death of one German soldier would result in one hundred Serbs being hanged in public. One day Vujnovich was walking down the street when he saw a crowd running toward him. They yelled at him to turn and run away, which he did without question. When he got the chance, he asked one of those fleeing what was wrong.

"There was a small fire at a gas station," the man answered. "The Germans assumed it was sabotage and started killing people. They took the first ten people they saw off the street and shot them."

Despite the danger in Belgrade, the gamble paid off. Not long after arriving, Vujnovich ran into his American friend Vasa Purlia, who told him that not only was it still possible for the Americans to get out, but they could take their wives as well. He was planning to marry his girlfriend, Koka, a local girl like Mirjana, and get her out with him. "Have you married Mirjana?" he asked eagerly. "Where is she? The American consulate can give you all the necessary documents for her to enter the United States," Purlia explained, "but only if you are married."

"But what about her passport? Will they give her an American passport?"

"No, they can't do that. But they can give all the papers to show that she is your wife and entitled to leave with you."

"Will the Germans and Italians accept that?"

"I don't know, George. But it is the only hope for Mirjana and Koka to leave."

To make matters worse, George found out that the Gestapo were looking for any Yugoslavian citizens with connections to Americans or British organizations, on the theory that they might be spies or at least disloyal. Mirjana was on the list, not only because of her relationship with George but because she had received a scholarship from the British Council and studied English.

That meant Mirjana was in extreme danger if she stayed, probably more than any risk involved with trying to get her out of the country. Vujnovich knew he had to try to get Mirjana out with him. If only he had known this before leaving her in Herzeg Novi. They could still be together and so much closer to leaving. Now he had to spend more time reuniting, and every passing day made their task more difficult. Vujnovich raced to the nearest telegraph office and sent a message to Mirjana in the coastal village. The telegraph operator warned him that the message probably would not go through because the war had disrupted all means of communication, but he tried it anyway. Vujnovich paid a small sum and the operator sat down at his desk, tapping out a simple message to Herzeg Novi.

As luck would have it, Mirjana was staying in the home of the village's telegraph operator, who was surprised to hear the system clicking out a message. He rushed to receive it and soon he came out of the room with a message in his hand, calling for Mirjana Lazic. He handed her a small slip of paper that instantly raised her spirits.

*We can get married and get documents for you. Come back to Belgrade.*

While she was thrilled to hear from George, she was not entirely sure she wanted to go back to Belgrade. She had convinced herself that the war would be concentrated in the big cities, and she had seen the devastation already wrought on Belgrade. Maybe if she stayed in the countryside she would be okay, she thought. And did she really want to leave Yugoslavia, even if she could?

Her brother, Mirko, an engineer who spoke English, convinced her to think clearly. The two of them set off by train for Belgrade, itself a dangerous journey as the Ustashe monitored all activity in the region now, looking for any opportunity to harass someone without the right papers. George thought Mirjana was on her way to Belgrade, but he didn't know when she might arrive. Realizing that the Germans might go to her Belgrade home looking for her—or a neighbor might report her arrival—he didn't want Mirjana to get off the train and go there. But if the train arrived after the six p.m. curfew, she would have to stay on the train all night and then get off at six a.m. So every day, George sprinted out of the house at six a.m. and down to the train station, hoping to catch Mirjana before she could walk into danger. She might get off the train at the same moment George was able to step outside, so every morning he was in a mad race to catch up with her. This went on for five days until he returned to his hotel and found Mirjana waiting there with Mirko.

After a tearful embrace, George asked how she had known to go to the hotel instead of going home. Mirjana told him that she and Mirko had, in fact, tried to return home that morning. When they approached the house, the family's maid rushed out and yelled at them to go away. Her frantic tone explained why. Mirjana knew that George had friends staying at the hotel, so she hoped to find him there also.

As soon as they were reunited, George took Mirjana to the American consulate and spoke with the consul, an earnest administrator who was working feverishly to get Americans and their loved ones out before it was too late. He had already given the proper documents to Vasa and Koka, who had been married earlier that day. He told George and Mirjana that they must hurry. But there was one important issue, he said. The Germans have forbidden any foreigners to marry.

"You have to go to this church at six o'clock in the morning," he said, handing George a paper with the location of the church. "Don't tell anyone except two witnesses. You have to bring two witnesses and the priest will marry you."

They were married the next morning in a quiet, simple ceremony attended only by one of Mirjana's cousins and an American friend of George's. They had a small meal at the cousin's home that morning, and that was the end of their wedding celebration. After taking their marriage certificate to the American consulate, they received the documents that they hoped would get Mirjana out of her rapidly worsening homeland. The main paper was surprisingly simple, just a letter really, from the American consul.

> *This affidavit confirms that Mirjana Vujnovich, nee Lazic, is a Yugoslav citizen married to an American. This affidavit is issued to her to enable travel to the home of her husband in the United States of America. Please extend to her all courtesy and offer any assistance you can.*

It was signed by the consul, with a seal and a big red ribbon. They thought it quite a handsome document. When the consul handed it to Mirjana, he explained that it would help her once they got out of occupied territory. If they could get to a country not controlled by the Axis, maybe Palestine, this document would enable her to get to the United States with George. But there was no telling if it would carry any weight with the Germans or other local authorities, he said. All three of them knew that the consul was being optimistic about that last part. It was very unlikely that the Germans would respect the consul's document, and Mirjana's Yugoslavian passport carried the same weight. Outside of Yugoslavia it could help her, but not in her own country.

The city of Belgrade was in ruins, with Germans and Ustashe watching everyone, so George wanted to move as quickly as possible. From his contacts with the American embassy, he heard about a boat that was going to evacuate Americans to Budapest, Hungary, via the Danube River. George made sure he and Mirjana were on the boat, and Mirjana's documents were good enough for her to blend in with the group of Americans as they evacuated. The newlyweds ended up staying with about a dozen Americans at a small hotel in Budapest, still firmly in German-occupied territory, the group talking nonstop about possible ways to get out. By this time, even an American passport could not guarantee an easy exit. If you could find a means out of German territory, the American documents would ease the way. But you still had to find a way out from a region that was rapidly falling into a state of confusion. The Germans prevented most travel through areas they controlled, and even in the rare situations in which someone like George would be permitted through, someone like Mirjana would not. There was no simple way out. Like the thousands of others trying to flee Yugoslavia, George and Mirjana had to be creative.

Some of the group wanted to try going to Switzerland through occupied territory and then on to southern France, the extreme southern part of the country not yet occupied by German soldiers. From there they might get a boat to Spain and to Portugal. But after some investigation, they realized the Germans would not allow them to travel to Switzerland through their occupied territory. The Americans didn't know where to go or how to get home. George and Mirjana were worried that they had waited too long to get out. Maybe George should have just gone on his own, Mirjana thought.

Their break came when George was exchanging his Yugoslavian money for Hungarian, thinking out loud about possible routes to the United States. The old man changing his money offered a suggestion that had not occurred to the Americans yet.

"Why don't you fly out of the country?" he said. "You can fly south to Bulgaria. Bulgaria is not at war, so you can get away from there easily."

If he was right, this could be exactly what George and Mirjana were waiting for. He made a few phone calls and found out that there was a regular Lufthansa flight that went from Budapest to—of all places—Belgrade, and then on to Sofia, Bulgaria. If they could get on that flight, they might escape occupied territory. He took Mirjana to the airport and tried to buy two seats on the flight, only to be told that there was only one seat available each day from Budapest. They were desperate by this point, so they discussed going separately, Mirjana one day and George the next. But the problem was that Mirjana really could not travel without George because they would check her papers in Belgrade and arrest her for trying to leave the country without permission. Even with George at her side there was doubt about whether her papers from the American consul would be enough to get her through; without George, they were almost certain she would be arrested. They were dejected again. They could not escape this way together, but it might be their only chance to get out. They seriously considered flying separately, with George going first and vouching for Mirjana along the way, telling the authorities that his wife was following him the next day. They still didn't like the idea, but they might have no other choice.

The next day, Saturday, July 12, George and Mirjana were in bed in the small Budapest hotel when the phone rang. It was Lufthansa, calling the number George had left just in case something changed. The airline said they had two seats open from Budapest that day instead of one. Would they like to book them?

George said yes, yes, please book those seats for us. He and Mirjana were thrilled that they might finally make it out of occupied territory. George hurried to find a way to change some money from Hungarian pengö, which would be useless after they left, to American dollars. He had to wake up the minister of finance in Budapest to make it happen, but he was able to convert about one thousand dollars. Mirjana, meanwhile, was trying to figure out what to take from the suitcases they had been lugging around since first leaving Belgrade. Lufthansa would allow only twenty-two pounds apiece. When George returned they took two small suitcases with them to the Lufthansa office in Budapest, leaving all their other belongings behind. The airline drove them to the airport, where they boarded a Lockheed Lodestar, a graceful twin-engine airliner with twelve seats in four rows of three across.

George and Mirjana were eager to get on the plane and make the final legs of their roundabout journey out of Yugoslavia, but they were anxious also. Mirjana's documents might not be enough to get them through, and they knew it depended mostly on who was checking. If they had only a cursory look by local authorities in Belgrade, there might not be any problem. But if German authorities wanted to take a closer look, Mirjana could be spotted as a wanted person by the Gestapo. They would arrest her and then . . . George couldn't stand to think too much about what might happen to her.

They were the last people to board the airplane, and the only two seats available were not together. One was open in the very front and one in the back. George and Mirjana didn't mind, as long they could get on their way, so they parted and George took the seat in the rear, knowing that might be the bumpier ride. Mirjana sat up front next to a somewhat plump but well-dressed woman. They both tried to relax as the plane taxied down the runway and rose into the air.

The plane hadn't been aloft long before George sensed something was amiss. From his seat in the rear he could see Mirjana moving about in her seat, restless it seemed, and the woman next to her appeared to be helping her. The woman had a wet cloth she was holding to Mirjana's head while she patted the younger woman on the back.

*Mirjana's airsick*, George thought. He had known this might be a problem because she had not flown much. George stood up and walked down the aisle to check on his wife. As he reached her seat, he bent down to see her and was surprised to see how pale and distraught she was. The woman in the next seat smiled at George and gave a sympathetic nod to Mirjana, taking the cloth away from the sick woman's forehead so the couple could speak. George immediately tried to comfort her.

"Mirjana, what's happening?"

She looked up at him, far more sick than he expected to see her, and said, "I feel terrible, George."

"Why are you so sick?" he asked. "It's just the plane. You won't be sick for long."

Mirjana didn't reply right away, and then she motioned for George to lean down closer. He did and Mirjana leaned in to whisper into his ear, hoping the sound of the airplane engines would prevent anyone else from overhearing.

"Do you know who this is next to me?" Mirjana whispered. George looked over at the woman, who was quietly reading a book. He shook his head slightly to indicate he had no idea. "It's Mrs. Goebbels!" Mirjana whispered intently, almost breaking into tears as she said it. "The wife of Joseph Goebbels! George, I'm going to be arrested when we get to Belgrade!"

There wasn't much George could say to Mirjana without causing a scene, so he just whispered to her that everything would be fine and to try to relax. He kissed her on the forehead and walked back to his seat, stunned at the incredible bad luck of his wife sitting on a plane next to Magda Goebbels, the first lady of the Third Reich, wife of the fiery and charismatic propaganda minister Joseph Goebbels, a top leader in the Nazi movement. Adolf Hitler was a witness at their wedding, and in the 1930s Magda bore six children for Goebbels. With Hitler remaining unmarried, she was promoted as "the first lady of the Third Reich," the Goebbels clan presented to the public as the model family for Germany. She looked like such a kind woman, Vujnovich thought, but he knew better. In Hitler's bunker at the war's end in 1945, this kind-looking woman would kill her six children one after another by crushing a cyanide capsule in their mouths.

As he took his seat in the back of the plane, George could see that Mirjana was growing more and more upset. Magda Goebbels was playing the concerned mother, putting the cool cloth to Mirjana's forehead and hugging her around the shoulders. George could only imagine how the woman's touch made his wife more ill. But more important, he kept thinking about what would happen when they reached Belgrade. Surely Joseph Goebbels's wife would be greeted by German guards, who probably would want to take a look at the passengers on this flight about to leave occupied territory. *Exactly what we were trying to avoid*, he thought.

There was nothing they could do to change what would happen at the airport in Belgrade. For the rest of the forty-minute flight, George could only sit and watch while his wife was comforted, to no avail, by the most revered woman in the Third Reich. As the plane touched down in Belgrade for refueling, it appeared Mirjana was near collapse, the stress of the moment about to overwhelm her. But he could do nothing without arousing suspicion, so he waited for the door in the rear of the plane to open and then he was one of the first to exit. His heart sank as he saw a German officer there waiting to check passports. He handed his over and the officer let him pass. George stood nearby, waiting for Mirjana, hoping this wasn't going to be the last time they saw each other.

All of the other passengers came out the rear door, the officer checking each passport, and then finally George could see Mirjana coming down the aisle, Magda Goebbels's arm underneath hers, helping steady the sick woman. As they came to the door, the officer called out, "Passports, please," as he had with everyone else. George looked at Mirjana and they both thought this was the moment they had been dreading. Then Magda Goebbels shouted crossly at the officer.

"What do you mean, 'passports'?" she said sternly, in the tone of a woman used to berating Nazi officers and getting away with it. "This is the wife of that man standing there next to you. She's sick. Help me with this woman or you will hear from me!"

The officer did as he was told and helped Mirjana out of the plane, forgetting all about the passports. Mirjana walked to George and they embraced, no one around them knowing why they were so relieved. Magda Goebbels wished them well and went toward the airport terminal, nonplussed. George and Mirjana couldn't believe that Magda Goebbels had just saved them.

After a half-hour wait for refueling, they reboarded the plane and took off for Sofia, Bulgaria. Mirjana sat next to Magda Goebbels again, more composed but breaking into tears as the plane flew directly over the house where she had lived in Belgrade. She knew she was looking at her home country for the last time. Magda Goebbels assumed she was airsick again and patted her hand gently.

**When the couple landed in** Sofia, Bulgaria, they found a country that was not yet in the full throes of Nazi occupation but nonetheless full of Nazis shouting, "Heil Hitler!" at every opportunity. They stayed for two days until George could change more money at a bank on Monday and then they took a train to Svilengrad, a village of no more than a dozen little houses. There was no hotel, and the only water in town was a single hand pump, where George and Mirjana took turns washing their faces. George had found that this little village was the only way to get from Bulgaria to Turkey, which was still neutral, because the Germans had destroyed all the bridges between the two countries. The only remaining way out was a little strip of land near Svilengrad. The only trouble was that the Germans didn't want anyone leaving Bulgaria for Turkey, so that strip of land was mined.

The locals had found a path through the minefield, and for a fee they would show George and Mirjana where it was. The villagers took their passports and luggage when they arrived, to make sure they wouldn't head off in search of the path on their own. When a local villager drove George and Mirjana to the border the next morning, he pointed out the ribbons marking the safe path and made it clear that they must stay between them. They could see evidence of where mines had exploded on either side. George and Mirjana were scared, but they knew this was what they came for, their way to freedom. George handed the driver the equivalent of twenty-five dollars, a tremendous sum of money for a poor villager in 1941, and received their passports and luggage in return.

Hand in hand, they gingerly walked the hundred yards from Bulgaria to Turkey, taking about fifteen minutes and hoping the villagers knew what they were talking about. As they got to the end of the path, Turkish officials were there to greet them. One officer took George and Mirjana's passports, looked at them and the other documents Mirjana carried, and handed them back.

"Welcome to Turkey," the man said.

## Chapter 8

# Man of the Year

**George and Mirjana knew the worst of their ordeal was** over as soon as they set foot in Turkey. They still had a long way to go, but they were out of German-occupied territory. After hearing about their successful escape from Yugoslavia, ten more Americans took the same path into Turkey. Once again, George and Mirjana found themselves in a group of Americans trying to find a way home, congregated this time in Istanbul. To the south, Syria was in the hands of the Vichy French, working with the Germans, so that meant the only route out was to the east, going to the Indian subcontinent and getting a boat around the Cape of Good Hope. Some of the Americans took that route and made it home in about two months, but George and Mirjana weren't sure they were up for such a long, arduous journey by boat. And besides, George was quickly running out of money and probably couldn't afford the passage anyway.

Istanbul was relatively safe and peaceful, so they stayed there for a while, during which time the British military attaché approached George. The British had heard of the couple's adventure and wanted to glean some information about the occupied territory. George told them all he knew and, in the process, became quite friendly with the British military officers. When they had been in Istanbul for a month, the free French invaded Syria and took control, which made it possible for George and Mirjana to travel through the country on a train called the Taurus Express, to Jerusalem, which was in Allied hands. But when they got there, the authorities would not let them go on to Cairo, Egypt. Too many refugees were taking that route and Cairo couldn't handle any more. So George and Mirjana were trying to figure out their next step, walking the streets of Jerusalem as they discussed options, when a man approached them. Mirjana was admiring a store's window display when the man came up and commented on her shoes, canvas sandals common in Yugoslavia. He then asked if she was from Yugoslavia, and after a short conversation the two refugees realized they had mutual friends. He asked Mirjana and George about their backgrounds and then said, "I need people like you. I'm the head of the Yugoslav section of the British General Service Intelligence [GSI], and I need someone to translate for me."

And thus another door opened for George and Mirjana. The man, Branco Denic, was in charge of broadcasting radio programs from the post in Jerusalem into Yugoslavia, first listening to the Nazi version of the news broadcast in occupied territories and then quickly writing another program that refuted the German lies and told the real news. Mirjana and George both accepted positions with the GSI, translating for the broadcasts, and Mirjana occasionally even went on the air herself to deliver the news. The couple spent a year in Jerusalem and in May 1942 they asked for visas to go to Cairo. Because they had worked with the British intelligence effort, the request was granted.

The plan was to go to Cairo and make their way down the East African coast to Cape Town, South Africa, where they should be able to get a boat back to the United States. But when they got to Cairo, they found the city was in a near panic. German Field Marshal Erwin Rommel, known as the Desert Fox, was making his way across the Libyan Desert and there was fear that he might cut off the entire Middle East. Many embassies were abandoning Cairo as people looked for their own way out. George went to the American embassy repeatedly, asking if there were plans to evacuate U.S. citizens. On three separate occasions, the consul personally told him there would be no evacuation of Americans.

The couple was trapped yet again. They were low on money and even lower on options. In his despair, George realized it was June 28, a major holiday in Serbia known as Vidovdan, which celebrates several historical events occurring on that date. To ease his mind and to pay his respects on Vidovdan, he made his way to a Russian church in Cairo and encountered several older men who were also praying. Some small talk revealed that they were with Pan American World Airways, the principal international airline of the United States at that time. The oldest man of the group was George Kraigher, a Serb who had flown for the Yugoslavian army in World War I. He was now head of Pan Am in Africa.

Kraigher asked if George knew another young American who had been fleeing Yugoslavia as well, and George explained that the man had already found a way home to America. Kraigher said that was too bad, that he was going to offer the man a job.

"In that case, I'd like to apply for the job," George replied.

Kraigher ended up offering George the job, but on one condition: He had to get a visa to go from Cairo to Sudan, then into Nigeria, and finally to Ghana, where the Pan Am job awaited. They had to get out of Cairo before the Germans arrived anyway, so George and Mirjana headed to the Sudan agency, an office run by the British to provide visas and other diplomatic services for countries in Africa. They found a crowd of four hundred people there clamoring for visas, agitated and yelling at the British guards, some trying to force their way in. The British were not giving out any visas.

Mirjana saw the situation and realized it was hopeless. She broke down. "We'll never get out of here," she sobbed. "The Germans are going to come in a couple of weeks and we'll be taken prisoner."

George held his wife as she cried and thought for a moment, staring at the crowd mobbing the agency gates, trying to come up with any solution. He knew Mirjana was right. If they just stayed in Cairo, they would be caught. He had to do something.

So far they had been the beneficiary of incredible luck and fortunate coincidences, but now it was up to George to make something happen, to dig deep and find enough courage to bluff his way through the embassy. He wasn't sure he could pull it off, but he had to give it a shot.

"Let me see what I can do," George said, pulling away from Mirjana. He walked off and, with all the attitude he could muster, marched up to a guard at the entrance.

"I'd like to see Her Majesty's consul," he said, trying to sound as if it were a given that he should be allowed entry.

"What for?" the guard asked.

"I can't tell you. It's confidential." George stood there just staring at the guard, trying not to look away. Then he pulled out his identification card from Jerusalem, which identified him as a member of the British GSI. The guard looked at the identification and pushed aside the other people trying to get to the gate, letting George walk on in. Once inside, George answered the receptionist's query with the same reply: "I can't tell you. It's confidential." When she directed him to the British consul, Phillip Reed, George was feeling pretty confident about his ruse. Reed asked what he could do for him and George explained that he needed to go to Ghana.

"What for?" Reed asked.

"I can't tell you. I'm in intelligence and it's confidential."

The consul paused for only a short moment and then asked for George's passport. He had a clerk stamp the passport with visas for both Mr. and Mrs. Vujnovich, wished George luck, and shook his hand before turning to leave. He had been in the building for only ten minutes when he returned outside to find Mirjana. When she saw him return so quickly, she was sure he had been unable to get the visas. She broke down in tears again.

"What's wrong?" George asked with a grin, holding up his passport as he approached. "I've got the visas!"

Mirjana was overjoyed and astounded. "How did you do it, George?"

He couldn't resist. "I can't tell you. It's confidential."

✻　✻　✻

**Kraigher was just as shocked** when George returned with the visas, but he was pleased. He gave George and Mirjana first-class tickets to Sudan on the first flight out of Cairo, and when they got to the airport on June 28, George was surprised to learn that the flight was the first evacuation of Americans from Cairo. In the middle of a crowd of thirty Americans milling about was the American consul who had assured George three separate times that there would be no evacuation of Americans. Looking at the crowd of executives from American companies—a sea of camel-hair coats, crocodile-skin shoes, and ten-gallon hats—George immediately realized that the consul had notified only the wealthy and influential Americans in Cairo of the evacuation. People like George were on their own. But they had tickets for this flight, if there was enough room. It looked to George and Mirjana that there were far too many people for the plane, and they were stuck in the back of the crowd. Plus, the consul announced that he would be calling names for boarding and George didn't expect to be at the top of his list.

They were waiting at the foot of the stairs leading into the DC-3 passenger plane, hoping to make it on the flight, when Kraigher walked up and onto the stairs. He looked over the crowd and said, "Employees of Pan American first. Mr. and Mrs. Vujnovich, please." They pushed through the crowd and George peered directly into the eyes of the American consul as they boarded the plane first, enjoying the surprised look on the official's face.

After a couple days of flying, they arrived in Accra, in the Gold Coast, where George took over duties as assistant airport manager, working under Kraigher. About three weeks after arriving, he put Mirjana on a plane that went from Accra to Fisherman's Lake, Liberia; then to Ascensión, to Natal, to Georgetown, and to South Africa. From there she went to Trinidad and Puerto Rico, and on to Miami. Then she rode a train for thirty-six hours to Washington, DC. With no previous arrangements, she walked into the Yugoslavian embassy and found someone with whom she had mutual friends. She was hired to work at the embassy, and her escape from Yugoslavia was complete.

**Vujnovich stayed in Africa, a** decision that Mirjana was not entirely happy with, because he enjoyed his job with Pan Am. Even after such a long ordeal to get out of occupied territory, Vujnovich was reluctant to go home because he felt that his job with Pan Am promised more than anything that awaited him at home. Besides, the war was on and chances were good that he would be drafted and sent overseas anyway. Better to stay here on his own terms, he thought.

The American war effort did reach out for Vujnovich before long. About the same time that Mirjana left, Pan Am was militarized for the war effort and became part of the Air Transport Command. Employees like Vujnovich were offered a military commission or a ride back to the United States with no job and the prospect of being drafted. So George accepted a commission as second lieutenant. Kraigher became a colonel. Vujnovich was soon transferred to Lagos, assisting with the delivery of planes to be used in the war, and eventually assumed command of the base. He excelled at his job, and then one day he was visited by two American civilians who asked him to join the Office of Strategic Services, or OSS. He would be useful because he spoke the Serbo-Croat language and knew the region well.

Vujnovich didn't even know what the OSS was, so the men explained that it was a special agency that reported directly to the president. He probably would be promoted if he joined the OSS, they told him. Vujnovich thought it sounded like the chance of a lifetime, so he said yes and found himself in Washington, DC, for a week. He had some time with Mirjana and then he was sent to the "Farm," the ultrasecret OSS training facility on a sprawling estate about twenty miles north of Washington, DC. This was where he learned close-combat skills, code work, and other espionage techniques. After a month at the Farm, Vujnovich was an expert in skills like reading maps and judging latitude from the sun. The instructor in close combat was a former police chief in Shanghai, and he taught Vujnovich how to break a man's arm or leg quickly, and how to make a man hurt so he would do anything you wanted. Once Vujnovich was fully trained, he had to take the final exam that was required of everyone leaving the Farm: a real-world assignment that would test what he had learned during his stay. His instructors gave him a challenging assignment: Go to the Bethlehem Shipyard in Baltimore, Maryland, and find out what ships were being built and how many. This was in wartime 1943, and such defense information was supposed to be closely guarded. He was given a small pressing tool for copying documents and a special phone number to call if he were caught and the police got too rough with him. If they didn't beat him too badly, he was supposed to maintain his cover as long as he could. Calling for help from the OSS because you received a standard police beating might mean you failed your exam.

Vujnovich set out on his task and decided right away to use a technique called "negative information," which involved stating information you know to be false in hopes that the other person will correct you and reveal secrets. The shipyard was in need of workers, so it was no problem getting a job there with a fake identification card he made himself. He befriended a coworker and joined him for a beer one day after work, casually mentioning that he had worked in another shipyard that was turning out one Liberty ship every five days, a pitifully slow rate during a war. "It doesn't look like Baltimore is much faster than that," he said.

This was Vujnovich's entrée into finding out exactly what the Baltimore yard was doing, because most individual workers weren't supposed to know details about production rates, and if they knew, they weren't supposed to talk about it.

The other worker was eager to brag about the shipyard's fast pace and told Vujnovich he was wrong, that, by God, they were completing a ship a day and they were damned proud of it. Vujnovich scoffed at the idea, so the man bet him a beer that he could prove it. He brought over another worker who confirmed the information. The man won his beer and Vujnovich became an OSS officer.

After his training, Vujnovich was able to spend a month and a half with Mirjana in Washington, where she was living with a naval officer and his wife on the west side of town. He had to leave before they found out that Mirjana was pregnant. Then the OSS flew him back to Cairo and on to Bari, Italy, where he arrived on November 20, 1943. The British Eighth Army had liberated Italy only about three weeks earlier. By the time he arrived in Bari, Vujnovich had been promoted to first lieutenant.

Vujnovich was back, and this time he was fighting the Nazis instead of running from them.

**When Mirjana wrote him from** Washington to ask if he could help the airmen stranded in the hills of Yugoslavia, he immediately set out to determine if his wife really did know something that had eluded the OSS post in Bari. A little investigation revealed that no one had been informed of any group as large as the hundred airmen Mirjana referred to, but there was reason to think she might be right.

If it proved true, the revelation in Mirjana's letter was surprising but not exactly shocking. It was entirely possible for so many airmen to be in Mihailovich's territory without word getting to him in Bari. Vujnovich knew quite well how the military bureaucracy and politics, not to mention the Communist moles that had infiltrated the OSS, routinely got in the way of his agents doing their jobs. But how the news got to him didn't matter as much as what he could do in response. He instantly felt a connection to the young men who just wanted to get out and go home. And he also felt a strong tie to the local Serbs helping them, any one of whom could be his own relative.

Not a man to stand aside and hope someone else acted, Vujnovich decided he had to get those men out of Yugoslavia. He knew the task would be challenging and he was not certain it could be done at all. But he was certain that it had to be tried and that the OSS was the right bunch of men for the job. While he tried to confirm Mirjana's message, Vujnovich started looking into rescue options and quickly found out that the task would be challenging on many fronts, not the least of which was all the political maneuvering over the Balkans. Vujnovich knew that the political situation in Yugoslavia was growing more complicated by the day, and the interaction among the United States, Great Britain, Tito, and Mihailovich was becoming a tangled mess of alliances, pseudo-alliances, outright opposition, and conflicting loyalties. In just the past year, the relationship between the Allies and Mihailovich had taken a dramatic turn for the worse, which Vujnovich knew was the primary explanation for why the messages from Mihailovich about the downed airmen were not acted on. Sure, the situation on the ground was more complicated and more dangerous than when the OSS had gone into Yugoslavia in 1943 to bring out some pilots, but that didn't explain all of the hesitation. Vujnovich knew that politicos were arguing back and forth about Tito and Mihailovich, juggling the reports from Yugoslavia—many of them questionable at best—to determine where the Allies should put their support. The facts about what was happening on the ground took a backseat to the political posturing and propaganda spewed by many parties with many different agendas. Vujnovich knew this and he knew that it would be as formidable a challenge for him as any Nazi trooper his agents might meet in Yugoslavia.

The first thing Vujnovich investigated was the reports from Mihailovich. When he looked into Mirjana's comment about the downed airmen, it didn't take long for him to confirm that Mihailovich had been sending detailed accounts of the airmen he was harboring. So why wasn't anyone doing anything about it? The answer, Vujnovich discovered, was that Mihailovich was officially persona non grata with the Allies now. By the time Vujnovich started working on the rescue, the Allies' position was that Mihailovich could not be trusted and should receive no support that might give him an advantage over his internal opponent, Tito. Or rather, that was mostly the British position and the Americans went along with it.

Vujnovich was no stranger to Yugoslav history and he was quite familiar with Mihailovich. This turnaround was shocking, though it fit into the pattern he was seeing within the OSS. There were so many Communists infiltrating the OSS and other military agencies, Vujnovich realized, that it was hard to trust any information disparaging an anti-Communist like Mihailovich. Especially one who had been such a loyal supporter of the

Allies since the war began, and one who had been hailed as a great freedom fighter by the West.

Only two years earlier, a flattering, dramatically rendered portrait of Mihailovich graced the cover of *Time* magazine, leading readers to an article that described him as "the greatest guerilla fighter of Europe." The first articles in the Western press had appeared in late 1941, a few months after the Germans invaded Yugoslavia in April and soon after the Yugoslav government in exile in London was able to make radio contact with the rebel general. The people of America and Great Britain were captivated by the romantic tales of this handsome guerilla who dared to stand up to the German invasion. The news from most other fronts in Europe was discouraging. German armies were advancing on Moscow and Leningrad, other countries had capitulated already, and resistance movements elsewhere were still fledgling. But the public was reading stories about this dashing general who refused to concede his country to the Nazis. The very idea that someone was fighting back gave people in the West reason to hope, and the press quickly realized that its readers couldn't get enough of Mihailovich. Before long, Mihailovich was one of the better known and most popular public figures in the West, his name becoming synonymous with resistance and dedication to one's country. *Time* magazine readers voted him Man of the Year.

The press reported on everything they could find about Mihailovich, painting a flattering portrait of a man who was at once intellectually gifted and possessed of a fierce fighting nature. He was of medium height, wiry, with blue eyes, horn-rimmed or wire-rimmed eyeglasses, and a look that reporters often described as pensive. Before the war, when he held positions in the Yugoslav government, Mihailovich was mostly clean shaven. During the war, he sported the bushy Old Testament beard common among the Serb peasants. In most photographs of Mihailovich, especially those taken before the war, it would be easy to mistake him for a university professor rather than one of the world's foremost resistance fighters.

Mihailovich had been a war hero in World War I and had achieved the rank of colonel in the Yugoslav army. Like many Serb officers in the army, Mihailovich was known as "a man of the people" who looked out for the peasants in the countryside. He was known throughout the military, and by some leaders abroad, as a brilliant strategist and theoretician, though his outspoken criticism of some military operations earned him official rebukes and even house arrest on more than one occasion. While there were those who differed with him on politics and military strategy, scarcely anyone could fault Mihailovich as a man. He was known by all as a man of great integrity, dignified and controlled at all times, and he consistently displayed an egalitarianism that others of his rank did not always share. Mihailovich always took his meals sitting on the ground with common soldiers, not in more comfortable quarters with officers, and he carried his own knapsack on long marches. This man of the people was always willing to sit down with local people and hear their concerns.

No matter what else his detractors might have said of Mihailovich, there was no disputing his loyalty to Yugoslavia and its monarchy. When the Germans invaded, Mihailovich led seven officers and twenty-four noncommissioned officers and soldiers who refused to surrender and retreated to the hills. After arriving at Ravna Gora, mountain country in the region of Serbia, on May 8, he started organizing parts of the splintered Yugoslav army into the Yugoslav Army of the Homeland, dedicated to driving the Nazis out of their country but also vehemently opposed to the Communists who were promoting Soviet-style government. In the first year after the fall of Yugoslavia, Mihailovich's forces didn't constitute much of a formidable force; he was mostly trying to consolidate the bits and pieces of the Yugoslav army that were still in isolated pockets throughout the country. A major challenge was gaining the trust and cooperation of individual commanders who were accustomed to working independently. Mihailovich had his hands full fighting the Germans, Fascist Italy, the Ustashe Fascists from Croatia, and anyone promoting a Communist future for Yugoslavia. As far as the Allies were concerned, and especially the Americans, Mihailovich was our man in 1941—opposed to both the Germans and the Communists, and having pledged his support to the Allied cause.

At first Mihailovich and his guerillas were able to concentrate on the German occupiers because he did not seek to directly engage any of the other enemies. In fact, he didn't seek confrontation even with the Germans on a large scale. Though he was well liked by the Yugoslav people and hailed as a hero by those in the hill country, Mihailovich did not try to incite a mass uprising against the Germans and others occupying their country. After seeing the catastrophic Serb losses in World War I, in which the Kingdom of Serbia lost a quarter of its male population, Mihailovich could not encourage the people of his country to charge German machine guns with their pitchforks and axes. His strategy, instead, was to gather men and materials and create a stronghold in the Serbian hills while he awaited an Allied landing that would liberate Yugoslavia the same way Italy had just been freed from German control. Mihailovich's plan was to prepare a large army that could be mobilized quickly at the right moment, attacking the Germans and Italians just as the Americans and British were approaching. To that end, he avoided any premature conflicts that could lead to the destruction of his fighting force. In particular, he avoided enlisting the local Serbs in espionage or overt sabotage against the German occupiers because he thought the risk was too great. Having seen almost three thousand civilians executed in the towns of Kraljevo and Kragujevac in October 1941 as reprisals for sabotage against the Germans, Mihailovich took a firm position that he could not expose the people of Yugoslavia to such risk unless the outcome was great enough to justify the inevitable deaths from reprisal. Until he knew the Allies were on the brink of invasion, he thought, it rarely was worth the lives of innocent villagers just to kill a German soldier or blow up a bridge. That conviction led Mihailovich's forces to concentrate their efforts on delayed sabotage that made reprisals less likely, but it should be noted that Mihailovich found protecting the downed American airmen to be so important that he was willing to risk lives and even see villages massacred rather than give them up.

The exiled King Peter supported Mihailovich, and the colonel who refused to surrender rose in rank in the exile government, becoming minister of war on January 11, 1942, and then general and deputy commander-in-chief on June 17. That prompted the *Time* magazine cover, and Mihailovich was lauded the world over for fighting the German war machine from within occupied territory.

Mihailovich's position was challenged in June 1941, after the German attack on the Soviet Union, when the Communist movement led by Josip Broz Tito—known as the Partisans—began actively resisting the German and Italian forces in Yugoslavia. A dedicated Communist even before the German invasion, Tito was a member of the outlawed Yugoslav Communist Party in the 1930s and became chairman in 1937. He and his fellow Communists were vehemently anti-Fascist but had been pushing to keep Yugoslavia out of the war until Germany invaded the Soviet Union in June 1941. With the Soviet Union, the motherland of Communism, under attack, suddenly the Yugoslav Communists felt it was time to fight the Germans occupying their country. Mihailovich wanted nothing to do with Communism, but like the Allies in the West, he didn't mind if Tito wanted to kill a few Germans. A problem soon arose, however, when Mihailovich realized that Tito was adopting a very different approach from his own. Instead of quietly gathering resources and waiting for the Allies to arrive, Tito was striking out at the German and Italian occupiers like a cuckold with nothing to lose. All-out resistance was Tito's strategy, and Mihailovich knew it would prompt vicious reprisals from the Germans.

The reason for the different approaches was crystallized by one of Mihailovich's senior officers, Lieutenant Colonel Zivan L. Knezevich, who had been chief of the Yugoslav prime minister's military cabinet and the former Yugoslav military and air attaché in Washington. He noted that Mihailovich's primary goals were saving the country and its traditions with as few civilian casualties as possible. Tito, he explained, wanted to Sovietize Yugoslavia and establish Communism, and he didn't care how much Yugoslav blood was shed in the process. "The Communist Partisans wanted immediately to lead the people into an open fight against the forces of occupation although the people were completely bare-handed and the fight could not have benefited anybody," Knezevich explained soon after the war. Mihailovich "thought that the uprising was premature and that, without any gain in prospect, it would have brought disproportionately great sacrifices. He was not able to convince the Communist Partisans that an open fight could have only one result, namely, the annihilation of the population."

Tito's open opposition prompted reprisals not just in his own territory but throughout Yugoslavia. The Communist actions led to punitive German expeditions in the region of Serbia, where Mihailovich operated, that led to the deaths of seventy-eight thousand Serbians between the ages of sixteen and fifty. And German reprisals weren't Mihailovich's only concern. Tito was committing his own crimes against the people of Yugoslavia in his quest for a Communist state.

In a telegram on February 22, 1943, Mihailovich reported on a recent Tito operation:

In their flight from the Bihac Republic the Communists forced the entire population to flee with them before the Germans and the Ustashe, in order to protect the Communists from attack. Because of this Communist terror, masses of people are fleeing from Mihac toward Glamoc. As soon as the Germans approach, the Communists abandon these unprotected masses and leave them to the mercy of the Germans and the Ustashe, who massacre them mercilessly. Those who succeed in escaping die in the snow and ice. Between Drvar and Glamoc, there are over five hundred frozen bodies of women and children. All this is more than horrible. That is the fight which the Communists wage, a fight which is directed by foreign propaganda with the aim of systematically annihilating our nation.

With each such incident, Mihailovich's resolve grew and the picture became clearer to him: The Communists were no better than the Nazis.

Though Tito and the Partisan leaders were staunch Communists and planned a Soviet-style postwar government that would gift wrap the Kingdom of Yugoslavia for the Soviet Union, many of those joining the Partisan movement had no such dreams. Some were pro-Communist, but many didn't care one way or the other. Many joined the Partisan effort because Tito made it clear he was anti-German; he could have been pro-anything and the people who wanted the Germans out wouldn't have cared. Many Yugoslavs also were directed to one camp or the other purely by geographical proximity. Mihailovich was in the hills where the peasants were his main supporters, and Tito was in the lowlands where city dwellers and others could join his movement. For many, the question was who was going to drive out the Germans, and Tito gave every appearance of doing that more aggressively than Mihailovich.

The animosity between Mihailovich and Tito also was tied to their ethnic and religious backgrounds, in a country that had a long, bloody history of clashes between rival groups that all called Yugoslavia home. Mihailovich was Serbian and Tito was Croat. The Croats had a deep-seated and long-standing resentment over how the Serbs had dominated the political structure in Yugoslavia for decades, and they saw this conflict as a chance to correct that problem. King Alexander, a Serb, had declared himself the supreme ruler in 1929 and abolished the country's parliament and constitution. For the next fifteen years, the Croat community seethed and grew ever more resentful that they lived under a Serb dictatorship. Italy, soon to join hands with Nazi Germany, took advantage of the Serb/Croat conflict and supported the Ustashe terrorist organization, which was pushing for an overthrow of the Serb dictatorship. The Ustashe were responsible for the assassination of King Alexander in Marseilles, France, in 1934, which led to the rise of Prince Paul, first cousin of the king. Prince Paul was considered a weak ruler who looked to the British for support and instructions. When King Peter took over from Prince Paul in 1941, he continued to rely on the British and lived in exile in Great Britain during the war.

The groups' religious differences only fueled the fires, the Croats adhering to Catholicism and the Serbs belonging to the Orthodox Church.

Adding varied loyalties to Communism, Fascism, Nazism, and Democracy to the mix only ensured that the groups would find good reason to shoot at each other eventually.

The two sides in this civil war hated each other as much as they did the Germans or the Italians, and they both felt fervently—and correctly, it turned out—that the outcome of their conflict would determine the future of Yugoslavia every bit as much as whether the Germans stayed. If Mihailovich prevailed, the country's future would be monarchist, anti-Communist, and largely democratic. If Tito won, the future Yugoslavia would be Communist, pure and simple. With such sharp contrasts in philosophy, and with the long history of merciless Balkan conflicts influencing their every move, Mihailovich and Tito waged a brutal civil war. When Tito's men captured Mihailovich territory, they publicly executed anyone even suspected of being sympathetic to the general. Mihailovich's Chetnik forces followed much the same pattern, though they tended not to be as capricious and put a little more effort into determining who really was a Partisan or Partisan sympathizer before cutting their throats.

Chapter 9

# *Abandoned Ally*

**In the early stages of the resistance, Mihailovich and** Tito both considered the advantages that could be obtained by combining their forces. But doing so would require one of them to compromise his political beliefs and neither was willing to budge. Better to fight the occupiers separately than give up your commitment to Communism, or your commitment to preserving the Kingdom of Yugoslavia. The two sides resisted the Germans in their own ways, with Mihailovich still receiving strong support from the Allies and Tito left to do as he pleased as long as he was undermining the Nazi effort to secure Yugoslavia.

Though Mihailovich was content to avoid direct confrontation with Tito, the same could not be said for the Communist leader. Tito aggressively attacked Mihailovich's forces in November 1941, bringing to a head all the differences that had been largely philosophical and theoretical up to that point. From that point forward, both Tito and Mihailovich were forced to divide their attention and their resources, fighting each other for control of Yugoslavia while they fought the Germans so there would be something left to control.

The growing civil war in Yugoslavia forced the British government's hand. Sending support to both sides was British policy for a while, but by late 1941, the Allies were beginning to realize that supporting both Tito and Mihailovich would not be productive if they were using the arms and resources against each other and not just the Germans. One or the other had to be the Allies' man in Yugoslavia, and so the British sent in a field agent named Captain Duane Hudson to investigate the situation. Hudson was an agent of the Special Operations Executive (SOE), the British equivalent of the American OSS. This would prove to be the beginning of the end for Mihailovich.

Communication between the parties consisted mainly of telegrams, radio broadcasts, and the personal reports of agents sent in to meet with Mihailovich, and the records indicate that while the British were annoyed by Mihailovich's apparent defiance of their orders, he was just as annoyed that they would presume to tell him how to run his insurgency. Hudson spent seven months in Yugoslavia, traveling between Mihailovich's and Tito's forces, meeting with both leaders and assessing their commitment to the Allied war effort. When Hudson reported back to his superiors in May 1942, he concluded that Chetnik leaders had collaborated with Italian forces in Montenegro and he confirmed that Mihailovich was taking a passive stance and not actively resisting the German occupation. Though he reported that Mihailovich might be willing to make a secret pact with the Germans or Italians if it would keep Yugoslavia from falling under Communism, he underscored that he thought Mihailovich much preferred an Allied victory. The general and his forces could be counted on to participate in a "grand finale against the Axis" if Allied troops arrived to liberate Yugoslavia, he said. The Chetniks were committed to the Allied cause, Hudson concluded, but they might be more committed to fighting the Communists than the Germans.

The enemy, on the other hand, clearly saw Mihailovich as a threat. In the latter part of 1941, not long after Yugoslavia fell, the Germans launched Operation Mihailovich to capture or kill the rebel leader. (They were equally interested in capturing or killing Tito.) The concerted effort to stop Mihailovich reportedly came after German leaders finally realized how strong his movement was and how much it was impeding the German invasion. When Hitler was informed in late 1941 that Mihailovich's guerilla movement had killed one thousand German troops so far, he announced that for every German soldier killed by Mihailovich, one hundred Serbs would be shot. For every German soldier wounded, fifty Serbs would be killed. Any village harboring Mihailovich or his men would be punished severely. Gunshots from any house would result in the home being destroyed and any male over the age of fifteen executed. The Germans carried out these orders ruthlessly, but Mihailovich evaded the German dragnet. On July 20, 1943, the Axis published a proclamation offering a reward of one hundred thousand gold marks for the capture of Mihailovich, dead or alive. Still, no one turned him in.

Another SOE agent followed Hudson in and returned with essentially the same conclusions about Mihailovich. He also reported that Mihailovich's forces in Montenegro were dealing arms with the Italians—a major concern for the Allies because it signaled a lack of loyalty to the Allied cause, or at least a lack of discipline within Mihailovich's forces—but the agent noted that Tito's Partisans were doing the same thing. Telegrams from Mihailovich to the exiled Yugoslav government indicated that he had ample opportunity to collaborate with the Germans but consistently refused. In a telegram sent from Mihailovich on March 2, 1943, he wrote of several instances in which he and his senior officers had been approached by Germans with offers of cooperation. Mihailovich reported that he consistently refused such offers, replying to one query with, "As long as you are shooting and arresting innocent Serbians and as long as you are in our Homeland there can be no negotiations of any kind." In another telegram on March 10, 1943, Mihailovich again reiterated his refusal to cooperate with the Germans and this time he voiced suspicions that the offers themselves were part of a plot orchestrated by the Communists and the Axis to discredit him and his National Movement with the Allies:

*The attempts of the enemy to get in contact with me continue. This time the offer came both from*

*the Germans and the Italians together, asking me*
*to get in touch with one of my collaborators at*
*least. This attempt I also refused emphatically*
*and I shall continue to do so in the future. The*
*constant attempts of the enemy to establish con-*
*tact with me, I am convinced, come from a desire*
*to take advantage of the campaign which is being*
*waged in the Allied countries against the National*
*Movement which is headed by the Central National*
*Committee. I do not exclude the possibility of an*
*intrigue on the part of the Germans and the Ital-*
*ians directed against the National Movement and*
*its integrity. Please, be careful.*

Mihailovich voiced those concerns throughout the war, but the British continued to focus on reports of collaboration with the enemy—mostly from their agents in Yugoslavia. There is reason to believe some of those reports of collaboration were well founded but that they missed the big picture. Some instances of collaboration can be found among many warring factions in any war, especially with a loosely organized guerilla movement, but by and large the evidence supports Mihailovich's loyalty to the Allied cause. Much of what the Allies considered collaboration really could be more accurately termed "accommodations," which are common and generally benign agreements between warring factions—pragmatic agreements that did not signal any alliance or any backing down from the overall intent to stop each other's military. An example would be exchanging prisoners or opposing units deciding not to fight each other at the moment because each needed a respite. While these accommodations were the opposite of what the British wanted from Mihailovich, they still did not represent any lack of allegiance to the West.

Nevertheless, the agents' reports cast doubt on Mihailovich as an ally to be trusted and played into the hands of British authorities who didn't like the idea of the general supposedly twiddling his thumbs in the hills of Yugoslavia while Tito was out killing German troops and blowing up train depots. The British concerns were increased when British troops caused Hitler's Afrika Korps to retreat in October 1942, and then Allied forces landed in North Africa less than a month later. Those events caused the Mediterranean to suddenly become a major theater of operations for the Allied and Axis forces, and the British thought it was imperative that German supply lines running through Yugoslavia be cut. When they looked at Tito and Mihailovich, they wanted to see active resistance and they told them so.

Tito's forces continued attacking German supply lines, but Mihailovich, though he was doing more than the British gave him credit for, did not increase activities in a way that satisfied the British. Authorities in Great Britain were growing increasingly frustrated because their first choice to support in the Yugoslav struggle had always been Mihailovich. They had no interest in seeing Tito establish a Communist government in Yugoslavia after the war. But as explained by author Kirk Ford Jr. in *OSS and the Yugoslav Resistance*:

> Obviously the bond of mutual self-interest which had for slightly more than two years held Mihailovich and the British together was beginning to unravel. As it did, the British had to choose between short-term military policy, which suggested the extension of military support to the Partisans, and long-term political interests, which implied continued support of Mihailovich.

Despite doubts about his loyalty, the British—and by extension the Americans—continued to support Mihailovich as their ally in Yugoslavia. That support was sometimes only on the surface, as material support was given to Tito in amounts similar to what Mihailovich received. Neither received much. In the spring of 1943, however, Mihailovich was beginning to lose all support in London. Concerns had been mounting about Mihailovich being less willing to engage the Germans than Tito, and the accusations of collaboration had gained a foothold. A final straw came on February 28, 1943, when Mihailovich delivered a speech to a local gathering of supporters. In that address, an obviously frustrated and candid Mihailovich said the Serb people were now "completely friend-less" and that the British were not willing to help then or in the future, and that, "The English are now fighting to the last Serb in Yugoslavia." Continuing in his ill-advised rant, Mihailovich stated that his enemies were now the Partisans, Ustashe, the Moslems, and the Croats. When he had dealt with them, he said, he would turn his attention toward the Ital-ians and Germans. He then stated, at least according to the British liai-son who reported back to London, that he needed no further contact with the Western democracies whose "sole aim was to win the war at the expense of others."

Such accusations, and the apparent declaration that Mihailovich was breaking with the Allies, could not be ignored. British Prime Minister Winston Churchill fired off a stinging rebuke to Slobodan Jovanovich, the Yugoslav prime minister:

> *I appreciate that words spoken in heat may not express a consid-ered judgment, and that General Mihailovich may feel himself tem-porarily aggrieved of a small amount of assistance which it has unfortunately for reasons beyond the control of His Majesty's Gov-ernment been possible to send him recently. You will appreciate however, that His Majesty's Government cannot ignore this outburst nor accept without explanation and without protest a policy so to-tally at variance with our own. They could never justify to the Brit-ish public or to their own Allies their continued support for a movement, the leader of which does not scruple publicly to declare that their enemies are his allies—whether temporary or permanent is immaterial—and that his enemies are not the German and Ital-ian invaders of his country, but his fellow Yugoslavs and chief among them men who at this very moment are fighting and giving their lives to free his country from the foreigners' yoke.*

Churchill went on to conclude with a warning:

*You will, I am sure, appreciate that unless General Mihailovich is prepared to change his policy both towards the Italian enemy and towards his Yugoslav compatriots who are resisting the enemy, it may well prove necessary for His Majesty's Government to revise their present policy of favouring General Mihailovich to the exclusion of the other resistance movements in Yugoslavia.*

The Yugoslav prime minister relayed the British concerns to Mihailovich with a sternly worded telegram that underscored how precarious the British support was and that words spoken in anger could be disastrous. But at the same time, he met with Churchill and explained that Mihailovich's comments were made in a relaxed state to a small circle of his followers and were not representative of the general's true feelings. "If there were a secret service to overhear what the Allies say about one another, much worse things would be heard than that speech by General Mihailovich," he told Churchill.

The warnings from Churchill and Jovanovich made an impression on Mihailovich. While he contended that his speech was greatly misunderstood and then interpreted with the most cynical preconceptions, he responded with a statement of unequivocal support for the Allies, reiterating that, "My only enemy is the Axis. I avoid battle with the Communists in the country and fight only when attacked." He also stated that he had made every effort to stop the civil war in Yugoslavia, including repeated requests for the British to intervene with Tito, to no avail. He assured the British that he was ready "to do everything I can for the mutual cause."

The damage had been done. Mihailovich's speech was just what the doubters in the British government needed to confirm that support should be thrown to Tito and withdrawn from Mihailovich. On June 1, 1943, the British Middle East Command sent a telegram to the Yugoslav prime minister detailing an "operational decision" concerning Mihailovich. "Execution is very urgent," it said. The telegram, the contents of which were soon forwarded to Mihailovich, explained the British conclusions that Mihailovich's forces did not represent a significant fighting force but the Communist Partisans did. The telegram instructed Mihailovich to go "immediately to Kopaonik with all his faithful officers and men; if necessary he is to force through with armed forces." The British were instructing Mihailovich to go to Tito's headquarters and submit to him, fighting through Germans and Italians to get there. The British position was influenced in part by reports from Randolph Churchill, Winston Churchill's son, who was at Tito's headquarters as the principal British liaison to Tito. Vujnovich had heard from the American OSS agents working with the Partisans that Randolph Churchill was uniformly seen as a bad-tempered, spoiled rich boy with a serious drinking problem. Apparently his main function was to send reports directly from Tito to his father, mostly reports of the Partisans' glorious victories over the Germans that the younger Churchill made no attempt to verify.

Mihailovich responded with astonishment that the British would order him to surrender. He categorically refused, saying, "My fighters and I did not recognize the capitulation which the enemy imposed upon us and we certainly will not accept capitulation from our Allies." His response only further enraged the British military leaders and politicians who had aligned against him. When Churchill met with President Franklin D. Roosevelt and Russian general secretary Joseph Stalin at the Tehran Conference on December 1, 1943, Mihailovich was one of the subjects of conversation. Churchill pushed the British view that Mihailovich could no longer be trusted to support the Allied cause, even though his own advisers were warning that Tito intended to establish a Communist government in Yugoslavia that would be controlled from Moscow. Churchill insisted that the war effort demanded a short-term focus and whatever happened after the war they would worry about later. He explained that his only goal at the moment was to find out "who was killing the most Germans and suggesting means by which we could help to kill more." As Roosevelt already knew, Churchill vigorously opposed Communism except when Hitler was involved. A year and a half earlier, on June 22, 1941, Churchill broadcast a message to the people of Great Britain explaining that the country was allying itself with Communist

Russia, which had recently been invaded by Germany. When his private secretary remarked that Churchill previously had called Communism a menace he would like to "strangle in its cradle," Churchill acknowledged the irony of the moment. But he replied that, "If Hitler invaded Hell, I would make at least a favorable reference to the Devil in the House of Commons!"

Depending on the British assessment of Tito's and Mihailovich's activities in Yugoslavia, and not realizing how skewed that assessment was, Roosevelt reluctantly accepted Churchill's argument. Before they left the meeting in Tehran, Iran, the big three had agreed that Mihailovich would receive no more support. Instead, the Allies would put all their efforts behind helping Tito win control of Yugoslavia.

From that moment forward, Mihailovich was cut loose, fighting alone in Yugoslavia with no support from the British and even open animosity from old friends in Britain.

Despite being abandoned, Mihailovich remained loyal to the Allied cause and particularly the American pilots who risked their lives flying over Yugoslavia to bomb the Ploesti oil fields. However, he continued to grow increasingly frustrated and disappointed by the actions—and inaction—of the British and Americans, especially now that the British had severed all ties. It soon became clear that not only was he not receiving any active support from the British (not that he had received much in the first place), but now he was being smeared by British radio. The Yugoslav general was enraged when he heard BBC radio broadcasts that extolled the anti-German efforts of the Communist Partisans while giving no credit to the work done by his own forces, sometimes even praising Tito for missions carried out by Mihailovich's men. As the British sided with Tito over Mihailovich, the authorities constructed their radio propaganda accordingly. The BBC radio broadcasts were vital sources of information for the Yugoslav people, and the British voices were telling people that Tito and the Communists were fighting valiantly for them. Almost no mention was made of Mihailovich.

* * *

**This was the situation that** Vujnovich found when he arrived at the Bari, Italy, office of the OSS and took over covert operations in Yugoslavia. He knew enough about the politics of the Balkans, and the influence of Communist moles in the American and British governments, to give Mihailovich the benefit of the doubt, but Vujnovich understood that the British were guiding the Allied position on Mihailovich. If they had decided that he was no longer a partner in the war, the Americans would go along with that. Besides, it was only recently that American operatives had any direct involvement with Mihailovich. Until 1943, the British had complete control over Yugoslavia as far as Allied operations were concerned, but the SOE and OSS agreed in July 1943 to allow limited OSS operations in Yugoslavia. The OSS was eager to get into Yugoslavia, seeing ample opportunity to fulfill its mission behind enemy lines and gain a foothold for operations in the Balkans after the war. The primary goal for the OSS in Yugoslavia was to slow down and interfere with the actions of as many German units as possible, to keep them from linking up with the twenty-six Nazi units already in Italy or redeploying to fight the Allied troops soon to land in Normandy.

At the beginning of World War II the British were considered the worldwide masters of subterfuge and clandestine warfare, and the SOE had been established in 1940 by the Secret Intelligence Service for the specific purpose of assisting local rebels fighting the German invasion across Europe. So it was with great reluctance that the Brits allowed the Yanks onto their turf. Though the British and American intelligence units were supposed to be coequal when working together in the region, American OSS agents reported that their British counterparts always seemed to regard themselves as the senior partner, a little more than coequal with the Americans.

Vujnovich knew from one of the key agents in Yugoslavia that the American and British forces did not always get along. They may have been Allies, but they weren't always allies, agents reported from the field. Some OSS agents felt that the British were every bit their enemy as the Germans, at least when it came to their intelligence activities.

Similar concerns were reported by George Musulin and George

Wuchinich, OSS agents who had recently been sent into Yugoslavia. Arriving in May 1943, the two Americans of Yugoslav heritage were sent into Yugoslavia through Cairo, with the goal of establishing an OSS presence that would facilitate other missions. A round-faced, robust bear of a man, Musulin was a former steelworker with a personality as big as his girth. He had joined the army in 1941 and was assigned to the 29th Infantry Division at Fort Meade, Maryland. By July 1942, his Yugoslav background and his ease with the Serbo-Croat language, not to mention his eagerness to take on dangerous assignments, made him an excellent candidate for an OSS agent. While on infantry maneuvers in Virginia, Musulin was approached by an OSS representative who asked if he would volunteer for dangerous work behind the lines in the European theater. Musulin immediately accepted the offer and soon found himself in parachute training, made possible only by a special waiver that gave him a nearly one-hundred-pound exemption to the usual 185-pound limit for parachute jumps. The training officers marveled at the huge soldier's willingness to jump, and each time he did, they made lighthearted bets about how many panels in his chute would blow out.

When he was dropped into enemy territory in October 1943, this former star tackle on the University of Pittsburgh football team was the heaviest American soldier to make a successful parachute jump in World War II.

After making his way to Mihailovich's headquarters in 1943, during the period when the British were officially supporting Tito and Mihailovich in equal measures, Musulin reported to his superiors in Cairo that Mihailovich claimed to have 57,440 men mobilized and that he could mobilize more than four hundred thousand if he had arms for them. The American agent's estimates of Mihailovich's men was somewhat lower at thirty-five thousand, but he described the general as having "a fairly well-organized army." However, he also reported that, "Mihailovich is now doing very little fighting against the Germans, although he did have a month of considerable activity after the Italian capitulation in September 1943." Mihailovich's forces appeared to have complete control over the mountainous region of Serbia, he reported, though he noted that the soldiers were remarkably lacking in military supplies. All of the arms were in "very poor condition," he said, most of them old Yugoslav army rifles, and the guerillas seemed as dependent on mountaineers' axes and knives strapped to their belts. Musulin saw many German machine pistols and Barettas in the hands of Chetnik fighters, along with the occasional light machine guns. Mortars and heavy machine guns were in especially short supply, and there were practically no artillery pieces at all. Worst of all, Musulin reported, was that there wasn't enough ammunition even for the few old weapons the Chetniks had. "I would estimate each soldier has an average of about twenty-five to forty rounds per rifle, and one hundred fifty to two hundred rounds per machine gun," he reported. He went on to say that the average Chetnik soldier "is extremely poorly clothed and has been living a hard, rugged, and miserable life for three years in the woods, suffering many hardships, living in dirty peasant huts, and eating what the peasant will give him. Many troops have not seen their families for nearly three years, or have lost them through German reprisals. Considering these factors, the morale and discipline of the troops in Serbia is good."

Musulin also noted that, "The Serbian people are tremendously enthusiastic for Americans. They refer to Americans as the only nation which has no ultimate designs on them." They did not have such warm feelings for the British. Musulin described a complete distrust of the British by Mihailovich and his leaders "who feel the British have now sold them down the river to Stalin."

The American agent was not in any mood to defend the British SOE. Musulin also reported back to the OSS post in Cairo that the British sometimes obstructed his operations, apparently not out of any disloyalty to the Allied cause or any interest in collaborating with the enemy, but as a matter of protecting their turf and making sure the British authority in the region was not challenged. Vujnovich saw the same interference on his end. Sometimes the interference was overt and sometimes it amounted to simply a lack of cooperation and a disregard for the aims of the OSS missions. Intelligence might be restricted so as to exclude the

Americans who could benefit from it, or messages might be passed along very slowly, eventually winding their way through the proper channels but with no urgency. The lack of cooperation, or outright interference, was even more pronounced when it came to operational missions in which the OSS needed to send agents behind enemy lines with specific objectives. These missions required great coordination and logistical challenges, and the Americans often had to rely on the British SOE because of its longer history in the region and more substantial infrastructure. In his short time in Bari already, Vujnovich had experienced the same frustration with the British that Musulin and the other agents in the field were complaining about. Missions that relied on British cooperation would be delayed over and over, critical supplies would not be dropped to agents and local guerillas, and perhaps most difficult of all, virtually all communications in and out of Yugoslavia had to go through British channels.

Musulin also complained that the Chetniks—and the airmen they were hiding—were receiving virtually no material support. Having already seen the supplies delivered to Tito, Musulin was outraged at the lack of airdrops to the equally loyal—and some would say far more loyal—Mihailovich in the mountains. Why should the airmen harbored by Mihailovich get virtually no support from the Allies when airmen lucky enough to bail out in Tito's territory could depend on a quick return to their Italian bases? Musulin became so enraged with the lack of supplies sent to Mihailovich that he sent an angry message to his OSS superiors in Cairo reminding them that, "We can't fight Jerry with bare feet, brave hearts, and Radio London."

The bottom line for Musulin was that Mihailovich represented a significant fighting force that was on the Allies' side. "Mihailovich keeps a certain number of German and Bulgarian troops immobilized. Withdrawal of all Allied liaison or labeling him as a traitor would undoubtedly free some of these troops for use on some other front." He also pushed for the Allies to exert more pressure on both Tito and Mihailovich to declare a truce with each other and concentrate on fighting the troops occupying their country, saying, "The Royal Yugoslav Government could make Mihailovich agree to a truce. It is up to the Great Powers to make Tito do the same by exercising sanctions they obviously possess."

That never happened.

**It would be decades before** Mihailovich's suspicions about a Communist plot to besmirch his reputation with the British was confirmed. Not until 1997 would the world understand that the switch of allegiance was orchestrated largely by a Soviet operative who convinced the British that Mihailovich could not be trusted.

The abandonment of Mihailovich was the culmination of a long series of suspicions and mistrust, not just the work of a single man, and Mihailovich's own missteps must be considered. But the information revealed fifty-four years later indicates that the general was right about the primary reason the British thought he was collaborating with the enemy and failing to fight the Germans and Italians in Yugoslavia. Communist moles had infiltrated both the OSS and the SOE, working to besmirch the name of Mihailovich to promote the postwar communization of Yugoslavia under Tito. In 1997 newly declassified secret reports on one of the most controversial British undercover operations of World War II showed a Soviet spy was responsible for the British switching support to Tito, confirming the suspicions of some experts who had been studying the case for years. The documents included transcripts of secret wartime signals to London and included evidence of the role played by James Klugmann, a confirmed Soviet mole.

Reports sent by Klugmann, who was closely associated with the infamous British traitors known as the Cambridge Five, for the first time confirmed that he was principally responsible for sabotaging the Mihailovich supply operation and for keeping from London information about how much Mihailovich forces were fighting the Germans and how much success they were having. The Cambridge Five was a ring of British spies who passed information to the Soviet Union during World War II and on into the early 1950s. Proven members were Kim Philby, Guy Burgess, Anthony Blunt, Donald Maclean, and John Cairncross—all high-ranking members of the government and secret agents. Klugmann was essentially the sixth member, though his role as a spy was not confirmed until after the rest of group was identified. Philby served as head of the Soviet counterespionage section of MI6, Britain's external security agency and top intelligence outfit. Burgess was secretary to the British Deputy Foreign Minister and able to transmit top-secret British Foreign Office documents to the KGB on a regular basis, secreting them out at night to be photographed by his Russian controller and returning them in the morning. Blunt was an art historian who had served the royal household as surveyor of the queen's pictures. Maclean worked as a diplomat for the British Foreign Office, serving as secretary at the British embassy in Washington, DC, during the war and sending messages to Moscow revealing British efforts to develop an atomic bomb. Cairncross was an intelligence officer working on ciphers at Bletchley Park and MI6. He passed documents through secret channels to the Soviet Union.

Klugmann spent two and a half years working in Bari on the staff of the Yugoslav section of the British SOE as an intelligence and coordination officer—the SOE that Vujnovich knew was favoring Tito over Mihailovich for no good reason, and which ultimately persuaded Churchill to side with the Communists in Yugoslavia's civil war. Klugmann's work with the Yugoslav section was so influential that his commanding officer, Basil Davidson, said—with admiration—that the time should be called the "Klugmann period."

The group of traitors was originally known as the Cambridge Spy Ring because all known members of the ring were recruited at Trinity College in Cambridge while members of the Cambridge Apostles, a secret debating society. They also were open Communists and Klugmann was secretary of the Cambridge Communist Party in the mid-1930s. Like the Cambridge Five, Klugmann could more accurately be described as a mole rather than a typical spy. The difference is that, unlike a spy who embarks on a mission with specific objectives, moles entrench themselves in key government roles or other positions that make them privy to secrets—or the ability to manipulate leaders—and then wait for the right time to act. Moles often are ideologically driven to betray their countries, as opposed to mercenaries who act for money. The Soviets recruited Klugmann because he displayed a sympathy to leftist causes and was well on the path to a career in government or other sensitive work, the same as Philby, Burgess, Blunt, Maclean, and Cairncross. Taking their orders from Moscow, their task was to direct British policy in a manner favorable to the worldwide Communist movement and Russia in particular. They did the job well. David Martin, the foremost historian on Yugoslavia during World War II, concluded that Klugmann was ultimately responsible for leading the British to abandon Mihailovich, and that he was responsible for the postwar Communist expansion in the Balkans. "Klugmann was a mole whose great accomplishment was to falsify information in a manner that resulted in handing over a nation of fifteen million people to Communist control," he wrote.

Klugmann was a bespectacled bookworm, warm-hearted and compassionate but so fiercely devoted to Communism that he had little time for personal relationships. Blunt, after he was exposed as a traitor and his knighthood for wartime service revoked, described Klugmann as "the pure intellectual of the Party," more dedicated than any other Communist in Britain. Even though he spent little time on personal relationships, while at Cambridge he was among the most effective in recruiting other students to the Communist cause, and he could channel his political energy into manipulating those around him. The recently declassified files reveal that, for instance, Klugmann had great influence over Colonel Sir William Deakin, the senior intelligence officer in Yugoslavia, who said Klugmann provided "invaluable service." The declassified files reveal that Klugmann used his relationship with Deakin to advance Tito's cause, always claiming to act in the best interest of Great Britain but in fact working to further the Soviet Union's goal of a Communist Yugoslavia after the war by exaggerating claims of Mihailovich's transgressions, minimizing reports of his accomplishments, and glorifying the actions of Tito. All of the Cambridge Five used other unsuspecting people to serve the Soviet Union's goals. While the Soviets had operatives in the British intelligence services, Martin notes that the actual number of Communists in the top ranks was small. "Far more numerous than the Communists, and infinitely more numerous than the committed agents, were the muddleheaded liberals who shared a nebulous feeling that they, too, were serving the cause of progress," Martin writes. The naïveté of these government officials, and their desire to feel important, made them susceptible to Communist efforts to disseminate disinformation about Mihailovich. Klugmann and his fellow traitors may have been driving the effort to defeat Mihailovich from abroad, but there were many more British officials who unwittingly helped them along the way. As in the OSS, a person's Communist beliefs did not necessarily bar one from serving in the SOE, and those around Klugmann knew of his party affiliation but overlooked it because he was so hardworking, amiable, and seemed to produce good results.

On March 15, 1944, Klugmann moved from Cairo to Bari along with most of the other SOE staff. One of his duties was to educate newly arriving SOE staff about the Mihailovich and Tito conflict, briefing them on the opposing sides in Yugoslavia and where the British stood. The most influential Communist spy in Europe was working practically right alongside Vujnovich and his colleagues, quietly but effectively sabotaging every effort to help Mihailovich and ensuring that Yugoslavia would be in the hands of the Soviet Union after the war.

One of the most active and overt British Communists of his generation, Klugmann became an influential left-wing journalist after the war, serving as editor of *Marxism Today* and writing the first two volumes of the official *History of the Communist Party of Great Britain*.


**So Mihailovich's suspicions were on** target.

Vujnovich had no idea at the time that such a well-orchestrated and far-reaching Communist operation was at work within the OSS and SOE, but he would not have been overly surprised. He knew there were Communists infiltrating the ranks, and he hated every one of them.

Meanwhile, Mihailovich and the peasants in the hillside who were loyal to him watched over the downed American boys with a stoic determination. Their abandonment by the Allies would not cause them to abandon these young men who were helping them fight back the Nazis.

# Chapter 10

## *Screw the British*

**A few months after the Allies officially turned their** backs on Mihailovich, in March 1944, the British ordered all Allied units attached to Mihailovich to return home. The OSS's man in Ravna Gora, Musulin, was ordered to leave the Yugoslav general's stronghold in the mountains and report to the OSS post in Bari, Italy, where Vujnovich was in charge. He was instructed to leave as soon as an evacuation could be arranged for him and forty American airmen who were in the immediate area at that time. Musulin did not want to leave the field and tried to stall by saying that he had heard of an additional dozen men who were expected to arrive soon and also could be rescued if he stayed a while longer. His superiors knew that Musulin was trying to resist orders and supported the effort, appealing to President Roosevelt for permission to let him stay with Mihailovich. But the British would not relent and Churchill personally intervened to reiterate that Musulin had to come out. Mihailovich was no longer to receive any cooperation from the Allies, and that meant Musulin had no more business with the Chetnik guerillas, Churchill explained.

In May 1944 a plane was sent to pick up Musulin and the

downed fliers, and it successfully completed Musulin's extraction and a noteworthy rescue of airmen. Meanwhile, the Allied support of Tito was on the upswing. In November 1943 only six men had been assigned to Tito's group, but by October 1944 that number would reach forty.

Musulin was one unhappy agent when he stepped off the plane in Bari, and he progressed into a rage when he heard what the SOE and the OSS had been saying about Mihailovich.

Musulin was dumbfounded that anyone could believe the accusations that Mihailovich had collaborated with the Germans and Italians. When he heard that airmen were being warned to bail out only in the Yugoslav territory controlled by Tito, he was outraged. Musulin had personally witnessed the unwavering dedication of the Chetnik soldiers and the local villagers to the downed American airmen, and now his colleagues in Bari were trying to explain to him how Mihailovich was no longer a friend. They actually tried to tell Musulin that Mihailovich's people would pretend to take in downed airmen and then turn them over to the enemy for a reward. He couldn't believe the words he was hearing. Only days earlier he had seen these very people giving up their last bits of food, offering their beds to strangers from another country, risking their lives with every act of kindness to an American. Musulin was furious and he argued at every opportunity with anyone who would listen, trying to convince them that he had personally experienced life with the Chetniks, had become a good friend of Mihailovich himself, had lived with them for months, and he knew that they were loyal beyond belief.

Vujnovich asked Musulin for details about how many more airmen Mihailovich was aiding in the region. Was it more than just a few stragglers here and there? He was looking for confirmation that the rumors from his wife back home were correct, that there were a lot of men awaiting rescue. Musulin's response was quick and certain: Yes, Mihailovich was harboring a large number of airmen. He didn't know exactly how many, but he guessed close to one hundred men were near Mihailovich's headquarters in Pranjane. Nearly all were American, with a few British, French, Russians, and Italians.

*So Mirjana was right.* Vujnovich had known he could trust his wife to have good information. He was glad he had trusted her and that he had already started pursuing a rescue attempt. The effort was much farther along than it would have been if Musulin's report was the first anyone in Bari had heard of all those men awaiting rescue.

Musulin could not be calmed, and he was a formidable sight when angered. Not only was Musulin not pleased to hear that Mihailovich had been abandoned, but he felt that the Allies had for all practical purposes abandoned *him* while he was behind enemy lines with the Chetniks. Despite his pleas for aid, virtually nothing was sent to Mihailovich and his men. The burly agent stormed into the OSS headquarters in Bari one day and demanded that someone listen to his complaints.

"Listen, you bastards! You think I went in and risked my life for almost a year for nothing?" he screamed, instantly gaining the attention of everyone in the room. He went on for some time, railing about how he had almost no contact with the British the whole time he was in Yugoslavia and that when he arrived in Bari, the Brits weren't even interested in hearing his report about Mihailovich. They were concerned only with dressing him down for bringing five members of Mihailovich's political staff out with him. The general had requested that the men be evacuated, and since there was room on the plane, Musulin had obliged. After all, he explained, these were allies and he was doing a favor for the man who was supporting the American cause in Yugoslavia. Musulin refused to apologize for bringing the men out and grew more livid every time the British complained about it. He finally became so angry that he asked to be court-martialed for the incident so the truth of the whole ugly situation could be aired beyond the cloistered walls of the OSS.

Wisely, his superiors did not take him up on the offer and the British backed down. But Musulin was still furious about how the OSS seemed to be turning Yugoslavia—and more—over to the Communists. He was so disgusted with what he found in Bari that he decided it was pointless to even write a report about his experience with Mihailovich. Referring to pro-Communists as Partisans, like the followers of Tito, Musulin complained that, "I came to Bari and saw Partisans all over the damn town. I saw them in our headquarters. They were packing supplies on our planes in Brindisi." And he was right. The OSS officers' mess in Bari had seven Yugoslav refugee girls working as waitresses who made no effort to conceal their pro-Communist politics, even wearing Partisan uniforms around Bari on their off hours. Musulin went on to complain that the OSS and SOE "forgot that I was even alive."

Musulin was a bitter man, dejected by the politically motivated betrayals and propaganda he found waiting for him in Bari. He eventually was convinced to write a nineteen-page report that declared Mihailovich was a loyal ally and that he saw no evidence of collaboration with the enemy. But his protests and his report changed no one's position. London and Washington had painted their own picture of Mihailovich and the truth didn't matter.

Vujnovich listened to Musulin and believed him. Unlike many OSS leaders, Vujnovich understood what it meant for the Allies to throw their support behind a Communist, because he had seen them at work in Yugoslavia before the war and he knew their ideology and their tactics. He tried to explain to Musulin why his protests were going nowhere.

"People in the OSS don't have any real political orientation," he said. "When they hear 'Communist' they just think of Russian Communists. When they hear 'Fascist' they think of Germany and Italy. They don't realize what Communism really is, the way it works to overpower a country's people and take everything from them. They don't understand that Communism is a cancer that can spread all over if you don't stop it. They just think it's Russia and right now Russia is our ally."

Musulin found some solace in knowing that Vujnovich at least was on his side. And Vujnovich knew that Musulin was a man he could trust. That might come in handy, as Vujnovich was under fire in Bari from some of the pro-Communists in the OSS who thought he was too pro-Chetnik. Several of his colleagues who were sympathetic to Tito and the Russians regularly harassed Vujnovich, making unfounded charges about the way he ran his operations and generally trying to create trouble for him.

He had recently spent a difficult five months in Brindisi, Italy, at the air base from which the OSS launched incursions into Yugoslavia and Greece. (The OSS base in Bari was focused on analyzing intelligence and planning operations. The actual missions launched from Brindisi.) Vujnovich found himself under fire the whole time from other OSS officials who filed anonymous complaints and kept him busy responding to his superiors about supposedly poor performance on the job. It didn't take long for Vujnovich to figure out that the pro-Communists were behind the harassment, which ended only when he was transferred back to the OSS post in Bari.

That the OSS was full of Communist sympathizers, outright Communists, and even some people who were secretly spying and working behind the scenes to further the Communist cause came as no surprise to anyone familiar with the unusual makeup of the OSS. This group of operatives and analysts was unique in the history of the American military. They were given great leeway and resources to get the job done in unorthodox ways, with just about anything acceptable in the cause of defeating the Axis. The men and women of the OSS were some of the most dedicated fighters in World War II, many of them among the most idealistic patriots, but they also were a mix of down-to-earth "regular Joes" like Musulin and effete intellectual types who tended to the leftist, Socialist political spectrum. The mix made for an effective system overall, but it also created inevitable conflicts among people who had a common enemy—Hitler and the Axis—but who differed sharply on their basic political outlook and what they wanted for the country after the war. In that way, the struggle within the OSS mirrored the struggle within Yugoslavia.

**Established in June 1942 as** the country revved up for full-scale war with the Axis, the OSS was charged with collecting and analyzing strategic information required by the Joint Chiefs of Staff and conducting special operations not assigned to other agencies. Right off the bat, however, those other agencies started to feel that the OSS was encroaching on their turf. The Federal Bureau of Investigation, under the direction of the fiery and extremely powerful J. Edgar Hoover, was insistent that this upstart bunch of academics and wannabe spies neither get in the way nor usurp its own areas of operation. The FBI retained all responsibility for fieldwork in Latin America and essentially shut the OSS out of work in the Western Hemisphere. But the OSS was nobody's meek little brother. The organization was conceived and developed by William J. Donovan, known as "Wild Bill," a charismatic, energetic leader and one of the few men who could stand toe-to-toe with Hoover and not be intimidated.

Born in Buffalo, New York, Donovan was a college football star at Columbia University, graduating in 1905. Donovan was a member of the New York City establishment, a powerful Wall Street lawyer and a Columbia law school classmate of Franklin Delano Roosevelt. Donovan first became known for his military exploits in 1912, when he formed and led a troop of cavalry of the New York State Militia that in 1916 served on the U.S.–Mexico border in the Pancho Villa Expedition. In World War I, Donovan led a regiment of the United States Army, the 165th Regiment of the 42nd Division, the successors to the famed 69th New York Volunteers, on the battlefield in France. He was awarded the Medal of Honor for leading a successful assault despite serious wounds. By the end of the war he was a full colonel.

The disaster at Pearl Harbor had underscored what many in Washington already knew: The country was terribly deficient in its foreign intelligence and special operations. Nobody in Washington or anywhere else had put the pieces of the puzzle together and figured out that Japan was about to strike, and intelligence in the ever-darkening Europe was no better. President Roosevelt was preparing for the next world war, and he was ready to take bold news steps regarding intelligence, ready to undertake operations that the country had never pursued before. He was looking for men who had already proven themselves, and Secretary of the Navy Frank Knox recommended Donovan. Roosevelt gave him a number of increasingly important assignments, trusting him absolutely even though Roosevelt was a Democrat and Donovan a staunch Republican. In 1940 and 1941 Donovan served as an emissary for Knox and President Roosevelt, traveling to Britain and parts of Europe that were not under Nazi control. When he persuaded Roosevelt in 1942 that the country needed a more extensive and aggressive network of spies, analysts, and secret agents across the world, the OSS was born and Donovan became one of the most powerful men in Washington.

This cloak-and-dagger society was housed in a nondescript government building a short distance west of the Lincoln Memorial in Washington, DC, in the former home of the National Health Institute. It was in a rundown section of town, far from the gleaming white Capitol and the other glamorous structures of the city. But inside, brainy academics were performing some of the most important work of World War II, and others were supervising the dangerous, nerve-racking work of OSS agents in the field halfway around the world. The National Health Institute had been hastily evicted to make way for the rapidly growing OSS, and they hadn't completely vacated the premises by the time the OSS moved in. The health researchers left behind an experimental laboratory full of live monkeys, goats, and guinea pigs, all inoculated with deadly diseases, and the OSS staff were none too happy about sharing their space with them. More important was the need for the space taken up by the menagerie. So Donovan, in the creative style that he would employ throughout the war, complained to the National Health Institute that one of the monkeys had bitten a stenographer and caused a rebellion among the staff, who were afraid that the plague would sweep through the building. The scientists doubted the whole story but were forced to remove the laboratory and give the space over to the OSS. Nazi propaganda seized on the incident to broadcast gleeful accounts of how the supposedly fearsome OSS was really nothing more than "fifty professors, twenty monkeys, ten goats, twelve guinea pigs, and a staff of Jewish scribblers." As soon as Donovan had taken the helm at the OSS, Nazi propaganda minister Joseph Goebbels focused on him, directing more hate toward him than any American other than President Roosevelt.

The OSS had been designed from the start as a different kind of government agency. Even the FBI, as powerful as it was under Hoover, adhered to a strict bureaucracy that was every bit as rigid as the bureaucracy in any more mundane government operation and sometimes more so. But with the OSS, the whole purpose was to do things differently. President

Roosevelt's order establishing the OSS had defined its purpose as being "to collect and analyze strategic information, and to plan and operate special services," which were described as "all measures . . . taken to enforce our will upon the enemy by means other than military action, as may be applied in support of actual or planned military operations or in furtherance of the war effort." Roosevelt and Donovan understood that to mean anything the country needed, anything that the regular military could not accomplish logistically or could not do ethically. When a task had to be performed out of the public eye and without any obvious ties to the United States, that was a job for the men and women working under Donovan.

Donovan's stamp was all over the OSS, never more so than in the type of agents it recruited. When the OSS structure was just being planned in 1941, a high-ranking officer in the British Naval Intelligence named Ian Fleming, later the creator of James Bond, advised Donovan to select agents who fit the bill of the quintessential gentleman spy. They should be between forty and fifty years old and possess "absolute discretion, sobriety, devotion to duty, languages, and wide experience," Ian advised. Donovan ignored the advice and instead told President Roosevelt that he intended to bring in young men and women who were "calculatingly reckless" and trained for "aggressive action."

The OSS attracted some of the best and brightest in the country, even though it was still an obscure agency known only to government wonks and military leaders. Donovan's extensive network of contacts in business, academia, and the military, along with his own stellar reputation and gregarious personality, enabled him to recruit the top players in any field, many of whom would go on to their own high-profile accomplishments after a stint in the OSS. Recruiting was a major task for OSS leaders because the agency needed a lot of bodies at desks and in the field. Analysts were chosen for their skill in languages, mathematics, codes, sciences—any specialty that could be of use. Field agents—spies in the truest sense of the word—were chosen on more esoteric but equally stringent guidelines. The most important qualification, Donovan declared, was strength of character. While some suggested recruiting petty criminals experienced in deception, Donovan refused. He wanted good men and women who had nothing to hide, who were upstanding people with no experience living a double life. The reason was simple, Donovan explained: It was easier to train an honest citizen to engage in subterfuge for the good of his country than it was to teach a dishonest man to be a trustworthy agent. The people who fancied themselves secret agents and wanted to live a glamorous but dangerous life behind enemy lines always raised red flags with Donovan and his subordinates. Donovan found that the staid businessman, the type who would have led a perfectly sedate and uneventful live if not recruited to the OSS, made the perfect field agents. The OSS also made a point of recruiting people who could get along well with others, especially people of other races and cultures, and conducted psychological testing to confirm that trait.

The result was perhaps the most unusual collection of spies and analysts ever assembled, a mix of wealthy blue bloods, sons and daughters of the rich and powerful, men and women who looked more like the businesspeople they were before the war and not the skilled killers they were training to be. Newspapers joked that OSS must stand for "Oh So Social" because the recruits looked as though they had been taken from the Social Register. The halls of the OSS were full of DuPonts, Vanderbilts, Roosevelts, Morgans, and Mellons. The cousin of Winston Churchill, a star polo player, worked in the OSS. So did Ilya Tolstoy, grandson of the famous novelist. A columnist for the *Washington Times* wrote of the new OSS that:

If you should by chance wander in the labyrinth of the OSS, you'd behold ex–polo players, millionaires, Russian princes, society gambol boys, scientists, and dilettante detectives. All of them are now at the OSS where they used to be allocated between New York, Palm Beach, Long Island, Newport, and other meccas frequented by the blue bloods of democracy. And the girls! The prettiest, best born, snappiest girls who used to graduate from debutantedom to boredom now bend their blond and brunette locks, or their colorful hats, over their work in the OSS, the super-ultra-intelligence-counter-espionage unit that is headed by the brilliant "Wild Bill" Donovan.

Other notable members of the OSS were Jumping Joe Savoldi, a fullback at Notre Dame and a professional wrestler, and John Ringling North, the owner of Barnum & Bailey Circus. Quentin Roosevelt, grandson of the president, died on an OSS mission in China. Julia Child worked for the OSS in Ceylon before becoming a world-famous chef, claiming she was only a lowly file clerk but nevertheless winning the Emblem of Meritorious Service. Actor Sterling Hayden, often called "the most beautiful man in Hollywood," was recruited by the OSS to command a fleet of ships that ran guns and supplies to Yugoslavia.

OSS recruiters were always on the lookout for anyone with a special connection that might be useful, so many people with no special ambitions to be a spy—like George Vujnovich—found themselves approached with a unique offer. If you had spent significant time in a European country, or if you spoke a language that was in demand—like George Musulin—the OSS might come looking for you. The military ranks were often screened for those with needed skills, particularly languages spoken in Europe. Sometimes the recruit's value was less obvious but could prove vital in wartime. The OSS recruited a former Paris bartender from the Yale Club, a former German sergeant who could help forge military passes, a Swiss mountain climber who knew the high passes of the Apennines, and a Catholic missionary who had lived with the Kachin tribesmen in northern Burma. When the OSS spotted someone who could add to the agency's skill set, one or two men approached without warning and explained that his country needed his services. Questions were met with cryptic responses that provided little detail, not even the name of the outfit that wanted him to join. The men emphasized that he would be making a great contribution to his country, but they also were clear that he would be participating in extremely dangerous missions with a good chance that he would never return. In the patriotic fervor of the early war years, few of those approached by the OSS refused.

Donovan's whole approach to the OSS mission was to employ real people in real situations. He had no patience for those who thought the spy game was nothing but shooting and knifing the enemy or conducting explosive raids, or for the dilettante diplomats and amateur detectives. Donovan knew that in wartime, advances were often made not by the dramatic charge of a thousand troops but by one lightweight, bespectacled former accountant asking the right question of a bored farmer driving his sheep down a country road. While the work of OSS agents was often extremely dangerous, until the agents got caught their work encompassed the pedestrian more than the exotic. After the war, Donovan explained: "Our experience showed us that a half hour spent with the brakeman of a freight train running into occupied France would produce more useful information than a Mata Hari could learn in a year. We did not rely on the seductive blonde or the phony mustache. The major part of our intelligence was the result of good old-fashioned intellectual sweat." In addition to their particular skills, field agents were selected for their idealism. Most were under thirty years old, and they had a clear conception that the Allies were right and the Axis was wrong. When they parachuted into villages in Europe and lived with the people fighting bare-handed against the Nazis, they developed immense respect for the plight of those people.

The OSS would employ some thirty thousand people by the end of the war, and its zeal for assembling a broad collection of resources meant that the particular skill or knowledge possessed by the recruit could overshadow nearly anything else that might make the person undesirable for an intelligence post. If a dishwasher in Chicago spoke fluent Italian and had worked on the railway in his home country, he might be recruited for the OSS even if he spent every Tuesday night at a meeting of the Communist Party USA. Donovan had no love for Communists, but he also did not hate them so much that he let their politics get in the way of a larger goal. After all, this was the 1940s, before Westerners recognized that Communism was more than just an extreme political movement and the very word "Communist" became synonymous with evil. Largely because of the number of upper-class Ivy League graduates in the ranks, OSS agents at desks in Washington and in the field around the world tended to share a social idealism, the same unwavering faith in the common man espoused by Donovan. This idealistic view of the working man was more common among those who had spent time at Yale and on yachts in Bar Harbor than the recruits from the regular military, but the blue-blood idealism often meshed with the thinking of the Italian immigrant who had fled Fascists in his homeland and was recruited while waiting tables in New York. It was not uncommon for OSS agents serving in Europe to be immigrants who had fled the Nazi onslaught and joined the Communist movement mostly because it was staunchly anti-Fascist. The result was an OSS that was not nearly as inhospitable to Communists as other branches of the military or the government, especially Hoover's FBI, where any Communist trying to infiltrate had to keep a very low profile.

Donovan regularly confirmed that Communists were found throughout his organization. When the OSS sent a group of four confirmed Communists into Italy to send back information, an American congressman investigated and angrily informed Donovan that one of the group was said to be on the honor roll of the Young Communist League. Donovan didn't deny the charge but made it clear that he didn't care as long as the men continued sending back useful intelligence from Italy. "I don't know if he's on the Communist honor roll, but for the job he's doing in Italy, he's on the honor roll of OSS." Donovan's attitude was, again, pragmatic above all else. When the FBI presented him with dossiers proving that three OSS employees were Communists and demanded their firing, Donovan scoffed and replied, "I know they're Communists. That's why I hired them." The agents in question had fought for the Republican Loyalists in the Spanish Civil War of 1936–39, in a brigade sponsored by the American Communist Party. As far as Donovan was concerned, they were good fighters with a healthy hatred for Nazis, and that was good enough for him.

That attitude permeated the OSS, with all involved adopting the idea that they could and should do whatever was necessary to achieve the end goal and not worry about meaningless details along the way. This approach grew out of the very freedom that the OSS was founded on, the idea that its reason for existing was to get things done creatively, without the usual restrictions that hindered other military units. To some extent that was an effective way to cut through the bureaucracy that could bog down such important work, but some critics said the OSS took it too far and became a rogue outfit, too undisciplined for its own good. Though the majority of OSS operatives held military rank, they ignored most military protocol, rarely saluting and by necessity eschewing military uniforms. Most agents in the field, and even those working desks in foreign posts, were allowed to dress however they wanted, growing beards and long hair if they felt like it. Insubordination was a way of life in the OSS. The same instruction that would have been considered a direct order in the army might be considered a mere suggestion in the OSS. If a superior annoyed a junior officer, a request for information might be "lost." This was not the regular army, in more ways than one.

**The OSS favored results over** drama, but there was no denying that OSS agents had the opportunity for more romantic roles in the war than most soldiers. Rather than fighting on the front lines with a rifle or in a tank, the OSS agent lived inconspicuously behind enemy lines, blending into the often exotic locales and charming his or her way into the lives of people who could provide important information. Instead of a foxhole in Belgium, the OSS agent might be living in an apartment in occupied Paris. Plenty of agents, however, like Musulin, spent their time out in the countryside with local people who were just barely getting by. OSS agents went where they were needed and blended in wherever they were.

The OSS was designed to be creative, and it led the way in developing some of the most ingenious devices and methodologies used in World War II. Propaganda was a major focus, with the OSS facilitating radio broadcasts into enemy territory, leaflet drops to lower the morale of Axis soldiers, and even some strategies aimed at convincing the people of Germany that the war was lost. Intelligence gathering was perhaps the primary activity for an agent, but sabotage also occupied OSS agents to a great extent, sometimes with the aim of softening up an area before conventional forces moved in, sometimes with the goal of harassing and slowing down enemy forces in a given area. Donovan thought that his men had to be clever and devious because the Germans were the eight-hundred-pound gorilla of international warfare. There was no denying that Hitler had the arms, the soldiers, and the ruthless attitude necessary to take what he wanted, so Donovan's theory was that his men would take the other tack, slipping in behind enemy lines to create mayhem. They could nip at the heels of the Nazis, slowing them down as they ravaged another country and distracting them until the big guns of American firepower could come in for the kill.

In addition to extensive training in hand-to-hand combat and conventional weapons, the OSS provided agents with an astonishing array of clever gadgets and innovative ways to kill. Most of them were developed by Stanley Lovell, handpicked by Donovan to head the agency's research-and-development branch. He was given free rein to be as devious and underhanded as he wanted, with a premium placed on unusual, creative tools that the enemy would never suspect. Lovell did not disappoint, equipping agents with special weapons like Aunt Jemima, an explosive that looked remarkably like regular flour and could even be used to bake muffins and bread. The surprise came when you stuck a fuse in the muffin and threw it at some Germans. There was also the Casey Jones, a device that could be attached to the bottom of a railroad car. It had an electronic eye that sensed the sudden decrease in light when the train entered a tunnel, which set off an explosive charge that filled the tunnel with a mangled mess of metal. The train was destroyed, the tunnel was blocked, and it took days to remove the wreckage by hand. As a final touch in case the device was discovered, the OSS added a sticker to the Casey Jones that played into the Nazi soldier's seeming inability to challenge authority. In German, the sticker said, *This is a car movement-control device. Removal or tampering is strictly forbidden under heaviest penalties by the Third Reich Railroad Consortium. Heil Hitler.*

Other weapons included miniature guns disguised as pens, tobacco pipes, and umbrellas, and bombs disguised as everyday objects. A favorite was the lump of coal that Felman had seen used against a train in Yugoslavia. Another was a candle that a female agent could light while spending time with a German officer, making sure she left the room before it burned down to a preset mark and exploded. Shoes had hidden cavities and corsets had stilettos hidden in the fabric. Anything that a person might normally carry without suspicion was reworked in the OSS laboratories to make it a weapon, a hiding place, or a way to collect information.

OSS scientists also produced huge volumes of forged documents, everything from identity papers to supply requisitions and Gestapo badges.

Some of the weapons that Lovell and his team designed were so dangerous that the OSS lost agents while trying to demonstrate them. One was the Beano grenade, designed to be much more deadly than the typical grenade, which was plenty deadly already. A key difference was that the Beano had a small butterfly-shaped fitting on it that caught wind as the grenade was thrown. The butterfly turned in the wind, which activated the grenade, causing it to explode the instant it landed on the ground or contacted anything else. This design meant that, unlike when using regular grenades that worked on a timer after pulling the pin and throwing it, the enemy did not have a second or two to run away—or to pick up the grenade and throw it back at you—before it exploded. The Beano carried twice the explosive power of a regular grenade and one of its first victims was an instructor who was making the point that the round Beano could be thrown just like a baseball. Without thinking, he tossed the grenade up in the air as he would a baseball to demonstrate. The Beano activated and exploded when he caught it on the way down.

OSS agents knew that they were risking their lives every single day they were in the field. If caught by the enemy, spies and saboteurs could be killed on the spot without even violating the conventions of civilized warfare. Not that the enemy gave a whit about following the rules, of course. OSS agents knew that once they were caught, a quick execution might be the best they could hope for. In reality, they were far more likely to be tortured for days or weeks as the Nazis tried to squeeze information out of them or "turn" them, forcing them to work as double agents to feed misinformation to the Allies and draw out useful intelligence. The smallest slip of the tongue or a careless moment of inattention could result in an OSS agent dying slowly and painfully in a Gestapo torture chamber. Every person the OSS trusted was a link in the chain, a link that could be broken and lead the Germans to you.

Of the 831 members of the OSS decorated for gallantry during World War II, a significant number received their medals posthumously. Many disappeared without warning, never making another radio call to Cairo.

When the radio remained silent for weeks, their contacts knew what must have happened. And on occasion, the agent would radio but provide a subtle signal, perhaps a slightly different code word, to let his superiors know that he was contacting them under duress. When that happened, the Allies would continue providing instructions and information to the agent, making sure that the transmissions were plausible enough to keep the agent alive but not actually useful to the enemy holding the gun to his head.

The brutality of the Nazis knew no bounds. The cruelty unleashed on captured agents was unspeakable, including every type of beating imaginable and the liberal use of instruments of torture. The treatment of captured agents was surpassed perhaps only by the punishment exacted on members of the local resistance, like the villagers helping hide the Allied airmen in Pranjane. If caught helping the Allies, these hapless local people felt the worst of the German military. The Germans were great believers in the public spectacle and the power of heinous acts to cow anyone who witnessed them inflicted on others. The Nazi SS often castrated members of the resistance and gouged their eyes out, and a favorite method of terrorizing the local populace was to impale members of the resistance on meat hooks in the public square. The prisoner's hands were tied and soldiers lifted him off the ground, positioning him so that the meat hooks penetrated the underside of his jaw. Then the SS would force the entire village to file past the man and see him writhing in agony. The prisoner could hang for more than a day before the jawbone finally snapped and the hooks were driven deep into his brain.

Knowing that horrors like that awaited them, many OSS agents carried "L" pills hidden somewhere on their persons. The "L" stood for "lethal." The rubber-coated capsule could even be carried in the mouth for long periods, ready to use if the SS came through the doors. Biting down on the pill would spill its contents and bring nearly instant death.

**Most of the field agents** had been recruited through the army, so they had substantial military training and often some experience in the war before joining the OSS. The OSS administrators, on the other hand, tended to be the businessmen, the overeducated and the well connected. They usually were recruited because they possessed skills that were of use to the OSS, and there is no disputing that they served their country admirably. But inevitably, the agents risking their lives in the field developed a disdain for the "bourbon whiskey colonels" in Washington and other OSS posts who thought they could tell them how to do their jobs. Even the field agent who had led a sedate life before becoming a spy quickly developed disdain for someone who was giving him orders from the comfort of London or Cairo while he infiltrated German units and slept in pigsties. Unfortunately, these disputes sometimes went beyond the typical griping that comes from all soldiers in the field who think their commanders are out of touch. Arthur Goldberg, who worked for the OSS and later became a Supreme Court justice, complained after the war that Donovan had made a major mistake by selecting "men for the higher echelons of the organization who by background and temperament were unsympathetic with Donovan's own conception of the necessity of unstinting cooperation with the resistance movements." The men and women in the field shared Donovan's enthusiasm for supporting the insurgents and guerilla movements throughout Europe, but the OSS administrators in between were not always as consistent.

The OSS also had an ongoing feud with the State Department that would rear its head later in the Mihailovich affair. Part of the dispute was an old-fashioned turf war, the type that can be found in a thousand permutations around Washington, DC, but the State Department did have good reason to fear Donovan and his clandestine army. The freestyling ways of the OSS were a sharp contrast to the hidebound, stodgy, protocol-driven ways of the State Department. Where the OSS did whatever it felt would work in a given situation, the State Department was hobbled by tradition and diplomatic niceties. An analyst moving from the OSS to the State Department would be moving from a politically liberal, dynamic, intellectually driven agency to one that was conservative and driven largely by the career ambitions of bureaucrats. State Department officials knew that meant Donovan could always come out ahead when the president looked for results.

**Musulin's confirmation about the number** of airmen with Mihailovich, and his outrage at the abandonment of Mihailovich, built on the emotions the letter from Mirjana stirred in Vujnovich. When he started looking into the possibility of rescuing the downed airmen in the hills of Yugoslavia, he knew immediately that political concerns would be the first challenge. A year earlier, the same rescue mission would have been a very different proposition. It would have been a question of logistics mostly, a routine sort of decision about if, how, and when such a large rescue could be made. The answer might be no, but it would be for realistic reasons, not political ones.

In the spring of 1944, however, the logistical question took a backseat to politics. When Vujnovich presented his plans for rescuing the downed airmen in Yugoslavia, his superiors in the OSS knew there would be trouble getting approval from Washington. Aside from the risks of the mission, the Allies were now locked into their stated position that Mihailovich was a Nazi collaborator and could not be trusted. All Allied aid was given to Tito's forces, which ended up using the guns and ammunition against Mihailovich as much as against the Germans.

If Vujnovich could not get past the political impediments it didn't matter whether he could come up with a way to get those men out. The mission could never take place without approval from very high up, especially a rescue this large and one that would have to be so daring. Vujnovich worked with other OSS leaders in Bari and started formulating a plan. The OSS met with General Nathan Twining, commanding general of the Fifteenth Air Force, and at that meeting Musulin emphasized the need for an immediate rescue. The group discussed how such a large rescue might be accomplished, and then they sent the request up the chain of command. The OSS in Bari and the Fifteenth Air Force were in agreement that they wanted to go ahead with a rescue mission, but every time the request went across another bureaucrat's desk, the response was the same: We'd love to rescue those men, but how can we do that now that we've written off Mihailovich as a Nazi collaborator? If he really can't be trusted, this would be a suicide mission. And what if it's all a trick? What if he doesn't have a hundred airmen waiting to be rescued?

Vujnovich suspected the real motivation was fear that Mihailovich *did* have the airmen and really was protecting them. That could create an awkward situation if the man that the Allies accused of collaborating with the Nazis actually was protecting the downed airmen. If they went in and rescued the airmen, how could the Allies continue calling Mihailovich a collaborator?

The British, still operating on the false information fed to them by their spy James Klugmann, were vehemently opposed to anyone going into Mihailovich's territory for any reason, as were the Russians. The British insisted that Mihailovich could not be trusted and that no rescue mission be attempted. It was easy for them to say that, Vujnovich thought. There were maybe a few British fliers among the downed airmen in Yugoslavia, but there were a hundred or more Americans trying to get out, and the Brits were willing to let them stay in Yugoslavia until the Germans found them, they succumbed to injuries and disease, or in some other way were no longer a problem.

Vujnovich and the others in Bari kept pushing and eventually the debate went all the way to the top. On July 4, 1944, Donovan sent a letter to President Roosevelt asking for permission to send in a team of agents to conduct the rescue, working the request into a larger discussion about how Donovan and his subordinates were not happy about losing their presence in the territory controlled by Mihailovich. He noted in the letter that Musulin had been withdrawn at the request of Churchill, but he explained that the changing fronts of the war made it imperative to gather more intelligence from the region. Donovan was careful to acknowledge the delicate dance that had to take place between the United States and Britain when discussing intelligence operations in Yugoslavia, noting that there was "a basic difference between clandestine agents sent in for the purpose of obtaining general information and operational reconnaissance directed to the preparation of military movements." His interpretation of the current arrangement with the SOE was that the first could be carried out by either the Americans or the British without each other's approval, while the second required coordination.

> *Further, the British intend to send (if they have not already done so) an intelligence team into that area. In view of the above facts, and particularly of the view of General [Henry] Wilson that we aid him in searching for American pilots now known to be in that area, I respectfully request that we be permitted to send in our intelligence team and also our search parties.*

Donovan's letter had been carefully crafted to convey the proper respect for diplomatic channels and the propriety of international relations during wartime, the bureaucratic language striking all the required notes. But he was much more direct when speaking to the president in person a few days later. As they were discussing the issue, Roosevelt made it clear that he wanted to rescue the airmen but was concerned about how the British would respond.

Wild Bill Donovan, a man known for mincing no words and doing whatever it took to get the job done, spoke plainly to the president: "Screw the British! Let's get our boys out!" This was a tactic that Donovan often used when he was fed up with the insanely political maneuvering between the OSS, the State Department, and anyone else who thought they knew better than he did: Just say it in plain English. Get right to the point.

Sometimes it worked, sometimes it didn't. Fortunately the president was in the same no-nonsense mood that day and agreed. Word was sent from Washington to Italy, and on July 14, 1944, Lieutenant General Ira Eaker, the commander of the Mediterranean Allied Air Force, signed an order creating the Air Crew Rescue Unit (ACRU). The unit was assigned two B-25 bombers to use as needed, and the Fifteenth Air Force was on call to provide whatever other air resources ACRU wanted. The order creating ACRU specified that its work would be carried out by OSS agents and that missions would be coordinated from Bari. ACRU was commanded by none other than Colonel George Kraigher, Vujnovich's old friend from Pan American.

Kraigher's involvement gave Vujnovich some degree of confidence that this was a team he could trust. Vujnovich and his men could go ahead with his risky plan. Whether they could pull it off was still very much in doubt.

# Chapter 11

## Goats' Milk and Hay Bread

**The British were none too happy when they heard about** the formation of ACRU and the impending mission to Mihailovich's headquarters, suspecting that it was really just an attempt by Donovan to reestablish an OSS presence in that part of Yugoslavia. They were at least partially right. Donovan wanted to rescue the airmen for humanitarian reasons, but he was far too savvy to overlook the strategic potential of sending in a mission.

Five days after the special ACRU team was created, Donovan sent an urgent message notifying its members that Mihailovich had contacted the Yugoslav embassy in Washington with the news that about one hundred airmen were waiting for rescue. This was not news to anyone by this time, of course, though it may have been the first time that one of Mihailovich's many pleas for a rescue officially made it to the desk of someone who could act on it. Aware that Vujnovich and everyone else in Bari already knew Mihailovich was hiding the airmen, Donovan nevertheless used the official communication from Mihailovich as an opportunity to move the rescue forward and to pursue his own goals with ACRU. Donovan forwarded the message from Mihailovich as if it were urgent news.

*You are requested, therefore, to act on this soonest, using this chance as a means of establish [sic] a clandestine intelligence team in Yugoslavia. In order that our colleagues may not take advantage of our present position, you must act soonest.*

In other words, get the OSS team in there fast, while we have this message from Mihailovich as our reason for going in right away, and before "our colleagues" the British can interfere.

Vujnovich didn't need to be persuaded. He was in agreement with Donovan's intentions and he was working hard with the ACRU team to organize the rescue. But as soon as he got the go-ahead from Washington, Vujnovich realized he was facing a big challenge. With the rescues that already had been carried out in Yugoslavia, the idea of going in to pick up downed airmen was not radical in itself, but the situation had changed a lot in the past year, and Vujnovich knew this rescue would not be like the ones before. There was no real support from the British and only a grudging acceptance of the president's order, unlike previous missions that had been carried out as joint operations between the Allies with complete cooperation. And the previous missions had brought out a few dozen airmen, mostly by shuttling them through Yugoslavia's underground railroad to a safe zone where they could be picked up in relative safety. As recently as December 1943, OSS Lieutenant George Wuchinich parachuted into Yugoslavia with two other agents and, while pursuing other mission objectives to gather intelligence, managed to rescue ninety downed airmen over a four-month period.

With everything changed in Yugoslavia, and with so many more men awaiting rescue than ever before, this mission would be different.

Musulin had told him there were about one hundred airmen waiting in Pranjane, Vujnovich thought. *One hundred.* That number alone meant that the rescue was exponentially more difficult and dangerous than any that had been carried out before. How do you get one hundred sickly, injured airmen out of enemy territory without the Germans noticing? There were far too many to just try to slip them out on a small plane, and moving them all to a border where they might sneak across was out of the question. They risked being caught if they ventured away from Pranjane, and Vujnovich knew that one hundred men can't move anywhere with stealth. He decided there was only one way to rescue these men. They would have to go in and pick them up from Pranjane, right where they were. It was the only way, he kept telling himself, partly to convince himself that he wasn't organizing a suicide mission. *It's the only way to get them out. We have to go pick them up.*

The numbers complicated everything. If it were a dozen airmen needing rescue, it wouldn't have been such a wild idea to just send an OSS plane to land somewhere nearby and then sneak back out of Yugoslavia. Or you might be able to move through occupied territory until they reached a border that could be crossed. But with one hundred men, how many planes would that take? How many times would they have to land, pick up the airmen, take off, and fly home without being caught? Once was risky, but more than that was just foolhardy, wasn't it? Maybe so, Vujnovich decided, but there was no other choice. So Vujnovich's plan began to take shape: The OSS would organize a rescue by first sending in agents to prepare the airmen, and then the Fifteenth Air Force would send in a fleet of planes to land in enemy territory and bring them home. When Vujnovich approached his counterparts in the air force, they had him coordinate with an air force officer who suggested the rugged C-47. The ubiquitous C-47 filled many different roles in World War II—everything from troop transport and cargo delivery to paratrooper drops and rescue missions. The plane's versatility led to the nickname Skytrain. The two-engine plane had a roomy interior that could be outfitted any way the user wanted, with seats, guns, or radios, or left empty to hold anything you needed hauled from point A to point B. They were the primary utility plane of the American military, serving all over Europe and playing a key role in the D-Day invasion of Normandy. In civilian life, it was known as the DC-1, DC-2, or DC-3. With a wingspan of ninety-five feet and a length of sixty-three feet, the C-47 was a big, bulky plane, but it required a crew of only four. When outfitted with seats as a passenger plane, a C-47 could carry only a dozen people in addition to the crew. The airmen in Yugoslavia would be picked up by C-47 cargo planes with mostly empty interiors, making it possible to carry more. But under the conditions of this rescue, the planes would probably carry no more than a dozen passengers per plane.

*That's a lot of landings and takeoffs to get one hundred men out,* Vujnovich worried. He didn't yet know that his challenge was even bigger than that. Because of the lack of intelligence coming from Mihailovich's camp after Musulin was pulled out, he did not yet know that the number of men in Pranjane had surpassed one hundred and was growing bigger every day.

"And another thing," the Air Force officer told Vujnovich. "Those boys in Pranjane will need to build an airstrip. There is no suitable landing area around Pranjane, so it will be up to the airmen and the villagers to build a landing strip big enough for a C-47."

Vujnovich knew the airmen and the villagers had no tools other than whatever farm implements might be around, so they would be building the airstrip pretty much with their bare hands. He had to hope they could find a flat enough area to make the landings possible, and that they could build the makeshift runway without attracting attention from the Germans just a few miles down in the valley. Nazi planes flew overhead all the time, prompting the airmen to dive for cover lest they be discovered, so it was going to be a challenge to build an airstrip for C-47s without being caught. And the consequences were substantial. If their efforts to prepare for the rescue gave away their location, Vujnovich knew the Germans would respond in one of two ways: Either they would come in immediately to raid Pranjane, kill the airmen and probably do worse to the villagers and Chetniks who helped them, or they would wait until the rescue attempt so they could do all of that *and* kill the rescuers.

Secrecy was paramount, so the C-47s would go into Yugoslavia just a few at a time, without fighter escorts, to keep the mission clandestine. A big pack of C-47s and fighter planes would only draw attention and invite attack.

As if that wasn't enough of a challenge, the air force officer informed Vujnovich of one last detail: "The planes will have to go in at night, landing on that rough little airstrip in pitch-black darkness. It's the only way to improve the cargo planes' chances of going undetected by the Germans."

Vujnovich understood the necessity of a nighttime rescue, but he could hardly believe how difficult this mission was becoming. Vujnovich was no pilot, but he knew that a dark landing on an unfamiliar makeshift runway would challenge even the most experienced fliers, and if one of the planes crashed in the dark, that would be the end of the rescue. No more planes could land; dozens would die in the crash itself; and the commotion would probably bring in the Germans to finish off the rest.

This was an audacious plan, a rescue attempt unlike any ever attempted by the OSS or anyone else. Vujnovich knew that his career was on the line with this mission because he had pushed so hard for it and because he was betting so much on what 20/20 hindsight surely would call a desperate, ill-advised folly if it failed. His own future was not a priority at the time, however. Vujnovich felt a great responsibility to get it right, to make sure he was working through every possible scenario, because so many lives depended on this rescue being completed smoothly. Not only were the airmen's lives at stake, but Vujnovich was putting a great many more on the line: the villagers in Pranjane, the Chetniks, and the dozens of OSS agents and air force fliers who would carry out the mission. Vujnovich went over the details again and again. There was so much risk involved, so many ways that the whole plan could fall apart, but there was no other way to get them out. They had to make this work. They had to.

**Vujnovich started putting together a** team for the mission to Yugoslavia. He was reluctant to hand over such an important and risky plan to someone else, not to mention that he might be sending agents to their deaths, so Vujnovich's first intention was to go into Yugoslavia himself. He was more of a desk officer by this point, but he was fully trained as a field agent and he knew the language. That plan didn't get off the ground, however. When Vujnovich briefed his superiors about his intention to lead the mission, word spread to the State Department, which was not happy that this mission was going forward at all. The idea of Vujnovich, known to be a die-hard anti-Communist, parachuting into Yugoslavia made them uneasy. Who knew what this brash Communist-hating OSS officer would do if he were allowed into Yugoslavia to meet up with Mihailovich?

So one day the State Department liaison to the OSS in Bari came to Vujnovich's office and handed him a telegram. The message said, *Former naval person objects to George Vujnovich going into Mihailovich's headquarters. Therefore he will not be sent.* It was signed by President Roosevelt.

Vujnovich knew that "former naval person" was a common euphemism for British Prime Minister Winston Churchill, who had served as First Lord of the Admiralty in World War I and the early part of World War II. The picture was clear to Vujnovich: The Communists had convinced Churchill that he was not sufficiently pro-Tito and anti-Mihailovich, so it was too risky to let him go. Vujnovich would have to find someone else to lead the mission, and he didn't have to look far. His second choice for leading the mission had always been the obvious one—Musulin.

Musulin was eager to go back into Yugoslavia. He hadn't wanted to leave in the first place and had done everything he could to avoid following orders, so he jumped at the chance to lead this critical mission. He knew how difficult it would be, but he also knew how much those men needed help. He had been with them already. He knew the Americans streaming into Pranjane were hanging on the hope that one day the Americans would come for them. Vujnovich didn't even have to ask. He knew how badly Musulin wanted to return, so he simply told him one day, "George, they're not going to let me go. You'll lead the mission." Musulin was overjoyed, a big smile piercing the bushy black beard he still sported. They needed three agents altogether, and Musulin worked with Vujnovich to pick the other two members of the team, looking for men who could speak the language and whom he could trust with so many lives.

To work alongside Musulin, they chose another OSS agent who spoke the local language. Sergeant Mike Rajacich, from Washington, DC, and of Yugoslavian descent, had arrived in Bari only days earlier, but he had served in Cairo since October 1943 and came highly recommended. Rajacich mentioned to Vujnovich that if he needed another agent with the right language skills he could count on Nick Lalich, a handsome young OSS officer with a big black mustache. The son of Serbian immigrants, Lalich was in the Cairo OSS post and assigned to the activities in Yugoslavia. Both of these men could be trusted with this important mission, and Musulin seemed comfortable with the idea of taking Rajacich in as the second agent. Lalich wasn't needed at the moment, but Vujnovich was glad to know he was available.

The team was not yet complete, however. This was to be a three-man team and every infiltration team like this needed a radio operator. Even though the OSS had access to the most advanced radio equipment available, World-War-II-era radios that could transmit from one country to another were bulky, temperamental devices that required a skilled operator, a far cry from the push-and-talk radios of the modern military. OSS agents often were hindered by the need to carry around a suitcase-sized radio, most frequently disguised as an actual suitcase, and not just any OSS agent could use the device effectively. For this mission, Vujnovich knew that it was crucial to have reliable communication from the field so that the difficult rescue could be coordinated properly, and that meant sending in someone with the best possible radio expertise. When he considered the agents available, Vujnovich was pleased to find one who not only had proven himself an excellent radioman but who also had been behind enemy lines in Yugoslavia before. Arthur Jibilian, a compact, amiable fellow from Toledo, Ohio, wasn't the most cocky of the OSS agents and didn't inspire fear at first glance—unlike say, Musulin, whom you wouldn't want to see charging toward you in anger—but Vujnovich knew he was a combat veteran who could take care of himself in Nazi territory.

Only a couple months earlier, Jibilian himself was on the ground in Yugoslavia running from the Germans and hoping he would make it back alive. He had spent two months gathering intelligence behind enemy lines, this time with Tito's forces, narrowly escaping death many times. The experience had taken him a long way from the Art Jibilian

Airman Clare Musgrove, on leave in Naples, Italy, after returning from Yugoslavia

Ball turret gunner Clare Musgrove, ready for a high-altitude bombing mission

Allied airmen sleeping in the hay loft of a barn in Yugoslavia, hiding from German patrols while awaiting rescue

American airmen waiting on a farm cart used to help transport them from one village to another in Yugoslavia

A typical Serbian village in the mountains of central Yugoslavia, with ox carts being readied for helping wounded American airmen travel to Pranjane

George and Mirjana Vujnovich in September 1943, when George returned from Africa to undergo OSS training in Virginia

OSS agent George Musulin, known affectionately as "Captain George" to his Chetnik friends, in the Ravna Gora region of Yugoslavia

Anthony Orsini in 1944, the year his bomber was shot down over Yugoslavia

OSS agent Nick Lalich (left) relaxes with Chetnik leader Draza Mihailovich.

"Wild Bill" Donovan, head of the Office of Strategic Services (OSS) during World War II

OSS agent Nick Lalich (standing, center), with OSS radio operator Arthur Jibilian (kneeling, left) and others in Pranjane, Yugoslavia

General Draza Mihailovich (second from right) meets with OSS officers conducting Operation Halyard. From left to right: Colonel Robert McDowell, Lieutenant George Musulin, Lieutenant Nick Lalich, Mihailovich, Sergeant Michael Rajacich

Navigator Robert Wilson in 1945

Nick Petrovich

Seventeen-year-old Nick Petrovich, one of the Serbian soldiers protecting the downed airmen in Yugoslavia

Robert Wilson

Airmen posing with their Chetnik guards. From left to right: Chetnik soldier, Robert L. Marshall, Anthony Orsini (in back), Donald E. Loehndorf, Robert Wilson, a Chetnik, Michael O'Keefe, Leonard M. Brothers, a Chetnik, Roy J. Bowers, Lawrence T. Norton, William Harwell, a Chetnik, Russell W. Burney

Chetnik soldiers protecting the downed airmen in Pranjane, Yugoslavia, pose with one of their .50-caliber machine guns salvaged from crashed American bombers.

Allied airmen marching to work on the improved airstrip in Pranjane, Yugoslavia

The field in Pranjane, a small village in central Yugoslavia, that was turned into an emergency airstrip for the evacuation of Allied airmen in 1944

Chetnik soldiers in charge of guarding the airfield take a moment to pose in front of a C-47 rescue plane before it takes off again.

A group of American fliers draped in Serbian national rugs given to them by the local Chetnik soldiers and villagers as a good-bye gift

Airmen inspect a C-47 rescue plane with wing damage from striking a haystack while landing on the improvised landing strip.

An injured American airman leans on a cane while waiting to board a rescue plane in Pranjane, Yugoslavia. He and the other airmen are using pieces of parachute silk as scarves.

Chetnik soldiers help fliers prepare for boarding a rescue plane.

A flier waves good-bye as he and others board a C-47 in Pranjane, Yugoslavia.

American fliers enjoy a snack on a C-47, on the way from Pranjane, Yugoslavia, to Bari, Italy.

American airmen on a rescue plane back to Italy, some warming their feet in canvas bags because they gave their shoes to local villagers before leaving Pranjane, Yugoslavia

American airmen settling in on a C-47 rescue plane about to leave Pranjane, Yugoslavia

American airmen huddle under blankets for the cold flight to Italy after being rescued.

Two Serbian men (third and fourth from the left, in dark coats) who were evacuated from Pranjane, Yugoslavia, for medical reasons, prompting the recall of OSS team leader George Musulin

OSS agent Nick Lalich (center) with some of the last fliers to be taken out in Operation Halyard, on December 27, 1944

Chetnik leader Draza Mihailovich (far left, with cape) assembles with his soldiers and local villagers for a formal farewell to a group of airmen departing Pranjane, Yugoslavia.

Back in Bari, Italy, Americans who just returned from Pranjane, Yugoslavia, await the next plane carrying more airmen.

George Kraigher (left) and George Vujnovich (right) celebrate with the Operation Halyard team returning on its final flight from Yugoslavia on December 28, 1944. Nick Lalich is standing in the center with mustache, and Arthur Jibilian is to the right of him.

George Vujnovich (standing, right) greets Nick Lalich (standing, center, with mustache) and the last group of downed airmen returning from Pranjane, Yugoslavia, on December 28, 1944.

Former OSS agent Nick Lalich (right) leads a group of veterans outside the Yugoslavian consulate in New York in 1946, protesting the trial of General Draza Mihailovich.

Former airman David O'Connell pickets the Yugoslavian consulate in New York in 1946.

Sixty years after he participated in Operation Halyard, former OSS radio operator Arthur Jibilian points to a photo of himself in a museum dedicated to the mission in Pranjane, Yugoslavia.

After a sixty-year delay, airmen and OSS veterans involved in Operation Halyard present the Legion of Merit to Gordana Mihailovich, daughter of Chetnik leader Draza Mihailovich. Standing from left to right: Clare Musgrove, Robert Wilson, George Vujnovich, Charles Davis, Arthur Jibilian.

that people knew before the war. A second-generation American of Armenian descent, Jibilian was raised by his cousins Sarkis and Oksana Jibilian because his father had fled the Turks during a Turkish/Armenian war, after his own father was beheaded. Jibilian's father came to America to escape a similar fate, leaving his mother, two brothers, and one sister behind in Armenia, but eventually the Turks drove the family out, with one brother and Jibilian's sister dying in the process. The mother and the surviving son escaped to the United States to join his father, and Arthur Jibilian was born soon after in 1923. The family had settled in Cleveland by the time he was born, but any dreams of an idyllic American life were shattered when Jibilian's mother committed suicide only eighteen months after he was born, the pain of losing her other children and the terror she experienced in Armenia too much for her to bear. Jibilian's father left soon after and so did his older brother, leaving the young American-born boy to be cared for by cousins in Toledo.

Jibilian—known as Jibby to friends—had only recently graduated from high school when Japan attacked Pearl Harbor. Like so many other men of his generation, he marched right downtown to enlist in the military, and like a great many of them, he wanted to join the Navy Air Corps to be a flier. But he missed a letter on the eye exam and was advised to come back and try again in a couple weeks. Before he could get back to the recruiting office, bad news came to the household. His cousin Sarkis, whom he looked to as a father figure, was diagnosed with lung cancer and Jibilian decided he had to stay with him instead of enlisting right away. Sarkis died on January 19, 1943, and before he could try enlisting in the Navy Air Corps again, he was drafted into the regular navy, not the air corps. With Sarkis's death, Jibilian felt all alone and saw the draft notice as an acceptable alternative to pursuing life in Toledo on his own. There was no longer anything to keep him there, so he was happy to arrive at boot camp on March 15, 1943. A series of exams revealed that Jibilian could be a good radioman, so before long he started learning Morse code and navy protocol for radio communications.

One day in boot camp, Jibilian heard that there would be a visitor from the OSS and that he wanted to meet anyone who spoke a foreign language. Jibilian spoke Armenian, but he wasn't sure how useful that would be when the country was fighting Japanese and Germans. He went to the meeting anyway and was interviewed by a lieutenant commander from the OSS who confirmed that, indeed, they weren't so interested in people who spoke Armenian. "But we are interested in radio operators. We're in desperate need of some good radiomen," he explained. "And who knows? That Armenian might come in handy someday." When Jibilian asked about exactly what a radioman would do for the OSS, the lieutenant commander explained that they accompanied other agents into the field, usually parachuting into enemy territory, and used the radio to relay intelligence such as troop movements. They also might take part in sabotage such as blowing up bridges. Jibilian was thinking about whether he should volunteer for that kind of assignment when the OSS man spoke again.

"Let me make one thing very clear," he said. "These missions are extremely dangerous. Every time you go out there's a good chance you won't come back. This is a volunteer assignment; you don't have to do this if you don't want to."

Jibilian appreciated the officer's candor and he continued pondering the possibilities while the other man sat and waited for him to decide. He took only a short moment before speaking up, saying, "I'm interested. I'll volunteer." The OSS officer was glad to hear it and shook Jibilian's hand, telling him he was making the right choice and doing a tremendous service to his country. Jibilian hoped so. He felt good about the decision, but he had just volunteered for something far more dangerous than anything he probably would have been assigned in the army. The danger actually was one thing that pushed him toward volunteering, not because he was a big risk taker but because he knew he was different than a lot of guys in boot camp who had families, wives, even children to go home to after the war.

*I'm more expendable. I don't have any immediate family and maybe it's better that I take a dangerous assignment than let it go to some guy who has people waiting for him at home. Shoot, I don't even have a girl. So if anybody is qualified for a dangerous assignment, it's me.*

*At least it should be more interesting than sitting on a ship out in the ocean and tuning a radio,* he thought.

**After the initial excitement and** anxiety about volunteering for the OSS, Jibilian didn't hear anything more about it until just before he had completed his training for becoming a radioman. He was beginning to think the OSS had forgotten about him or didn't need him anymore, but then he received orders stating he was on "detached temporary duty with the Office of Strategic Services." So Jibilian was in the OSS after all. The orders said he was to report immediately to the Farm outside Washington, DC, the same place that Vujnovich and scores of other agents had been trained in spy craft. There he underwent the same training as every other agent, learning to kill and avoid being killed, but the OSS also provided specialized training in the use of the radios that spy teams took into the field. The radio set consisted of a transmitter, a receiver, and a power pack, all fit into a small suitcase that, the agents hoped, could let them mingle into a crowd of refugees or at least look reasonable as you were walking down a road in Europe. After that training, Jibilian and some other agents in training were sent to Fort Benning, Georgia, where they spent a week—instead of the typical four to six weeks—learning how to parachute out of a plane. Not long after, he found himself at the OSS post in Cairo where, in his downtime, he managed to make contact with members of his family from Armenia.

Jibilian was still waiting for his first mission when he heard that OSS Lieutenant Eli Popovich was looking for a radio operator to join him and Colonel Lynn Farish on a trip behind enemy lines in Yugoslavia. Farish had already made one trip into Yugoslavia, but he had been unsatisfied with having to rely on British radio operators to get his reports out. He insisted that for this mission they should take an American radioman. There weren't that many available, so the rookie Jibilian got the nod. He was thrilled to be selected, as he was eager to actually put his skills to use. The mission, code named Columbia, was launched from Brindisi on the night of March 15, 1944. Popovich, Farish, and Jibilian parachuted into

Yugoslavian territory held by Tito's Partisans. When Jibilian hit the ground, the most grueling two months of his life began.

Once they landed in the wooded hills at the base of a mountain range, the team made sure the area was safe and then Jibilian set up his transmitter to try to contact the OSS post. He was eager to prove himself and do his job, but he was also nervous. The adrenaline coursed through him and his heart pounded as he manipulated the controls of the radio, trying to get a signal through to Cairo and listening for a response. There was nothing despite repeated tries. He kept sending the signal over and over, waiting for a call back, and when nothing came, he decided he had to use more antenna. Popovich and Farish watched with concern as he unreeled more of the wire antenna hidden in the suitcase, hoping it would boost the signal strength but also knowing that he was increasing the chances that the Germans could use a direction finder, known as a DF to radiomen, to electronically home in on the broadcast and find the trio of spies. It was risky, but it worked. Jibilian finally got a signal to Cairo and felt he had redeemed himself with the other two more experienced agents. They were surprised to find out why it had been so difficult make contact. It hadn't been Jibilian's fault at all. His radio signals were going through just fine, but no one was listening for them in the Cairo OSS post because they thought the mission had been cancelled.

After straightening out the mix-up, the team was getting comfortable in their hiding spot and Jibilian continued transmitting some information to Cairo. Suddenly he heard planes overhead.

"They put a DF on us!" Jibilian called to the other two, instantly realizing what had happened. He turned off the radio's power supply and hastily packed it all away. Popovich and Farish grabbed their gear and prepared to run as Jibilian slammed the radio suitcase shut and grabbed his own bags. They were already sprinting deeper into the woods when the Messerschmitts and Stuka dive bombers opened fire on their location, strafing them with large-caliber machine guns that would tear them apart instantly. The planes continued strafing, climbing, turning, and coming back for another attack. The trio narrowly escaped being killed as rounds hit the trees and the ground all around them, and then they thought they had made it up high enough in the hills so that the pilots didn't know where they were. They were exhausted from running uphill, scared for their lives, while hauling all their gear. Jibilian fell on top of his radio suitcase, his chest heaving, gasping for air. But they had only a brief respite before the planes were on them again. The pilots must have guessed that they ran uphill into the more dense wood cover, and they were repeatedly strafing the area in hopes of a lucky hit. The men started running again and it wasn't long before Popovich and Farish dropped their gear bags. Jibilian hung on to the heavy radio set as long as he could, but he couldn't keep up. One of the other men looked back and yelled at Jibilian to drop the radio, and he welcomed the order. The radio set fell away like almost all of their other gear as they continued running, dodging trees in the dark and trying to outpace the plane attacks.

The OSS team remained on the run for five days and six nights. After escaping the initial attack on the first night, they knew the Germans were onto them. That was confirmed the next morning when they saw planes overhead looking for any sign of the spies, and they could see ground units moving into the area to hunt them down. They had no choice but to run and keep running, to get higher into the hills where it was harder for the German troops to follow and where they might find more hiding places. Their mission to gather intelligence had been abandoned for the moment and they were in the most basic of all mind-sets: running for their lives. Dressed only in their summer khakis, which had been appropriate at lower altitudes, they ran higher and higher into the snowy mountain trails, the air growing colder with every step. Eventually they ran into snowdrifts, some so deep that they had to pull each other out before continuing on. When they stopped to catch their breath, their sweat-soaked clothes froze to their bodies, thawing again once they started to move on.

As they reached higher elevations the trio thought the Germans were not quite so close on their trail and they slowed their pace. They would have slowed anyway, since they were all exhausted. Making their way along mountain trails used by the locals, they ran into local villagers who were pleased to see Americans. Though these were not Mihailovich supporters, like those harboring the airmen in Pranjane, these villagers were just as gracious and welcoming to the needy Americans. Jibilian and the other men lived on only what the local peasants could spare, a bit of goat cheese and bread made with hay to extend the meager flour on hand, perhaps a pear picked from a tree. The hay bread was tough and dense, but it was filling. The strange food and exertion gave all three men a bad case of diarrhea.

After about a week, the Germans gave up on finding the spies and the OSS team felt they could make their way back down the mountain to a lower elevation. As they made their way down, some of the local people told them of American airmen who were hiding from the Germans and awaiting rescue. These were not the same airmen being aided by Mihailovich in a different part of the country, but rather a smaller group of only a dozen. Their original mission compromised and all their equipment lost, Jibilian and the other agents decided it would be better if they accomplished something before they simply tried to escape from Yugoslavia. So they gathered as much information as they could from the sympathetic locals and determined where the airmen were. If they could, their plan was to go find the airmen and somehow get them out with them.

The distance to the airmen was not great, but there were plenty of Germans in between. Popovich, Farish, and Jibilian figured out that the best way to get to the airmen was by going through a German checkpoint at a bridge. The only alternative was an eight-day march around the checkpoint, and the trio wasn't up to that, what with their exhaustion, diarrhea, and lack of food. And besides, finding a way through a German checkpoint with subterfuge or cleverness was exactly the kind of task at which OSS agents excelled. Jibilian had never done it, of course, because this was his first mission, but he remembered his training from the Farm and trusted the other agents to know best. With no radio to use, Jibilian relied on a submachine gun instead. The weapon was considered a good choice for a young, inexperienced agent like Jibilian, the thinking being that you didn't have to be accurate if you could throw enough lead at the enemy in a hurry. He was ready to do whatever Popovich and Farish needed to make this rescue happen.

About eighteen of Tito's Partisans joined up with the OSS agents to help with rescuing the airmen, and after some discussion, the agents decided that good old-fashioned bribery was the best way to get through this checkpoint. The Partisans told them that the guards could be bought off, and Farish still had some twenty-dollar gold pieces he had brought for just such an occasion. Using a go-between that the Partisans trusted, the group made contact with the German guards at the checkpoint and offered to pay them if they would allow passage. The Germans agreed, the gold pieces were delivered, and the group planned to cross the bridge the next night at a specified time. The agents knew they were taking a gamble, but bribery had proven quite effective in such situations before. If the guards were satisfied with their gold pieces, the deal was that they would know the group was coming at the appointed time and simply let them pass unmolested.

It was pitch-black as the group headed toward the bridge, the three Americans leading the way. They wanted it dark so they could travel without being noticed, and as they approached the bridge everything looked fine. Jibilian, Popovich, and Farish hid in the bushes near the bridge for a while to watch and see if anything was amiss, and then they checked with the Partisans to ensure that all seemed right to them. Everything did, and as the designated time approached, the group moved out onto the road and headed toward the bridge. They moved in a quick trot, eager to get over the bridge but also wary of surprising any Germans at the checkpoint. The moment of truth came when they approached close enough for the guards to see them. The Americans froze, everyone else waiting behind them and ready to bolt at the first sound of gunfire. But then Jibilian saw the two guards look directly at them, look at each other, and then turn their backs. The bribe had worked. They were letting the Americans and the Partisan fighters through.

The group hustled on up to the checkpoint and started across the bridge, needing to go only a few dozen yards to relative safety. But just as Jibilian and the other agents reached the middle of the bridge, flares soared into the sky and a spotlight came on that lit them up like daylight, followed immediately by machine-gun fire. Either the bribe just didn't work with these Germans or the go-between the Partisans trusted had double-crossed them. Bullets hit all around the group and some of the Partisan fighters went down. Men were pushing and shoving, no one really knowing which way to run, everyone trying to get out of the search-light's beam. In the frenzy, Jibilian kept getting glimpses of the river below the bridge and prayed that he wouldn't end up there. The look of that dark water at night, so far below, was about as scary as the idea of being shot. Jibilian and nearly every other man on the bridge opened fire on the spotlight, which soon went out, allowing them to sprint off the bridge and into the darkness again.

Over the next month, Jibilian and his team eventually found the dozen airmen and made contact with the OSS post in Cairo. The OSS men took the airmen, many of them weak and injured, from the villagers who had harbored them, traveling on foot and by oxcart for days to a spot that intelligence had identified as a possible pickup point. Popovich, strong but not especially large at six feet tall, carried one wounded man on his back for nearly two days. On June 16, 1944, a plane landed on an open field and picked up the agents and the airmen, ferrying them back to Bari, a small-scale rehearsal for what would come later in Pranjane.

Jibilian was awarded the Silver Star for his work on this mission, and those two months turned him from an expendable novice to a seasoned OSS agent. He was immensely proud of having helped retrieve those twelve airmen from Yugoslavia, and when he heard there were at least a hundred more, he knew he had to go back.

# Chapter 12

## An All-American Team

**When Vujnovich explained the plan for rescuing the** downed airmen in Pranjane, now known by the randomly assigned code name Operation Halyard, not one of the three men chosen for the mission batted an eye at the enormous risk they were taking. Parachute into enemy territory and organize the most daring rescue ever? Sure, can do. Build an airstrip right under the German's noses? No problem.

But they did have one question for Vujnovich. Will we be working on our own or with the British?

The answer, unfortunately, was that Operation Halyard would be a joint operation with the Brits. Predictably, the British were not pleased with Roosevelt's approval of the rescue mission, but the complex agreements governing joint Allied operations in Italy required British and American spy teams to work together when putting agents in Yugoslavia. In many cases, the British were responsible for actually getting American agents into enemy territory, and until recently they had been responsible for all radio communication on the ground. The OSS had only just begun sending in their own radiomen, so Jibilian would fill that role instead of a British agent. At least they had that going for them. Vujnovich had his doubts about letting the British help at all, but he went along with it because he didn't want to jeopardize a mission that already was on weak support.

The Operation Halyard trio also were warned not to interfere with international relations while on their mission. Your mission is to go in and get those men out, *nothing more,* they were told. A lieutenant commander from the Fifteenth Air Force specifically ordered them not to make "any military or political commitments on behalf of the United States of America or other Allied nation, or to make any commitments or promises for the furnishing of supplies or other material aid to any political or military group." In other words, this wasn't their opportunity to set right anything they didn't like about the way the Allies worked with Mihailovich and Tito. They trusted Musulin to follow this order, and Vujnovich had been kept out precisely because they didn't think they could trust him to comply.

As much as Musulin rankled at the continuing betrayal of Mihailovich, he was focused more on making this mission work. Vujnovich worked with Musulin, Rajacich, and Jibilian to plan their entry, thinking at first that they would have to make a blind drop into Pranjane, meaning they would arrive without Mihailovich's forces knowing they were coming. This was always a risky move because even the friendlies on the ground might shoot you if they didn't know who was dropping in without calling first. But as the planning proceeded, Vujnovich learned that the British had reestablished radio contact with Mihailovich and arranged for the trio to arrive between July 15 and July 20. Mihailovich's men would be looking for them on those days. As that window was almost closing, the rescue team caught a break with the weather on the evening of July 19 and drove to Brindisi, about an hour south of Bari and where most mission flights originated. There they climbed into a C-47 painted black to make it harder to see at night. They were eager to go in and get the rescue started, so their adrenaline was pumping as they neared the drop zone. The trio checked their gear, double-checked their parachutes, gave one another hearty slaps on the shoulders and stood in the dark body of the cargo plane, waiting for the jump light to switch from red to green, followed by the British jump master's signal to go out the door and into the dark night over Yugoslavia.

And they waited.

Musulin finally asked the jump master what was wrong, and he relayed the pilot's report that there was a problem with the ground signals.

"No ground signals over the drop zone!" the jump master shouted over the airplane noise, in a British accent. "We're sending, but there's nothing on the ground!"

He was referring to the way Allied planes confirmed that they were over the right drop zone and that the friendly guerillas on the ground were there to receive the agents. When the time and location of the drop was arranged, the air force had informed Mihailovich that the plane would send a specific signal of light flashes and that the men on the ground must respond with another light signal. The plane was sending its designated signal, but there was no return flash on the ground. Without the confirmation signal, the agents could find themselves alone once they hit the ground, or worse, the Germans may have found out about the drop and were waiting for the spies to land. No ground signal meant no drop. The jump master informed Musulin that the plane was heading back to Brindisi, and the trio had no choice but to abort the mission.

Vujnovich was not happy to see the agents return that night, but it was not an uncommon sight. Missions often were aborted at the last minute when something went wrong with equipment, or the plane got lost, or intelligence revealed new information. Better to come back and try again later than throw the agents out over the wrong drop zone or right into the hands of the Gestapo. The agents planned their next attempt, and on another night they again drove to Brindisi and boarded the C-47, flying into Yugoslavia.

This time the plane had to turn back because of a fierce storm over the mountains in Yugoslavia.

The next time, it was flak on the way to the drop zone. Too much antiaircraft fire to get through safely.

So far it seemed like just the routine reasons a mission can be aborted. But then Musulin and his team started getting suspicious about the British who were supposed to be flying them in. Musulin, Rajacich, and Jibilian soon realized that the British were not just unenthusiastic about the mission. They were actively sabotaging it, or at least that's how it appeared to the American team.

The outright hostility of the British was made evident on the next attempt to jump into Pranjane, a few days later. Musulin learned that on the first attempt, when there were no ground signals, the problem actually was that the pilot had flown to the wrong coordinates. They were in the wrong place, so that explained why there was no welcoming party. Knowing that, Musulin wanted to double-check the coordinates soon after they took off on their fourth attempt to go rescue the airmen. He went forward and asked the pilot to confirm their destination. The pilot read out the coordinates he intended to take the men to and, as soon as he checked the spot on his own map, Musulin exploded in anger.

"That's Partisan territory!" he yelled. "Where the hell did you get those coordinates?"

The pilot, visibly intimidated by the large and very angry American, explained that he had been briefed on the mission by his British superiors and he was just following orders. That answer did not satisfy Musulin, and then his blood pressure went a few ticks higher as he noticed a Partisan soldier sitting in the back of the plane.

"What the hell is he doing here?" Musulin screamed, incredulous that a Tito supporter was sitting on the plane that supposedly was going to take them to Mihailovich territory. *What in the world is going on here? Are they trying to sabotage this mission?*

The pilot's answer did not improve the situation. He explained that the Partisan was assigned to act as the jump master for this mission. He would be the one who told Musulin, Rajacich, and Jibilian where and when to jump. *Oh, hell no.*

"No son-of-a-bitch Communist is going to push me and my men out of this plane," Musulin boomed. "We're aborting this mission. Forget it!"

The three Americans were astounded that the Brits had so completely fouled up their efforts to get into Pranjane, but they still had a hard time believing that their tea-sipping allies were actually trying to sabotage Operation Halyard. Could they really be so opposed to Mihailovich that they would jeopardize the lives of these agents, not to mention preventing the rescue of a hundred airmen? The answer came on the next attempt.

All three of the men were on high alert when they boarded the plane the next time, watching for any sign that the British were undercutting their mission in any way. Musulin checked the coordinates and they seemed right. There was no damned Communist on the plane, at least none that was actually wearing the red-star cap of a Tito Partisan. All seemed well and the trio thought they might finally get into Pranjane this time. The jump site neared and the team again double-checked all their gear, confirmed their plans once they landed, and then they watched the red light and waited for the jump master to tell them to go.

Finally it happened. On the fifth attempt to get into Pranjane, the light turned green and the British jump master gave them the signal and the trio walked over to the open door of the plane. Musulin took the lead as the mission commander and was bracing himself in the doorway, pausing for the Brit to check that his rip cord was securely fastened to the cable over their heads that would pull his chute out. Rajacich and Jibilian were in line behind him, ready to leap out immediately afterward. The jump master had his hand on Musulin's back, ready to give him a hard shove that would help him clear the plane. All Musulin had to do was to let go of the doorframe and Operation Halyard would be underway.

But then he saw something. *What the hell is that?* He couldn't tell for sure what he was seeing on the ground, but it didn't look right. He held on to the plane's doorframe while he looked and then, suddenly, he realized what he was looking at in the darkness below. *Son of a bitch! You goddamn Brits are trying to kill us!*

Musulin pushed back hard from the doorway, knocking Rajacich and Jibilian off balance. The jump master looked at him quizzically and yelled to ask what was wrong.

"We're right over a damn battle! Look at that! Look!" Musulin screamed. He wanted to dangle the jump master out by his feet so he could get a good view, but he resisted the urge. Rajacich and Jibilian went to the door and peered out too, and they were shocked at what they saw: the flashes of light from heavy weaponry, vehicles, and soldiers in an active gun battle below them. The British were trying to drop them into the middle of a full-fledged battle. They would never have made it to the ground alive.

Musulin couldn't be sure whether the British were actively trying to kill them and stop the Halyard mission or whether they were just completely incompetent. But he was leaning toward sabotage as the explanation. He knew about James Klugmann in the British SOE post at Bari, knew him as a Communist with way too much influence over British operations, and he suspected Klugmann and the other Tito supporters were manipulating the Halyard mission. Jibilian didn't even doubt it. He was sure the Brits were trying to kill them. *They were hoping we would just drop into the battle and disappear.*

No matter what the explanation was for the Brits' actions, the OSS agents had had enough of this. Musulin marched into Vujnovich's office and demanded an American plane, an American crew, and an American jump master. They weren't going back into Yugoslavia without an all-American team.

Vujnovich was happy to comply.

# Chapter 13

## SOS . . . Waiting for Rescue

**In Pranjane, the Americans had no idea that the ACRU** team was working so hard to rescue them. The plight of the downed airmen was getting worse every day and in every way. Food was in short supply even for the local people, who shared all they could with the downed Americans, and some of the fliers were in desperate need of medical care for the wounds they suffered on their ill-fated bombing runs. Richard Felman, the leader of the airmen who had watched the Germans burn a Serb village when the Chetniks would not give up the fliers, decided that it was only a matter of time before the Germans found the hidden Americans. When that time came, it would be a bloodbath. Not only would they probably kill all the Americans instead of taking them prisoner, but they would kill all of the innocent Serbs as well. Or the Germans might even do something worse than killing them as punishment for helping the airmen.

Felman met with some other ranking officers of the Americans in Pranjane and started debating whether to do something to facilitate their rescue. Up this point they had been just waiting, hoping that the Allies knew they were there and were planning some way to get them home. And they assumed that Mihailovich, who was protecting them so diligently, had made contact with the Americans. But nothing was happening. Weeks and months had passed with no word of any way they might get out of Yugoslavia.

Felman and the other airmen wanted to do something to help themselves, but what? Some of the airmen wanted to send a radio message telling the Allies where they were and that they needed rescue. It was possible, because the Chetniks routinely salvaged anything they could use from the crashed bombers, including radios. With a little repair work they probably could get a radio working well enough to broadcast a message back to Allied territory. But it would be a risky move. So far their survival depended on the Nazis not knowing exactly where they were. Though the Germans knew that American airmen were being hidden in the hills of Yugoslavia, they didn't know that so many were concentrated in the small town of Pranjane. Even with Mihailovich's forces surrounding them, the Germans could launch an air strike that would devastate the entire town, killing the Americans and all the local people as well. It was crucial that the Germans not find their hidden sanctuary.

A radio message could change all of that. Just as Jibilian and his team had found out earlier, a radio message could allow the enemy to zero in on your exact location. The longer the message, and the stronger the broadcast, the easier it was for the enemy to determine where you were hiding. If they got on the radio and started calling to their bases in Italy, the first response could be a fleet of German fighters and bombers unleashing hell on them.

Everyone agreed it was a huge risk, but it was one they had to take. Felman and other ranking officers in Pranjane decided they had to send a message to the Fifteenth Air Force base in Bari, Italy. They asked Mihailovich's forces to send them a radio from one of the planes, and Mihailovich agreed, knowing that the risky message might be the only way to get help for the airmen. Thomas Oliver, the airman who parachuted down onto a family's picnic, was part of the group pushing for the message to Italy and he worked closely with radio operators and others in the group to devise the right way to call Italy. Everyone knew they had to be cautious.

At first the group decided to just be quick about it. They would send short, simple radio messages to Italy in hopes that the Allies would pick up the transmission but that the Germans wouldn't have time to zero in on where it was coming from. When it was time to send the first call for help, there were dozens of airmen gathered around the radio, set up on a farmhouse table. A radio operator took the controls and put his finger on the Morse code key. He looked at the other men and took a deep breath before sending the first message from the downed airmen. He began to tap.

SOS . . . SOS . . . One hundred fifty members of American crew have been waiting for rescue . . . There are many sick and wounded . . . Call back . . . SOS . . . SOS . . .

That was it. That was all they were willing to send out at first, lest they give the Germans plenty of time to trace the radio call. So they sat and waited, their eyes on the radio, hoping fervently to hear a message tapping in return. They waited for hours. There was no reply. Slowly the men left the room, a few at a time, dejected as they realized that no one had heard them.

As the radio sat silent, Felman and the other officers discussed the situation and decided to keep trying. They would send the same message every few hours and maintain a vigil by the radio, waiting for someone to call them back.

They waited two days and heard nothing.

Then they realized that, in all likelihood, the Fifteenth Air Force in Bari, Italy, was hearing them after all but just not replying. They probably suspected this was a trick, some sort of trap set by the Nazis to lure in a rescue mission. *Of course,* Felman thought, *they're not going to just get on the radio and arrange a rescue without knowing for sure that the message is legitimate.* They had to develop a code that would convince the Allies their message was trustworthy, that it really was coming from the airmen and not some Nazi intelligence unit.

Oliver volunteered to work with some other airmen to develop a code. American slang would be a good idea, they thought, because it would confuse any Germans listening in. But more important, they had to code their message with information known only to those back at their air bases in Italy. That inside information would serve two purposes: It would show the Allies that the senders were really American airmen, and it would confound any Germans trying to break their code.

The airmen came up with two codes. The first was a simple letter transposition that required the receiver to know key information unknown to the Germans. Instead of the letter "A," the code letter would be the third letter of the place of birth of a bartender at the Officers' Club in Lecce, Italy. Instead of "B," they would use the fourth letter of the name of the intelligence officer stationed in Brindisi, Italy. The airmen worked out an entire alphabet code with similar keys. Sending this much information would mean staying on the radio far longer than anyone had been comfortable with so far, but the airmen saw no other way to jump-start the communication process. They prayed for the best and transmitted the alphabet code to those listening in Italy. Once they were done, both parties had a code they could use to send specific information back and forth regarding a rescue without letting the Germans know what their plans were.

The alphabet code would be good for specific bits of information, but using it for all communication would be tedious and confusing. So Oliver and some of the other airmen came up with a slang-based code that could be used to quickly convey information that probably wouldn't make much sense to any Germans listening in. Once all the senior officers approved the plan, Oliver used Morse code to tap out another plea for help.

*Mudcat driver to CO APO520.*

Oliver had piloted a bomber called the Fighting Mudcat, and CO APO520 was the command of the Fifteenth Air Force.

> 150 Yanks are in Yugo, some sick. Shoot us work-
> horses.

The workhorse of the American Air Force was the C-47 cargo plane, so the airmen were asking that some C-47s be sent to them.

Oliver then went on to provide the "challenge" and "authenticator" that both parties could use to verify identities if a rescue party were sent. The challenge—the signal that the rescuers would send to prove they were friendlies—would be the first letter of the Fighting Mudcat's bombardier's last name and the color of the scarf worn by Banana Nose, the nickname of Sam Benigno, an airman in Oliver's squadron who always wore a white scarf. The authenticator—the signal the airmen would send to prove they were friendlies and in on the plan—would be the last letter of the "chief lug's" last name and the color of "the fist on the wall." Those items referred to the commander of the 459th Bomb Group, who referred to all his crews as lugs, as in lug nuts or key parts of the machinery. On a wall at the Officers' Club at their base, the commander had written, "Each lug in the 459th sign here," and signed it, "M. M. Munn, Chief Lug." The fist on the wall referred to the Fifteenth Air Force emblem, with a red fist.

Oliver also transmitted the serial numbers of himself and crewmates from his plane and one other bomber from the same group, cleverly adding them to the numerical coordinates of their location in Pranjane so that the string of numbers seemed meaningless. But he hoped that someone on the other end would figure out that the serial numbers confirmed his crew's identities, and the remaining numbers pointed the rescuers to their exact location.

To ensure that the message would get through to the right people who could understand that code, Oliver signed off by saying, *Must refer to shark squadron, 459th Bomb Group, for decoding.* His squadron had shark teeth painted on the noses of all its B-24 bombers. Then he said,

*Signed, TKO, Flat Rat 4 in lug order.* TKO were his initials, and he had signed the wall under Munn's signature with *T. K. Oliver, Flat Rat 4,* a reference to how he and his bunkmates called their tent "the poker flat" and numbered themselves as flat rats one through four.

That complex code might save their lives, the airmen thought. Or it might mean they were on the radio too long and the Germans had already zeroed in on them. Or the damn thing might be too complicated for anyone to figure out.

All they could do was wait and hope someone had heard it and was tracking down all the right information.

**The messages were heard in Italy,** where a Royal Air Force radio operator picked up the curiously coded pleas for help. He struggled for two hours to determine the location of the caller, finally recording them, and forwarded them on to the Fifteenth Air Force headquarters in Bari. There an intelligence officer locked himself in a room with the strange message and ordered that no one without a higher rank bother him. After a few hours of consternation, he started seeing patterns and bits of code that made sense. He was able to pull out the serial numbers and then he realized the remaining numbers must mean something. The longitude and latitude then became apparent. But he still couldn't make sense of some of the more arcane references in Oliver's code, and he understood the part that said, *Must refer to shark squadron, 459th Bomb Group, for decoding.* So he took the message to a Major Christi, commander of the 459th Bomber Group, from which Oliver's crew flew. Christi was stymied for a while but intrigued by the unusual code and determined to figure out what it meant. The two officers sat for a long time, staring at the message, not saying much lest they interrupt each other's thoughts. As he kept staring at the code, Christi had a sudden realization. "Mudcat Driver" and "Banana Nose Benigno" were his men.

"That's Oliver's crew and Buckler's crew!" Christi yelled excitedly, standing up and looking at the intelligence officer with astonishment. "My God! Go get them!"

**The code worked.** With the help of crew at the air bases where the missing men had been stationed, air force officials decoded the rest of the message and understood that the men were asking for a rescue operation. The intricate code convinced them that the message could be trusted.

Only some of this information was a revelation. The air force leaders weren't surprised to hear that American airmen were hiding in the hills of Yugoslavia, but they had not realized that the airmen were grouped together and organized enough to send a coded message requesting rescue.

The airmen in Pranjane continued sending their coded pleas— SOS . . . *Call back . . .* —and waited for a reply. There was nothing for days, and then the radio crackled with a Morse code message from Bari. It was brief, but it said everything they wanted to hear:

*Prepare reception for 31 July or first clear night following.*

They were going to be rescued! The Americans were coming to get them! The news kept the airmen jubilant for days, but they became quiet again as there was no more communication. They started to worry again that maybe a rescue wasn't forthcoming, that maybe the message had been a trick by the Germans. While they held out hope that July 31 would bring good news, they fell back into their usual pattern of waiting, helping the villagers with their chores, and listening to the radio for any more word of an impending rescue. Despite the one encouraging message, the airmen were slowly getting used to the idea that maybe the air force couldn't get them out. Maybe it just wasn't possible to come into enemy territory and take home hundreds of weary, sick airmen. The men's spirits sank lower and lower with each passing day. They played cards, swapped stories, anything to make the days pass.

Maybe July 31 would change everything. But they were wary about getting their hopes up. How could the Americans rescue so many of them? Even if some sort of rescue happened, what were the chances that you would be among those taken out before the Germans interrupted the operation? Not so great, many of the airmen thought. A big gamble.

**As the airmen waited for** help, they could at least be confident that they were relatively safe in Pranjane. Germans were garrisoned only thirty miles away, down in the valley, and Nazi patrols routinely rolled in villages all over the area. But unlike most of the countryside in the hills of Yugoslavia, this particular area was secured by almost ten thousand of Mihailovich's forces. Their job was to protect not only the American airmen but also Mihailovich's headquarters nearby. Within this area, Serb villagers could be assured that a German patrol would not cavalierly drive in and do as they pleased, but they also knew that the presence of Mihailovich and the airmen made the area a hot target if the Germans ever decided to launch a full assault. Until that day came, however, the day-to-day security was in the hands of young men like Nick Petrovich, a seventeen-year-old in Mihailovich's army. He had grown up listening to the stories of his grandfather and father who fought in the Turkish wars and in World War I, so when the Nazis invaded his country Petrovich knew he had to fight. He had revered the Serbian medieval heroes Kraljevich Marko and Milosh Obilich since he was a child, and in 1940 when he was only fourteen he altered his birth certificate so he could enter the Yugoslav gliding school, while also putting himself through a rigorous physical development program of his own design. When the Germans showed up a few years later, Petrovich felt ready to fight.

Petrovich joined Mihailovich's forces at about the time Mihailovich was abandoned by the Allies, starting first with underground work such as information gathering and stealing firearms from the Germans. One of Petrovich's methods was organizing small groups of children around ten years old to play marbles around parked German vehicles, watching for the opportunity to pilfer hand guns, ammunition, binoculars, or any other valuable items. They stuffed the booty in a flour sack and dragged it along behind them playfully. Petrovich became so bold that he once swiped a 9-mm submachine gun from an SS officer who lived in his girlfriend's family home. He was beaten and interrogated by the Gestapo for hours but would not confess, and they released him the same day. As he proved himself more to the Chetniks, Petrovich took on more and more responsibility, soon assigned to helping the American airmen falling out of the sky on a regular basis.

The duty was one of the most important that could be assigned to Mihailovich's troops, and it carried a great responsibility. As more Allied airmen gathered in Pranjane to await rescue, Mihailovich issued this stern warning to the officers commanding the guard in Pranjane:

"Take good care that nothing happens to these men. You must defend them, if necessary, with your lives. If any one of you comes to me with news that anything has happened to a single one of these airmen, I shall have the man who bears this news executed on the spot." Mihailovich may have been exaggerating to make clear his dedication to protecting the airmen, but no one could be sure.

A typical operation for Petrovich involved blocking a road leading to the area where the airmen had bailed out by placing large rocks or trees in the path, then waiting for the German patrol to stop and remove them. Once the Germans exited their vehicles, Petrovich and his colleagues opened fire. Their weapons of choice were the big fifty-caliber machine guns salvaged from downed American bombers, which they took to local blacksmiths who would secretly fashion metal stands so the guns could be used on the ground against German troops. Then they would take the deadly guns and hide in the trees, waiting for German patrols to come by. The machine guns designed to shoot down German fighter planes shredded the Nazi soldiers who dared try to get too close to Pranjane.

Knowing the price the villagers might pay for the deaths of German soldiers, Petrovich and the other guards conducted such attacks only when they had no choice but to engage, such as when a German patrol threatened Allied airmen or Mihailovich himself was in the area of Pranjane. Petrovich knew how to hold his fire and not provoke German retribution unnecessarily, but when he had to fire, he did so with gusto.

Like the Germans who would kill the American airmen rather than be bothered with capturing them, Petrovich had no time for prisoners.

## Chapter 14

# *Sure to Be a Rough Landing*

**July 31 came and the airmen in Pranjane eagerly** scanned the skies for any sign of a plane coming to rescue them. As night fell they gathered in a field near the village, the presumed drop zone for anyone parachuting in to help them. Dozens of eyes looked to the horizon, through the tree-covered hills, for any hint of Americans coming to take them home. They always had a red-lens flashlight ready to signal the plane with the predetermined code. They waited all night and into the morning. The weather was clear and they saw no reason the rescue had not been carried out as promised. Their hopes were dashed as the sun rose on another day in Pranjane, another day in which the Allies would not come and help them. They were crushed with disappointment, and more than a few vowed they would not get their hopes up again.

But what the airmen did not know was that Operation Halyard was still a go. They had no way of knowing that Musulin, Rajacich, and Jibilian had already made repeated attempts to reach them in Pranjane but were stymied by everything from bad weather to bad Brits. The mission would have arrived on July 31 if only the weather had been clear between Bari and Pranjane. Unfortunately, the airmen could see only the starry night above them and had to assume the mission was not really coming. Their despair knew no bounds, made all the worse by the fact that it was unnecessary. Not only was help on the way, but the radio messages the airmen sent so bravely, risking hundreds of lives in the process, would be the real catalyst for getting the Americans on their way to Pranjane. The rescue plan was well underway, spurred by Mirjana's letter to Vujnovich and Musulin's report from the field, but the coded messages from the men in Pranjane threw some momentum behind the effort. An actual request from these men, their plea for help spelled out in a way that made their desperate situation crystal clear, seemed to light a fire under anyone who held that message in their hands.

Once the message was decoded by the Fifteenth Air Force, excited intelligence officers there forwarded it to the ACRU team in Bari. Vujnovich, Musulin, Rajacich, and Jibilian all gathered around to read the message together. The words made their mission seem more real, more personal.

> There are many sick and wounded. . . . Call
> back. . . . SOS . . .

They felt it in their gut, the dire straits these men were in, and they knew they were the only ones who could help them.

Now they had some solid information. They had confirmation about where the men were, that they were all gathered in one place, and that they were eagerly awaiting rescue. And the message provided Vujnovich and the rescue team with one more vital piece of information: The number of airmen was up to one hundred fifty.

Vujnovich didn't like hearing that. Every extra man meant the mission was more difficult. He had thought one hundred airmen were a lot to bring out, and now they were dealing with one hundred fifty. But still, the message from the airmen pumped a new vigor into their efforts, overcoming the frustration and dejection they felt from their experience with the British. Seeing the desperation in the message convinced them anew that they had to get in there soon, and they had to make this mission work.

*　*　*

**On August 2, 1944,** the weather was good over Brindisi, the base from which the missions would launch, and also in Pranjane. Musulin had his all-American crew ready to take the ACRU team in and rescue those men once and for all. By now everyone was antsy from having been on standby for so long, eager to go and do this risky job. The words of the downed airmen's plea for help kept running through their minds. SOS . . . *Waiting for rescue . . .* Jibilian couldn't get that message out of his mind since he had first heard of the coded distress call, understanding that the men must have been in a desperate situation if they were willing to send such a long message and risk having German planes home in on their signal. He knew all too well how effective the DF could be.

Musulin, Rajacich, and Jibilian were focused and ready when the word finally came that today would be the day. They had tried so many times before, but they all felt that this time would be different. None of those crazy Brits to get in the way. An American crew to get them in there quickly and safely. Vujnovich personally drove the team down to Brindisi for the mission launch, and he could tell the men were focused.

In Brindisi, Vujnovich shook each man's hand and wished them good luck, looking them in the eyes and wondering if this would be the last time he saw them. He admired their willingness to go into such a dangerous situation, and at the same time, he wished he was going along with them.

The flight out was just like every other attempt, except that this time Musulin had checked the coordinates with the pilot and found them correct, and there was no Partisan sitting in the plane with them. They felt good about this one. They were really going in this time. When the plane reached the jump site, Musulin was on high alert, looking for any sign of trouble that might spoil this attempt as well, but none materialized. The pilot signaled that the jump site was approaching and the three agents stood up, double-checked their gear, and lined up at the door. This time when he looked down, Musulin saw no battle below, no cloud cover. Nothing that would stop their mission. But then he did see something. *Are those flare pots?*

On the ground, Felman and the other airmen had been waiting in the bushes on the edge of that large clearing in Pranjane, the spot they assumed the Americans would use for a landing zone if they were to be rescued. Just as they had been every night since July 31, as the message from Bari had instructed, they were waiting for the arrival of the rescue team. With each passing night, they had become less and less certain that the promise would be fulfilled. But still they waited, every sense on alert for a sign that something was finally about to happen. When they heard a plane in the distance, everyone thought the same thing: Is this it? Could it be? This wasn't a normal time for flights to Ploesti to pass overhead, so they feared that a German plane might be scouting for their location. Or maybe, just maybe, it was the Americans looking for them. Felman and a few other men stepped outside and looked up in the dark sky but they couldn't see the plane yet. *But damn if that didn't sound like a C-47,* Felman thought. He couldn't be sure, but the more he listened, the more that sounded like an American plane! He asked a few men around him what they thought, and no one was willing to commit, but Felman could tell from the look in their eyes that they also thought this could be the Americans coming to rescue them. Was the plane looking for them? What if they couldn't find the right drop zone? Felman thought quickly and he decided they couldn't just stand there and risk having their rescuers pass right over without finding them. He made a decision that, like the radio call, could bring Nazis instead of Americans if he was wrong.

"Light the flares!" Felman shouted. "Go! Now! Get the flare pots going!"

The men went running for the flare pots they had placed around the field for exactly this moment, pots of rags and wood that would burn brightly as a signal to the plane overhead. Felman was nervous as he watched the men light signals that would give away their position, but he was ready to signal this plane, whoever it was. These airmen couldn't wait any longer.

The flare pots roared to life and lit up the perimeter of the field, a clear signal for a drop zone. Felman and the other airmen crouched in the bushes around the field and watched the sky eagerly, listening as the plane drew closer.

Musulin saw the flares, as did the jump master, who was already sure they were in the right location. Then the pilot saw the three red flashes from the ground, the correct signal that these were friendlies waiting for the OSS agents. The jump master checked that Musulin's line was secured and then yelled, "Go!" with a strong push on the big man's back. The static line ripped Musulin's oversized thirty-two-foot parachute out of his pack and then Rajacich and Jibilian followed him quickly, the three men trying to stay as close as possible so they would land near one another. As soon as the men were in the air, the jump master pushed out several crates of medical supplies and clothing, which Musulin had insisted on taking back to these people he had lived with before.

The team had jumped from only eight hundred feet, which is very low, but makes it more difficult for the enemy to spot you and kill you on the way down or to meet you at your landing place. From that altitude the agents came down fast and hard, with only about thirty seconds from leaving the plane to hitting the ground. Musulin was the first to land, not only because he was the first out of the plane and starting from a low altitude but also because when this former football lineman parachuted, he tended to fall out of the sky like an angry rock, his parachute merely providing some drag to slow him down. Musulin landed on a chicken coop, smashing it to pieces and sending startled chickens flying in every direction. Rajacich followed soon after, landing in a tree near Musulin and the chickens. He was uninjured but had to call for Musulin to help cut him down from the tangled chute lines in the tree.

Jibilian was the last on the ground, realizing on the way down that he also was headed toward trees. The usual procedure in that circumstance is to cross your arms and legs tightly, with your elbows across your face to protect it from the tree limbs, but he barely had time to react when he saw the trees. That turned out to be good because he landed in a cornfield instead of the trees, and he probably would have broken both legs if he had crossed them as he intended. The cornstalks helped cushion his fall and Jibilian ended up with one of the best landings of his career.

As soon as the three men collected themselves and their gear, they saw a peasant woman in a long dress come rushing up to them. They instinctively tensed and readied their weapons, but it quickly became clear that this was another enthusiastic greeting by a grateful Chetnik woman. She charged right past her demolished chicken coop without seeming to notice and proceeded to kiss the three men on the cheek repeatedly, calling them "liberators" and saying over and over that she was so glad the invasion had begun. Apparently she was under the impression that the trio were the beginning of a full-scale parachute invasion as had just happened in Normandy, so Musulin had to break it to her that there would not be anyone else coming that night. She was grateful to see them nonetheless and insisted that they come to her house for something to eat. Musulin politely declined on behalf of the team and gave the woman fifteen thousand dinars, about ten dollars, to cover the cost of the chicken coop he had so thoroughly smashed. The woman accepted the money and pointed the men in the direction of the Mihailovich camp, with more thanks and more kisses.

The trio walked down a road in the dark, wary of being found by a German patrol but also confident that they were firmly in Chetnik territory. It was not long before they ran into a group of bearded men wearing the royal insignia of Mihailovich's army on their caps, and some of them recognized Musulin right away. The leader of the group yelled, "George the American!" and ran toward him. Some of the Chetnik men wept with joy at the sight, running to give their favorite American a big bear hug. Jibilian and Rajacich were amused by Musulin's celebrity, but soon they, too, were experiencing the bearded kisses and hugs of these fierce-looking guerilla fighters.

As soon as he could get a word in amid the celebration, Musulin tried to tell his Chetnik friends that his return did not signal any change in diplomacy by the Allies. Trying to adhere to his orders, Musulin explained that they were here to help the downed airmen and that their presence should not be construed as any signal that the Allies were more favorable to Mihailovich now. The Chetniks said they understood, but Musulin could tell they didn't really believe him. The way they saw it, the Americans had returned.

**Soon after lighting the flares** in a risky move to make sure the rescuers could find them, Felman and the other airmen in Pranjane saw parachutes popping out from behind the plane. They counted three good chutes, followed by a few more that looked like supply drops. And then just at that moment the plane flew directly over their position, low enough that the men could see the white star of the United States Army painted on the tail. The mountains of Yugoslavia were filled with a hearty cheer as the airmen felt for the first time that they might really, really be going home.

There was only a short while before Chetnik men started coming out of the surrounding woods with crates full of desperately needed supplies, a welcome sight to the airmen and villagers alike. But then the village erupted in celebration when they saw a very large man in an American uniform emerge from the tree line. Felman was watching, but he had no idea who this fellow was. The Serb villagers certainly knew him, and apparently they loved him.

"Captain George! Captain George!" they shouted, welcoming back the big American who had left them months earlier after spending so much time in the village and with Mihailovich. Men and women alike ran to embrace the returning American, grabbing his round face with both hands to kiss him hard. Tears streamed down the faces of men, women, and children as they saw Musulin emerge from the forest like a savior, followed closely by Rajacich and Jibilian, who received the same exuberant greeting as soon as the villagers spotted them, carried heroically on the shoulders of Chetnik soldiers. Felman and dozens of the airmen were standing nearby, eager to greet their rescuers but feeling like they should let the villagers have this special moment with a man they knew and loved. It took a short while for Musulin to peel himself away from the adoring crowd and walk over to Felman.

Musulin walked right up and somehow sensed that Felman was the leader of the group. He put out his hand and said, "I'm George Musulin."

The airmen welcomed the trio as angels dropping out of the sky, and one of the first things the rescue team noticed was the huge number of airmen greeting them. They had been told to expect one hundred fifty airmen, and Vujnovich was hoping that number had been exaggerated. The rescue team, however, found themselves surrounded by no fewer than two hundred fifty American airmen, and they were told that more were streaming into Pranjane every day.

The daunting numbers could be put aside for a short while, though, while all of Pranjane celebrated the arrival of the rescue team. In the Serb fashion that the airmen were getting used to, the village erupted into jubilant celebration with plum brandy and music, capped by a visit from Mihailovich himself. Jibilian was in awe of the already legendary general, feeling awkward in front of the charismatic leader, especially because the OSS was so informal, with little attention paid to military protocol. He almost never saluted his OSS officers, but Jibilian felt that he was an enlisted man in the presence of a famous Yugoslav general, so he snapped off a sharp salute when introduced to Mihailovich. The young American was pleased to find out that despite his reputation as a fierce guerilla leader, Mihailovich was as down to earth as anyone he had ever met.

Like every other American who met Mihailovich personally, however, Jibilian was taken by the way a man of such simplicity could at the same time give such an impression of grandeur. Jibilian and the other Allied soldiers were most impressed by Mihailovich's sense of dignity in the face of extreme hardship and insurmountable odds, and the humble way he received accolades from his followers, consistently coming away with the same unshakable impression that they were standing in the presence of greatness. More than one airman reported that meeting with Mihailovich actually made them feel physically small, though Mihailovich was merely of average height and build. Mihailovich was known to be even-tempered for the most part, despite his recent outburst about the British, and though he was not necessarily considered a great intellect by most of his peers, his sense of duty to his country and his people was unquestioned.

He was a man of great warmth and personality, kindly and paternal to everyone around him, though he was also a strict disciplinarian with his troops. Mihailovich was renowned for his simplicity, his insistence that he be one of the common people, never above them or his soldiers. He always preferred eating a meal on the ground with his troops to sitting inside a dining room with other officers, and everyone around him knew that his greatest joy was to live among the common people in their own communities—eating with them, dancing, joining in their festivals, singing folk songs, and playing a guitar. He dressed as his soldiers dressed, ate what they ate, and refused anything that even implied a privileged status. His followers loved him for it and commonly called him Chicha, the Serbian word for uncle.

The Americans saw Mihailovich at his best whenever the local villagers came to see him, always bringing gifts of wine or flowers, the women eager to kiss him on the cheek and pose for a picture with the general. Mihailovich was extremely fond of children, and whenever he passed through a village the local schoolmaster would declare a holiday so the children could swarm Mihailovich, eager to touch the hero. Mihailovich often would tease the boys in the group by saying he had heard that one of them was a Partisan and then ask which one was loyal to Tito.

*"Ne ja, Chicha!"* Not I, Uncle! each boy would yell in return. Mihailovich continued teasing them, eyeing them suspiciously, pointing to first one and then another, saying, "I have definite information. Is it you?" The boys would continue laughing and yelling, *"Ne ja, Chicha!"* until finally Mihailovich relented and patted the boys on the back, saying, "I see that you're all good Serbs. I shall have to tell my intelligence that they were wrong!"

The stories Jibilian had heard of Mihailovich were confirmed when he saluted the general and received a salute in return, then hung around for a while to exchange a few pleasantries and listen in as Mihailovich talked with Musulin and the other Americans about the upcoming rescue. Followers were always crowded around, seeking close proximity to this local celebrity, a celebrity without pretense who didn't mind a farmer suddenly giving him a bear hug and insisting on sharing a cup of plum brandy.

When the celebration died down, Felman and Musulin conferred at length about the plans for getting all these men out. Musulin was reluctant to admit that the OSS had not anticipated so many men, but he did tell Felman that the rescue plan was audacious, bigger and riskier than anything that had been attempted before, and he gave him a basic rundown of how it would work. C-47s would come in and pick up a dozen men at a time and fly them back to Italy, he told Felman. Exactly how that would happen was still a little uncertain, and that was one reason Musulin and his team were there in advance: They had to figure out how to accomplish the airlift of so many people, using whatever resources they found here. The first order of business: Build an airstrip. On this rugged hillside. With virtually no tools. Without the Germans finding out.

Musulin soon checked with an old friend in Mihailovich's army for an update on the Germans in the area. What he heard was not encouraging. Only twelve miles away in the village of Chachak was a garrison of forty-five hundred German troops. Only five miles away on the other side of the mountain was another garrison of two hundred fifty Nazis. Within thirty miles in all directions there were a half-dozen cities and other centers important to the Germans, each with a number of troops stationed there. In Kraljevo, only thirty miles away, a *Luftwaffe* unit was stationed at an airfield just a very short flight from Pranjane. The meaning was clear for Musulin: This had to happen quickly.

"If the Germans find out about this and attack, they're going to bring superior firepower and overwhelm the Chetniks," he told Felman. "Our friends will hold them off as long as possible, but eventually they will be forced to retreat through the mountains. All these airmen, especially the sick and injured, will never make it. We've got to do this evacuation before the Germans find out that my team is here."

Felman assured him that the airmen were ready to do whatever they were asked to make this rescue happen. Musulin knew he could count on the same from the villagers as well.

Meanwhile, Jibilian set up his radio and made contact with Bari, letting them know the ACRU team had arrived safely and were proceeding as planned. The airmen set up a field hospital with the medical supplies that were dropped, calling on the services of an Italian doctor who had escaped from a prison camp in Belgrade.

Jibilian was amazed by the number of airmen in Pranjane and by the generosity of the villagers risking their lives to help Americans. He was more determined than ever to get these men out safely, but actually seeing two hundred fifty men in one place was challenging his confidence. When Jibilian was asked by desperate airmen if the plan could really work, he always said yes. But deep down he was thinking, *Only God knows.* It was the same response he had when the airmen and villagers asked why the Allies had abandoned Mihailovich.

**The next morning, Musulin and** his team wasted no time in setting about their tasks. Job one was clear: Get to work on the landing strip. They knew this would be tough work for the airmen and the local villagers to build an airstrip big enough to land C-47 cargo planes using nothing more than their bare hands and the occasional hoe or pitchfork, but there was no other way. The airmen had already begun clearing the field near Pranjane, the one where they had waited for the rescue team to arrive, but there was still a great deal more work to be done. And as Musulin kept reminding everyone, it had to be done quickly and without the Germans catching on. He confirmed that the site chosen by the airmen was the best option because it was relatively flat and clear, at least for the mountains of Yugoslavia, but it wasn't much of a landing strip. It was just a small, narrow plateau halfway up the mountainside, about fifty yards wide and nearly seven hundred yards long. The field was surrounded by dense woods on one side and a sheer dropoff on the other. Farther out, the plateau was surrounded on all sides by mountain ranges that were less than two miles away. It looked like a pilot's worst nightmare.

Musulin knew from what the air force had told him in preparation for the mission, and plenty of the airmen on the ground confirmed it also, that the minimum distance required for landing a C-47 is seven hundred yards.

"And that's just the *minimum*," he emphasized to the airmen. "God help us if there's wind during the rescue attempt, or if the pilot comes in too fast. We could have a real mess out here if one of those planes runs off the end and bursts into flames. We're going to lose American men, and the crash might bring Germans to investigate too. It could get real bad, real quick." He repeated the same thing to the villagers gathered around, this time in Serbian. They all nodded in understanding, aware that the consequences of failing in this task were severe.

He turned his attention back to the airmen and made sure they understood that their lives depended, in a very direct way, on whether they could build this airstrip.

"And don't forget you're going to be on that plane when it tries to take off on this short little runway," he said. "If I were you, I'd make that airstrip as long as we can possibly make it before those planes come."

He didn't really have to pound home the point. These were airmen and they were very skeptical that they could make this plateau into a landing strip and not just a death trap. But they had no other choice, so they got to work right away, glad to have work with a purpose. They looked at the airstrip construction as another mission assigned to them, just like getting orders for another bomb run to Ploesti. The able-bodied carried the worst of it, while the sick and injured contributed in whatever small ways they could, by hauling off the smallest rocks or bringing water to the others. The airmen worked practically nonstop, breaking from their labor only when they heard a German plane overhead, which sent the men sprinting into the woods to hide. They hoped that, without a few hundred people visible working on it, the landing strip would look like a farm field. If a German pilot saw that many people out there toiling at once, it wouldn't take long to figure out who they were and what they were doing. At the call of "German plane!" even the most exhausted men would sprint for the tree line. The work continued well into the evenings because of the need to finish quickly and also because it was harder for planes to see the work in the dark.

The two hundred fifty airmen were joined in their work by three hundred villagers and Chetnik soldiers, using sixty oxcarts provided by the peasants for hauling rocks out of the field and moving dirt around to make the airstrip more level. Stones and soil were harvested from nearby streams to level the field. With very few tools to use, the airmen worked with bare, bloodied hands, digging up rocks and tamping down the earth with their feet to make the field solid enough for a plane to land. Every one of them was a flier, so they knew how important it was to do the job right. One soft hole or rock left in the field could mean a plane full of dozens of airmen cartwheeling across the airstrip and bursting into flames. Some airmen concentrated on cutting down trees at the end of the field and ripping up the stumps so the landing strip could be extended, while others hauled gravel and stones from a nearby streambed to use as makeshift paving. Their goal was to extend the length of the field by seventy-five yards. Every extra foot was another little bit of hope, another margin of safety for pilots who would be pushing their skills to the limit with this crazy mission.

Meanwhile, Musulin was more skeptical about the airfield than he let on to the airmen. He knew it was up to him to approve this site and not just bring those C-47 crews in if they were certain to die in a pointless crash. He wanted to see if there was anywhere else to carry out this operation, so he dispatched two teams of airmen to go look for other, more suitable landing sites. Several days later, both parties returned with reports of better landing areas, but the closest was fourteen hours walking distance from Pranjane. Moving everyone to that site would mean shifting away from the relatively well-guarded, secure area of Pranjane and being more vulnerable if the Germans attacked. And asking all the sick and injured to travel fourteen hours was not a good option.

So Musulin reluctantly accepted Pranjane as the rescue site. He didn't like it, but he didn't really have a choice.

**Each day, more airmen arrived** and the newbies heard what was going on in Pranjane, why they had journeyed so long to get to this little village that looked like every other village they had passed through. And each new arrival greeted the news with the same reaction—a wide grin that quickly faded into a look of skepticism. C-47s here? On this mountainside? Won't the Germans come and kill us all after the first plane crashes?

Jibilian knew the men had good reason to be skeptical. Their lives depended on this plan working and no one could be sure it would. But Jibilian had no intention of leaving Yugoslavia again without taking as many of these airmen with him as possible.

They had to make it work. Six days after arriving in Pranjane, Jibilian and his teammates thought it could. The airstrip was coming along well, looking smoother and longer every day as the trees came down on the far end of the field. After surveying the work on the landing strip one last time on August 8, Musulin told Jibilian to send a message to Bari.

"Jibby, tell Bari we're ready. We'll start evacuation tomorrow night."

# Chapter 15

## Red. Red. Red.

---

**Jibilian tapped out his Morse code message to Bari**, requesting six planes for the following night, and when he received confirmation that the rescue would finally happen
the next evening, word spread among the airmen in Pranjane like a bottle rocket skittering through a field of school-
children. This was the news they had been waiting for. They
were finally going home. Well, they were going home if this
crazy plan actually worked. No one was forgetting that the
whole idea was a big risk.

The airmen understood that they wouldn't all be able to
leave at the same time. They would be going out a few dozen
at a time, starting with the wounded and then leaving in order
of their longevity on the ground, with no distinction between
officers and enlisted men. Those who had been in Yugoslavia
the longest would be at the front of the line, and bomber crews
would go out together. Musulin drew up a list of seventy-two
airmen, most of them wounded, and told them to be ready to
evacuate the next day. He was playing it safe by assigning only
twelve men to each C-47, even though they typically carried
twice as many troops. Musulin had specified that the rescue
planes carry only half a load of gas, just barely enough to get to

Pranjane and back, to keep their weight to a minimum. They already were asking the rescue pilots to take off in the dark on a bumpy airstrip that was just barely long enough, so Musulin figured they should keep the planes light by assigning no more than twelve passengers. Plus, there would be fewer casualties if one of the planes didn't make it.

Hardly anyone slept that night. Like the rest of the airmen, Tony Orsini and Clare Musgrove, who had arrived in Pranjane about two weeks earlier, were way too wired to sleep. They alternated lying down for short stints until they couldn't stand it anymore with sitting outside in the chilly air talking with each other. Musulin, Rajacich, and Jibilian were up well into the night double-checking their plans and conferring with the Chetnik soldiers about defenses around Pranjane for the following night. They wanted to be sure that if the Germans came roaring up the mountainside to investigate the C-47 landings, the Chetnik soldiers could hold them off long enough to at least let them get the planes loaded and back in the air. "If we're going to be attacked," Musulin told them, "let's make sure we get some of these boys in those planes and on their way out before it all falls apart. We might not all make it out, but let's make sure *somebody* does."

The air was crackling with excitement and anxiety, so it was no surprise that most of the men were still awake when the machine-gun fire started. All over Pranjane, Americans jumped out of the haystacks and barn lofts where they had been trying to sleep, throwing on the rest of their clothes as the rapid staccato of a large-caliber machine gun carried through the damp night air. They were ready to bolt into the darkness and run for their lives. Musulin and his team sprang into action at the first sound of gunfire, grabbing their weapons and heading toward the firefight. *This could be it. They're onto us and they're not going to let this rescue take place.*

The OSS agents were making their way toward the sound of the gunfire, led by the husky former linebacker, when they met a Chetnik officer coming toward them. Musulin immediately was surprised by the man's calm demeanor. The Chetnik waved his hands at the Americans as if to indicate everything was okay and shook his head from side to side with a look of chagrin on his face.

"Is no problem. No problem," he said. "One of my men saw something moving and challenged it. When it did not say anything, he fired his machine gun."

"Oh, so there's nobody out there," Musulin said, lowering his weapon.

"Only cow. Now dead cow."

**The agents and the airmen** slept fitfully that night if they slept at all, and when they awoke on the morning of August 9, their first thought was of the rescue. For seventy-two of the men, they knew this was the day they would finally get out of Yugoslavia or die trying. For the others, this was the day they would see if this crazy plan would work and there was an end in sight for their time in Yugoslavia. The plan was to bring the cargo planes in at night to make them less of a target for German fighters, so there was still one more long day in Yugoslavia to get through. There was still work to do, however, so the men could focus on putting the final touches on their improvised airstrip, as well as setting up the flare pots that would help guide the planes in.

Late in the day, Orsini and Musgrove joined more than a hundred airmen and villagers working on the field, looking for soft spots and rocks, pushing carts of dirt here and there to even out the ground as much as possible, while Musulin and Rajacich oversaw the work. Musulin was on horseback, looking for any last-minute problems or areas that could be improved, when he spotted two or three tiny specks off the horizon, coming from the direction of Belgrade. He knew at once they were German planes. Once again, he thought the jig was up, the Germans were onto them and coming in to strafe them just as they were close to rescue. Rajacich saw them too. Simultaneously, both men started shouting to the airmen and villagers.

"German planes! German planes! Run! Get off the field! Hurry!"

Everyone scurried like field mice from an approaching hawk, sprinting and hobbling off the airstrip and into the closest tree line, squatting down in the ground cover to hide from the planes. Musulin and Rajacich joined them, watching the specks get closer and louder. It didn't take long to see that the planes were a Stuka dive bomber and two JU-52 Junker planes that were similar to the American C-47s expected later that night, only more angular and boxy. The Stuka dive bomber struck fear in the hearts of the airmen, who easily recognized it on sight. Though it looked more like a small fighter plane, airmen and infantry the world over knew the Stuka as a fearful plane to encounter when you were helpless on the ground beneath it. In addition to strafing, which most any plane could do, the Stuka was specially designed for precision bombing of critical ground targets—including airfields. One of the most advanced and successful planes used in World War II, the Stuka had a dedicated autopilot system that put it in a steep controlled dive, allowing the pilot to aim the bomb with great precision, and then the system automatically pulled the aircraft out of the dive and back to level flight when the bomb was dropped. The extreme G-forces of such a near-vertical dive often caused pilots of other planes to temporarily lose consciousness during the pull out of the dive, resulting in a crash, but the Stuka's autopilot prevented that from happening. The Stuka pilot also had an excellent view from the cockpit and special indicators to inform him of his dive angle and when he reached the optimal bomb release altitude, allowing him to focus entirely on precise aiming during the fast, steep dive. The sight and sound of a Stuka diving right at you should have been plenty frightening enough, but Hitler wanted to maximize the terror. So he ordered the *Luftwaffe* to equip the Stuka with a screaming siren that made the sound of its dive far more frightening, even rattling some antiaircraft gunners so much that they did not fire at the plane.

While they were primary transports of one type or another, like the C-47s, the German Junkers were armed with machine guns and could make slow lazy circles around the airmen, strafing the men on the ground until the bodies were heaped in piles. On this day, it was likely that the Junkers were on a routine mission and the Stuka dive bomber was accompanying them for protection. It might have been pure chance that their path had brought them right across the Pranjane airstrip, but Musulin and Rajacich couldn't be sure. They were only a few hours away from carrying out this mission, and German planes were flying right toward the field. . . .

All around the airstrip, tended lovingly with bloodied hands and improvised tools, the hearts of the American airmen sank as they watched the planes approach. When they saw the Stuka dive bomber, they all had the same thought. Musgrove looked at the planes with anger. *Damn, they're going to bomb our field. A few bombs on this airstrip and it'll take forever to repair it enough for C-47s to land.* Even if the Germans hadn't sent the planes specifically to foil the rescue attempt, they all knew that the pilots would notice something amiss when they spotted the freshly cleaned strip of land and the extension into the woods. Having the pilots see that big stretch of land near Pranjane with nothing happening on it, no farmer plowing or tending a crop, would look almost as suspicious as seeing the Americans working on it. But it was too late to send a villager out there with a plow in an effort at looking normal. They could see the planes coming in right toward the field at about one thousand feet and very slowly, slow enough that the pilots would get a good look if they just glanced down at the right moment. Everyone tensed in their hiding places, watching the planes get closer and closer.

Then Musulin noticed a most providential herd of cows sauntering onto the airstrip. The bovine pack's attention was drawn to the fresh grass on the airstrip, which had been denied them while the workers were busy all day and into the night for weeks prior. The cows waddled up into the field and didn't seem to notice when the three planes flew directly overhead at low altitude, giving the field exactly the look the airmen needed at that moment—that of a normal farm field in the mountains of Yugoslavia.

Musulin, Rajacich, and the rest of the airmen watched intently as the German planes continued on their path past Pranjane, never turning to come back and take another look. Everyone started breathing again as they realized that the German pilots who could have put an end to Operation Halyard didn't notice a thing, perhaps due in part to the impromptu cow camouflage. They were all talking about how sure they had been that the Germans were onto them. But apparently not, they said. Just a random flight.

Musulin wasn't so sure. He was keenly aware that the success of this mission depended on operational security. The mission was so risky to begin with that he could only hope for success if the Germans didn't get wind of it too early. There was no way he could carry out this rescue and engage in an all-out battle with the Germans simultaneously, so Musulin was worried that those three planes weren't just a random overflight. The enemy might have intercepted a message from Bari and sent that seemingly random flight over Pranjane to take a look at the airstrip and check for defenses. If it was a reconnaissance flight, it would make sense that they didn't attack or come back for a second look. With just hours till game time, this ex-linebacker was getting his game face on; Musulin was suspicious of everything.

*If they're onto us, that was just recon for an attack later. They might have been checking us out in the daylight so they'll know how to attack us tonight when the planes come in.*

Musulin considered calling off the rescue, postponing it for another night. But he realized it was probably too late. The planes were probably already taking off in Brindisi, and besides, every day they waited just made the risk worse. He asked one of the Chetniks to check on the German garrison in the valley below, using a secret telephone line, to see if there was any unusual activity that could signal an impending attack. The Chetnik supporters in the valley reported that all was normal.

The big brawny American stood in the field, the wind blowing through his bushy black beard, and watched as the men got back to work, looking for any way to make the airfield just a little bit safer for that night's rescue. As he looked over the men, ragged and scrawny but still working hard, Musulin knew they were willing to risk everything to be rescued.

*We're on. We've got to start getting them out. Tonight.*

✳   ✳   ✳

**The airmen and the villagers** continued toiling on the makeshift runway throughout the day and well into the evening, some bringing carts of dirt to level out another dip in the field, others wielding crude farm axes to bring down just a few more trees on the end. If they didn't have any specific task to do, many of the airmen roamed the field methodically, their eyes cast downward looking for any bump or soft spot, any rock that had been overlooked. Even if they couldn't do much more in the hours before the rescue attempt, they couldn't sit still. Orsini felt that he had to be out there, doing something, anything, to give himself just a bit more hope that this wild plan could actually work. They were all doing their damnedest to make sure this little farm meadow on a plateau in the mountains would be the last place they touched the ground in Yugoslavia.

As night fell and forced the men to stop working, they retreated to the homes in Pranjane for what seventy-two of them hoped would be their last meal in the village, their last cup or two of plum brandy. They were tired from the day's work and from living for weeks or months in Yugoslavia on little food, and the wounded were suffering from their broken bones, lacerations, dislocated shoulders, and myriad other injuries. But on this night, no one was eager to bed down in the haylofts and small cottage rooms. The men were anxious to see if this rescue could really happen, seventy-two of them realizing they were the most fortunate to be going out that night, but also the most at risk because they would test the details of this plan with their lives. But there wasn't an airman in Pranjane who wouldn't trade places with them and willingly take that risk.

The night was clear but dark, exactly what Musulin wanted for this operation. Though it greatly intensified the challenge for the pilots of the rescue planes, the night landing would help protect the lumbering C-47s from German fighters. All through Pranjane, downed American bomber pilots asked themselves the same question: *Could I pull this off? If they asked me to fly into some strange country and land on a little airstrip in the dark, could I do it without killing myself and a few dozen men?* No one ever had a clear answer. They told themselves they could do it if they had to, and they assumed that the pilots on their way to Pranjane were saying the same thing to themselves.

The airmen awaiting rescue didn't know it yet, but the rescue had already begun. Six C-47s were in the air and on their way to Pranjane. When the planes took off from Bari, George Vujnovich knew it would be hours before he heard anything about the mission, good or bad. But like the airmen in Pranjane, Vujnovich would not sleep that night. He occupied himself as best as he could, shuffling paper and writing letters, anything to keep him busy so he didn't just sit and worry about the mission. After all the bureaucratic infighting and resistance from the British, Operation Halyard was in the air. Vujnovich thought again of his last days in Yugoslavia and how much he had yearned to get out and be free of German oppression. He knew the men in Pranjane must feel the same way, and he was right. They could think of nothing else, every sense on alert as they waited for the appointed time. A couple of hours after darkness enveloped the airfield, Musulin sent the word: He ordered the first seventy-two airmen to gather at the airfield and prepare to leave.

The chosen seventy-two made their way to the airfield just outside the village, many of them hobbling with their injuries, and waited in the cold night air. The rescue planes were not due for another two hours, but Musulin did not want to run the risk that the planes would show up early and the men would not be ready. The makeshift airstrip was crowded again, just as it had been during the day, because most of the other airmen had come along to see what would happen. They milled about in the darkness in an imitation of their last-minute runway inspections before losing the sun, but this time the men said good-bye to those who were chosen to leave that night, and the talk was all about whether the planes actually could land out here in the dark. And whether the Germans might crash the party.

Dozens of villagers and Chetnik soldiers also converged at the airfield with the Americans, some of them with a specific task to aid the rescue and some just wanting to see this great event that everyone had been talking about for so long. Everyone who had been aiding the airmen for months turned out to see the final act, and they were as excited as if the circus were coming to town. And in a way, it was. The mood was jovial at first, but it grew more and more somber as the hours passed and the time for the rescue grew near. Conversations died down and even the most exuberant of the men became quiet, sensing that the coming hour would bring something momentous to this tiny village in the mountains, and that whatever it brought would deserve some respect. Either dozens of men would be saved tonight, with the promise of many more soon after, or dozens of men might be killed and along with them the hopes of all the rest. What was about to happen in Pranjane would be profound, in one way or another.

Musulin and his air force contacts in Bari scheduled the rescue to begin at ten p.m. on August 9. Musulin checked his watch obsessively and nearly every other airman who still had a watch followed suit, all of them reflexively making sure they were in place, that they were ready on their end as soon as the planes arrived. As ten p.m. grew nearer, Musulin ordered everyone off the airstrip. The men made their way to the tree lines on either side, just as they had done many times before when a German plane flew overhead, leaving the makeshift runway empty. Then Musulin spoke with the Chetnik officers at the field and made sure that the soldiers manning the flares, improvised out of oil cans and hay bales donated by the villagers, understood what to do. As soon as Musulin gave the order, he wanted the Chetniks to light the flares and hay bales lining either side of the runway, giving the incoming pilots some rudimentary indicators of the landing field's parameters. The Chetniks were ready. The airmen were more than ready. Musulin, Rajacich, and Jibilian were scanning the skies looking for any sign of an incoming plane.

Hundreds of airmen crouched in the brush and trees along their newly made airstrip. They were eager and hopeful, but they were worried, too. Then, at exactly ten p.m., they heard the drone of a plane. A wild cheer arose from the trees, shattering the silence in the pitch-black night.

Musulin and his team heard the plane at the same time, the cheers quickly drowning out the welcome sound. *Right on time*, Musulin thought, looking at his watch again. *Okay, this is it. Let's get this done.*

He yelled to the men in the trees, giving final orders before the planes came in.

"Stay where you are!" he yelled, trying to overcome the sounds of celebration. "If you are not going out tonight, stay off the field! I don't want a madhouse out here when the planes land!"

The airmen understood Musulin's orders and remained in place, scattered all along the sides of the runway so everyone could see what happened, the cheers steadily dying down and giving way to silence again. The young men crouched in the bushes could hardly breathe as they waited to see their fate played out on this makeshift airfield.

As the roar of the planes grew louder and came closer, Musulin and everyone else realized that it was more than just one plane. The planes made their way toward the airfield at low altitude and began to circle Pranjane.

That's when Musulin saw there was a problem. There were only four planes, not the six he had requested. He didn't know that two had been forced to turn back because of engine trouble along the route.

Musulin ordered Rajacich to go ahead with the signal that would tell the rescue planes they were in the right place. He rushed out onto the airfield with an Aldis lamp, a highly focused lantern that produced a bright pulse of light. Most commonly used on naval vessels and in airport control towers to signal planes, the OSS team had brought the Aldis lamp along for exactly this purpose. Rajacich held up the round lamp in one palm, using a sight on the top to aim it at the lead C-47 circling overhead and squeezed the trigger three times to send the predetermined signal: Red. Red. Red.

Using the same device, a crewman on the C-47 signaled the appropriate response: Red. Red. Red.

Then Rajacich sent the next message that would confirm all was ready on the ground and the planes could come in. This time he used the lamp to blink a predetermined code word: -. .- -. *Nan.*

Everyone waited a long moment for the plane's reply. And then everyone on the ground saw the flashes: -..- - ....- .-. .- -.--. *X-ray.*

The airmen in the trees could see the signal and knew what it spelled, but they didn't know the code words. Likewise, the villagers knew what the signaling was about, but they couldn't tell if all was going as planned. All of them, the villagers and the airmen alike, looked intently at Rajacich and Musulin. Rajacich let the Aldis lamp drop to his side and began trotting off the field. Musulin stepped out to address the airmen one last time.

"We're on, boys! This is it!" Musulin's last words were drowned out by another joyous roar from the airmen and the villagers. He yelled to the Chetniks to light the flares and hay bales, and within seconds, the field was ablaze with fiery orange markers. The night took on an eerie appearance and the crowd grew silent again as they watched the planes circle. When he was sure everything was in order, Musulin marched out to the middle of the airfield, raised a flare gun high over his head, and pulled the trigger. A green flare screamed skyward like celebratory fireworks, the final signal that the landings should begin. The excited airmen let out another cheer as the flare erupted and then quickly quieted down again.

The night was deadly quiet except for the crackling of the burning hay bales, and all eyes were on the first plane in the group. The airmen watched as it dropped out of the circling formation and positioned itself for a landing on their airstrip. Every airmen in Pranjane knew what a risk this crew was taking for them, and in the air, the C-47 pilots from the 60th Troop Carrier Command especially knew what a difficult task lay before them. The airmen on the ground watched the plane come closer and closer and then, finally, they could see the white star on the tail. They knew by now that the planes were American, but still, the sight of that white star added another layer of jubilation for these men who weren't sure they would ever see home again. The Americans were coming to rescue them!

But the plane still had to land, and that was the tricky part. Everyone waiting in the woods had spent many hours in planes just like that C-47 and they knew that landing at night on such a rough airstrip wouldn't be easy. They all watched, wondering if they would have the nerve to make the same landing attempt if the roles were reversed. And just as the men on the ground suspected, the pilots coming in for this first landing were terrified. They didn't know what to expect of this hastily made landing strip and they feared they would crash, either dying in the wreckage or joining the other men in their limbo behind enemy lines. Both on the ground and in the air, scarcely a breath passed the men's lips as they waited for the C-47's wheels to touch down.

The plane came in lower and lower. Musulin, Rajacich, and Jibilian were left to watch just like all the airmen, the same thoughts running through everyone's mind as they focused intently on the incoming plane.

*It looks good so far. You're lined up on the runway nice and straight. C'mon boys, you can do it. . . . Looks good . . . looks good . . . Hold it steady, boys. . . .*

First there was the thump of the wheels; then the pilot cut back on the throttle and the engines changed pitch. The plane raced down the airstrip, nearly silent now, hundreds of eyes watching intently. Maybe this plan would work, after all. The men crouched in the brush were just about to breathe a sigh of relief when they heard the plane's engines roar back to life.

The plane lifted back into the air, over the trees, and into the darkness.

The field was quiet again, the only sound the crackling of the burning hay bales.

The airstrip was too short. The pilot just couldn't do it.

Musgrove and the rest of the men were crushed. The dark, quiet night hid hundreds of broken hearts. Musgrove thought that was the end of it all.

"Too short, too short," he heard another airman say quietly. "They can't do it. This will never work."

# Chapter 16

## *Going Home Shoeless*

**Everyone feared the same thing: The mission was a fail-**
ure. No one had been sure that the airstrip was long enough
or that the C-47 pilots would have the nerve to land here in
the dead of night. Seeing the plane touch down and then roar
off again was a terrible disappointment, but not necessarily a
surprise.

The despair, however, was quickly pushed aside by another
glimmer of hope. The second plane was coming in! The airmen had feared that the first plane, presumably the lead C-47
carrying the pilot in charge of the whole group, had told the
other planes that the airstrip was too short. They fully expected
the planes to regroup and just fly back to Italy. But here was a
second C-47 coming in for this dangerous landing. Again, all
eyes were on this plane as it lined up in the darkness to try and
hit this little airstrip just right. Once again, the plane came
down at a steep angle, slammed its wheels on the ground and
cut the power. But this time, the pilot hadn't overshot the runway. He dropped in hard on the leading edge of the field so he
could use every single foot in front of him to stop the plane,
braking hard and taxiing all the way down to the end of the

runway, then maneuvering off to the side as much as possible so the next planes wouldn't hit the first one.

Musulin, Rajacich, and Jibilian joined the airmen in letting out a wild cheer as they saw the airplane come to a safe stop. *This is like Babe Ruth hitting a home run to win the Series*, Musulin thought.

Airmen and Serb villagers rushed the plane, screaming in celebration and urging the crew to hop out so they could be welcomed to Pranjane. Musulin and his team, along with some of the Chetnik soldiers, worked to keep the airstrip clear, pushing the crowd away from the parked plane and off the airstrip. Other planes were coming in, or at least Musulin hoped they were, and each landing was going to be just as risky as the one before it.

Musulin crouched by the airfield again, and with everyone else, watched as the second and third planes came in for landing, ignoring his previous orders to wait for the previous plane to take off and clear the field before coming in. The OSS team was on edge, wondering if they would end up with a pile of planes running into one another on the small field. Each landing was nerve-racking, but the planes made perfect landings—all except one that ran into a haystack near the airstrip and ended up with a severely dented wing tip. The planes taxied off the airstrip as much as they could, the wings of one plane sometimes passing over the wings of another, clearing by only a few inches. Then the first plane, the one that had overshot the runway, came back in for another attempt. Musulin felt for the crew, having to make this frightening landing more than once. But on the second try, the pilot knew exactly where to find the sweet spot. The last of the planes was on the ground and everyone could relax again. At least for a moment.

The airmen shook the hands of the C-47 crews, who all looked tremendously relieved to be on the ground, and the villagers greeted them with the same over-the-top show of hospitality to which the downed airmen had become accustomed. Burly men and stout women gave the rescue plane crews hearty bear hugs and kisses on both cheeks, while others threw flowers on them and pressed cups of plum brandy into their hands. Women and young girls rushed the C-47 crews to drape garlands of flowers around their necks. The moment was joyous, with the villagers singing songs in celebration and also as a farewell party for some of their American friends.

In the midst of the celebration, Musulin, Rajacich, and Jibilian were pleasantly surprised to see Nick Lalich step out of one of the C-47s. Vujnovich had thought it a waste to keep Lalich in Bari when he was so eager to help with this mission, so he sent him out on one of the first planes. He knew the OSS team could use another experienced hand on the ground, and he was right. As soon as they could make their way through the throng of airmen and villagers surrounding the planes, Musulin welcomed Lalich with a strong handshake and said he was glad to have the help.

As usual, Musulin was a favorite of the villagers and everyone wanted to sing and dance and drink with him, but the big American had to demur, for he still was in the middle of carrying out the most dangerous part of this mission. The planes were on the ground, and now he had to get them back in the air. He also kept worrying about whether the Germans would show up at any minute.

*Four American planes circling, signal lights, flares, burning haystacks, and a green flare to top it all off. Could we do anything else to invite the Germans in?*

**Nick Petrovich, the young Chetnik** soldier who was among the thousands of Mihailovich's fighters around Pranjane, was on guard duty during the rescue. He was stationed about half a mile away on the one road leading up the mountain and into the village, crouched in the woods waiting for a German patrol to investigate the air show they must have seen from below. Petrovich was manning a fifty-caliber machine gun taken from a downed bomber, which he knew from experience acted more like a small piece of artillery than a machine gun. He had torn through German troops, trucks, and cars with the big gun already, so he was confident that if the Nazis came up the mountain to stop the rescue, he and his fellow soldiers could hold them off long enough to let the planes get back in the air. As they had many times before, Petrovich and the other Chetniks chose a spot on the road that was slightly elevated to give them a firing advantage, and on a curve so that the vehicles could be surprised when they came around the bend. If a patrol came near, the ambush team would hold their fire and let the first one or two vehicles come by, then open fire with the big fifty-caliber and their other weapons. Several soldiers were ready with hand grenades to throw at any Germans who tried to flee the vehicles.

But for the moment, the road was empty. No sign of Germans. Petrovich was trying to concentrate on watching the road, but he couldn't help staring off in the distance at the airfield, which he could see clearly from his elevated hiding place. The airstrip danced with the flickering lights of the flares and burning haystacks, illuminating the hundreds of figures dancing in the open field and pressed close to the four big planes that Petrovich saw come in earlier. He had watched in awe as the C-47s came down at treetop level, just barely clearing the surrounding woods and then dropping down sharply onto the airstrip. Petrovich was sure the planes were going to crash, especially when he saw the first plane go down and right back up again. When the next planes went down and taxied to a safe stop, Petrovich and his fellow soldiers were overjoyed, letting out a cry of celebration that echoed the cheers rising from the airfield, waving their rifles high in the air and hugging one another with joy. *The Americans are here!*

Petrovich couldn't take his eyes off the spectacle below, and he longed to be with the rest of the Chetniks celebrating on the airfield. But he was also immensely proud to be part of the operation, and he knew it was vital that he guard the road. There was still every reason to think the Germans would come investigate this outlandish incursion into their territory.

He tried to keep his eyes on the road, but he kept going back to stare at the airfield in the distance. It was such a sight.

*It looks like a movie. Just like an American movie.*

**The celebration on the airstrip** continued as Musulin conferred with the pilots of the rescue planes and discussed plans for the next rescue flights that would come in. He wanted to know if the field was suitable for more rescues and if they could count on more of the men going out in the next few days. The pilots assured him the field was okay, though it made for a dicey landing. The first plane just overshot the runway, touching down too far down the runway, and then the other pilots knew where they needed to aim.

Once he had the information, Musulin didn't want to waste any more time. About ten thirty p.m., Musulin ordered the men to clear the field so the planes could be readied for takeoff. Then he called for the predetermined seventy-two men who were going home that night, and the group ran and hobbled toward the planes at the end of the field, some helping the injured airmen along. Musulin divided the men up into groups of twelve to assign them to planes, and then had to break the bad news to the last twenty-four on the list.

"You boys won't be going tonight," he told them. "The other two planes couldn't make it in, so you'll have to go out tomorrow."

The twenty-four men were disappointed to have come this close only to be told they would still have to wait. One of the C-47 pilots spoke up and told Musulin that he could take more than the twelve he was assigned, but the boss vetoed that idea.

"You'll be lucky to get over those trees with just twelve," he said. "We can't let you take any more."

That was the end of the discussion, and the airmen began loading up on the planes. Thomas Oliver, the airman whose complicated code helped set the rescue in motion, was among the lucky ones going out on this first night. One of the C-47s was mired in the soft ground at the end of the airstrip, so a couple dozen airmen manhandled it back onto solid ground before the men loaded. As the four planes were loading, those going home said their good-byes to the other airmen, shouting, "See you in Italy!" and those staying behind yelled, "Tell them to have chow ready when I get there!" The airmen leaving Pranjane knew they would not be apart from their friends for long because they were all going to the same base in Italy to be debriefed and receive medical care, but the situation was different with the local Serb villagers who had sheltered them and risked their lives to protect them. These people had tears in their eyes as they watched their American charges board the planes, and more than a few Americans began to tear up as they hugged the men and women who had done so much for them and who had to stay behind in German territory. As much as Musulin wanted to load the planes in a hurry and get them airborne, he couldn't deny people the chance to say good-bye. The embraces were long, and even though most of the villagers and airmen could not speak more than a few words of each other's language, the expressions on their faces said everything. The villagers were happy for the airmen but sad to see them go, and the Americans were so grateful that they had to keep saying, "Thank you, thank you, thank you," and hope that their hosts understood. Some of the villagers presented the departing airmen with homemade Serbian national rugs, a unique handcraft of the region, draping them around the men's shoulders and kissing them on the cheeks. After long emotional moments, the embraces ended and the airmen clambered aboard the four airplanes, waving a final good-bye to everyone outside.

They were going home. They were finally getting out of Yugoslavia. The airmen sat on the hard metal seats lining the edges of the plane's interior, facing the center of the plane, and readied themselves for the most dangerous takeoff they would ever experience. If they could get off the ground safely, and avoid German fighter planes for several hours, their journey out of Yugoslavia would be complete.

But as they sat there waiting for takeoff, the airmen in the four planes, almost as a group, had a sudden realization. The airmen and locals gathered outside saw one of the plane's doors open again, followed by another, another, and then all of the doors were open. Musulin wondered what was going on. *These planes need to get in the air. They barely have enough fuel to get back to Italy, so we can't keep them here much longer.*

And then he saw the first airman at the door bend down and unlace his army boots. He held the boots up high and yelled to a local villager he had befriended. "Radisa! Here! For you! Take these!" Then another man was at the door of another plane shouting the same thing. In seconds, the doors were crowded with airmen shucking their boots and throwing them out the door to the astonished villagers, many of whom were making do with nothing but traditional felt slippers even when the weather turned cold and snowy. The airmen were glad to have some way to show their appreciation, some even tossing their flight jackets, socks, and shirts to the villagers, who cheered and shouted their thanks, their eyes filling with tears all over again.

With the doors finally closed for the last time, the crowds moved away and Musulin gave the order for the first plane to take off. He wasn't at all sure the celebration would last, because he knew the C-47s were going to have a hard time getting in the air again.

*This could all be for naught if they crash trying to take off. This isn't over by a long shot. Not yet.*

Everyone else knew the challenge facing the pilots, too, and the mood quickly turned from celebratory to anxious again. The hundreds of airmen and villagers spread out along the sides of the runway and prayed for the best, all knowing that this moment was every bit as risky as the landings that had scared them so much a half hour earlier. Musulin stood with Rajacich and Jibilian, watching as the plane's engines roared to full throttle and the pilot started off down the airstrip, bumping along the uneven ground so much that the airmen in the back struggled to stay in their seats. In a reversal of the landing they had just witnessed, everyone in Pranjane stared intently at the plane as it picked up speed, its nose pointed high as it rumbled along toward the trees at the end, hundreds of prayers following it along. In what seemed slow motion, the rear of the plane left the ground so that the body was horizontal and the nose pointed forward; then finally the plane's big front wheels left the ground. Slowly, slowly, slowly, the plane rose into the air and those watching on the ground tensed with anticipation. The trees were so near, and the plane was not gaining altitude quickly . . .

A long moment passed as the plane struggled upward . . . and then the plane roared over the treetops, pulling its wheels in just in time to give it the few inches of clearance that made the difference between success and failure. From his guard post in the woods, Petrovich watched with wonder and admiration as the plane nearly brushed the treetops and flew right over him. He turned to watch the plane fly on and climb ever higher. Then within a few minutes, another C-47 repeated the same feat with about the same margin of error. Before long, all four planes were back in the air, circling Pranjane as they climbed higher and higher for enough altitude to get over the nearby mountain range.

Onboard the planes, the airmen were excited to be going back to Italy, and relieved that they hadn't died on takeoff. They settled in for a long, cold flight, many of them shoving their bare feet in canvas bags and wrapping themselves in anything else they could find on the plane.

**Musgrove and the other men** left behind were overjoyed at the sight of the four planes flying off and disappearing into the inky black night. All of the waiting and worrying, all the hard work they had put into this airstrip had paid off. Those men were on their way, finally, and every other airman could finally let himself think that he too would be back in free territory before long.

Felman and Musulin were thrilled to see the planes get off the airstrip, but they were worried. It all seemed too dicey to do it over and over again. Everything about the rescue was on a knife's edge, requiring nothing but a gust of wind or a pilot's uncertain push on the yoke to turn the success into a disaster. The two men conferred and ultimately it was Musulin's decision as the OSS team leader. He called Jibilian over and told him to send a message to Bari.

"Tell them this was too much, Jibby. We're pushing our luck. Tell Bari we're not doing any more night landings. Let's try again at dawn."

Jibilian sent the message as instructed, but the OSS team didn't know what would happen next. He kept looking for a return message from Bari that would confirm the landings for the next morning, but there was no signal. Did that mean Bari disagreed and wouldn't send the planes again? Or were they just not hearing the radio reply?

Musulin wasn't sure yet what the army would decide to do if night landings were too risky, so he was waiting to see. The army had insisted that night landings were necessary to keep the rescue planes safe from

German attacks, and Musulin knew that they were right. Those planes were lucky to get in and out without running into a Messerschmitt even at night, and it would be asking even more of them to come in during the day when German planes were everywhere. How much could they ask of these C-47 pilots? Was it too much to think that tonight's rescue could be repeated over and over? Surely those C-47 pilots were going to report that the landings and takeoffs were death-defying feats. Musulin and Felman worried that, as exhilarating as it was to see those forty-eight men rescued, it might have been a lark. They were incredibly lucky tonight, but what would happen next time, and the next time after that? They had to consider the idea that, as much as they hated to even think it, maybe those forty-eight men were the only ones who would be rescued in Operation Halyard.

Word spread throughout the airmen that the night landings had been canceled. Felman did his best to keep the men's spirits up, assuring them that the planes would be back, but the airmen's emotions were on a delicate balance now. The least thing could send them soaring into euphoria or plunging into despair. The news that tonight's feat would not be repeated made more than a few conclude that the operation was over and they had not been lucky enough to get out on the first night. Surely those C-47s wouldn't stroll right into German territory like this in broad daylight.

No one left the airstrip that night. They huddled in the woods or out under the stars, unwilling to leave the field in case the planes returned unexpectedly. Some were optimistic and scanned the skies for any signs of an incoming plane, but many grew depressed at the idea of remaining behind enemy lines for God knew how long.

But at eight a.m., as the men huddled in the cold, everything changed. A few men heard it first and perked up, standing to scan the horizon. They heard planes. Others joined them in looking for the source of the sound, a loud rumble that signaled more than just a lone German scout plane. Had last night's debacle tipped off the Germans to their location? Was a whole wave of German planes about to bomb and strafe them?

Many of the airmen, along with the OSS agents, at first thought the sound might be another sortie of bombers passing overhead on the way to bomb Ploesti. They saw the overflights regularly, and this sounded big enough to be a bomb run.

Then they saw them. They weren't German planes. They were American, but not bombers. And not just another C-47 willing to risk landing on their little airstrip. The airmen saw a beautiful sight in the morning's blue sky: a whole swarm of American P-51 Mustangs and P-38 Lightning fighter planes, well known to the airmen for their ferocity and the ability to strike fear in any German pilot. And right behind them, the C-47s. Not just one. It looked like half a dozen. The sky was full of planes.

They had returned—in daylight, with fighters! The men couldn't believe it. The doubters went from the deepest depression to uncontrollable joy in an instant. The men counted six C-47s and about thirty fighters— a buzzing cloud of American spirit headed for their airstrip. The P-51 Mustang, a single-engine fighter, and the P-38 Lightning, a two-engine twin boom fighter, routinely escorted bomber planes on their missions over Europe, so every one of the bomber crews on the ground in Pranjane knew them as one of the most welcome sights when they were in trouble. The fighters were a good match for the *Luftwaffe*, and the downed airmen instantly felt protected. The C-47s would take them home, but by God, those Mustangs and Lightnings were the cavalry coming in to save the day.

The airmen cheered and jumped up and down, waving their caps and blankets at the planes as they drew nearer. As they passed over the airstrip, the fighter planes wagged their wings in salute and made a few dramatic stunt maneuvers for the airmen before breaking off, diving down into the valleys to attack German camps and keep them busy while the cargo planes landed. The fighters attacked anything German within a fifty-mile radius of the airstrip as the C-47s circled and positioned themselves for landing. The airmen could hear the fighters strafing the German encampments and zooming back up to circle around for another run. They were giving the Germans hell, and the airmen couldn't have been happier.

Lalich was on the radio serving as air-traffic controller for the C-47s coming in. The airstrip was just as short and bumpy as it had been the night before, but in the light of day, the big planes were able to get down safely. It was nonetheless still the kind of landing that the pilots would talk about over beers for many years to come. To make sure they didn't run off the end of the runway and into the trees, some of the pilots even used a potentially disastrous technique called the "ground loop," a rapid horizontal spin on the ground. This quick U-turn solves the problem when running out of runway, but only if the pilot avoids the tendency for the inside wing to rise and the outside wing to scrape the ground, which happens more if the ground surface is soft like on an improvised airstrip. If the outside wing digs in, the aircraft will skid violently or even cartwheel. The ground loops amounted to a dramatic flourish for the airmen on the ground, who knew the danger in pulling such a maneuver in a big plane like the C-47. The airmen let out another hearty cheer of appreciation when they saw the risky maneuver completed successfully. Musulin admired the bravery of the C-47 pilots and thought they must be the best around, but he also thought they might have more guts than brains.

Everyone involved with preparing the field was elated at the success of the landings. The Mihailovich soldier in charge of guarding the airfield strutted around with his chest puffed out, a big grin on his face.

"Tell me," he asked an airman standing nearby, "is LaGuardia airfield anything like this?"

The scene from the previous night was repeated, with cheers and celebration every time a C-47 touched down, but today there was more of a sense of urgency. Once the six planes were on the ground, Musulin and Felman quickly hustled the chosen men onto them, usually twelve at a time. Seeing that the planes could take off safely, if not easily, Musulin eased up a bit on the twelve-man limit and allowed a few more men on some planes. The first men on the planes were the twenty-four sick and wounded who hadn't made it onto the previous night's planes, followed by other injured men, including Felman. As he boarded the C-47, Felman was overcome by the way the airmen wanted to show their gratitude to the Serb villagers who had helped them. Like those on the planes the previous night, many of the men on the rescue planes were shoeless and shivering in the cold, having given everything they could to the peasants who had kept them alive for so long.

In a repeat of the previous night's dramatic departures, the planes rumbled down the runway as fast as possible and slowly climbed to just barely clear the surrounding woods, more than one brushing the treetops with its wheels as it soared away. Musulin was astounded at the skills of the C-47 pilots and concluded they were some of the hottest fliers he had ever seen. A half hour after landing, the first six planes were off again, circling Pranjane to gain altitude and then forming a clumsy V formation for the return to Italy. When the rescue planes were assembled, the fighter escorts regrouped around them and the American planes dipped their wings in a farewell salute before heading toward the horizon.

Half an hour later, at nine a.m., another group of six C-47s and twenty-five fighter planes arrived for the remainder of the airmen, including Musgrove. They repeated the same scene again with cheering airmen, jubilant villagers, and more fighter attacks on the surrounding German forces.

One of the last planes became mired in the mud and Musulin worried for a while that it might have to be left there. Leaving the plane was in itself not a huge concern because the crew and passengers could be spread among the other departing planes. But leaving a big C-47 sitting out in the open would be a glaring sign to any German planes flying overhead later, and the villagers of Pranjane would pay the price after the Americans were safely back in Italy. They couldn't let that happen, so Musulin organized a hundred Serbs to push the plane out of the muck.

As the planes lined up for the takeoffs that would take out the rest of the airmen currently in Pranjane, Musulin checked his records and saw that one was missing. No one knew where he was and Musulin wasn't about to hold up the planes to look for him. Just as the last plane out of Pranjane was about to take off, the missing man came stumbling out of the woods, rushing to the plane in a stagger. He had overindulged in plum brandy during the night and almost missed his flight.

\* \* \*

**The Americans were so thankful** to the local Serbs for their help in saving the airmen that they offered evacuation to two who needed urgent medical attention. One was a man going blind, and the other had a serious leg injury. Musulin, as the rescue team leader, found it hard to shun these men when the Serbs were doing so much for the Americans and he gave approval for these two men to be evacuated on one of the first C-47s to arrive that day. But by the end of the morning he found out that he had stepped on some toes back in Italy. The Serb fighters were still officially seen as Nazi collaborators, no matter what they had done for American airmen, so army leaders in Bari were not pleased to see them step off the plane with the rescued airmen and considered their evacuation a grave indiscretion by Musulin. The error might have been overlooked except that several of Tito's Partisans were at the airfield in Bari when the plane landed and they recognized the two Serbs as Mihailovich guerrillas. Musulin soon had orders to get on one of the rescue planes and return to Italy. He argued with his superiors by radio, hoping to change their minds and stay to help rescue more airmen, but his immediate concern was whether Germans were soon going to attack Pranjane.

Assuming that there was no way the Germans didn't notice what happened in Pranjane, Musulin and his team retreated ten miles into the mountains to wait. While hiding out and keeping an eye on the village below, Jibilian received radio communications from Bari congratulating the team on a successful mission. As they hid in the mountains, villagers brought them five more Americans who had arrived in Pranjane only hours too late. The airmen were furious that they had come so close to rescue but missed their ride.

After several days in the mountains with no evidence that the Germans would attack Pranjane, Musulin decided to take the OSS team and the five airmen back down into the village. Though they found it hard to believe, the only conclusion that made sense was that the American fighter planes had so effectively attacked the German garrison that the troops dug in for protection and never saw the C-47s.

The team remained in Pranjane and greeted more American fliers, but the urgent messages from Bari kept ordering Musulin out. Reluctantly leaving Yugoslavia for a second time, Musulin returned to Bari on August 26. Initially there were calls to court-martial Musulin for refusing the order to offer no aid to Mihailovich during the mission, but the furor soon died down.

Rajacich and Jibilian stayed behind but didn't know how long they would be permitted to stay in Yugoslavia. Nick Lalich took over the OSS team and concluded just as quickly as Musulin had that the Serbs were completely loyal to the American cause. Lalich obtained permission for the team to stay in Yugoslavia, soon reporting that he had met with Mihailovich, who said he could funnel many more men to be rescued. *We can take more,* Lalich reported. *There are a lot more men to be rescued.* Despite ongoing misgivings about whether Mihailovich could be trusted, the authorities in Italy gave permission for Lalich, Rajacich, and Jibilian to stay in Yugoslavia and coordinate more rescues.

The airmen were surprised to hear from the crew members on the C-47s that some of the rescue planes had dropped supplies to Tito's forces, the enemy of the man who had harbored the airmen, on the way to Pranjane. In one of the later rescue flights, a crewman stepped out of the C-47 and happily announced that they had made a successful drop to the Partisans on the way over. The unsuspecting airman nearly had his throat slit by the Serb fighters before the Americans intervened and bundled him back into the plane.

**Two hundred and forty-one U.S.** airmen were rescued on the night of August 9 and the morning of August 10, along with six British, four French, nine Italians, and twelve Russians—a total of 272 men rescued, when Vujnovich and the other OSS leaders thought it would be a stretch to retrieve one hundred. Still, these airmen were only the first of hundreds to be rescued through Operation Halyard. All made it safely back to the U.S. air bases in Italy.

A mission that was supposed to last a couple of weeks went on for six months, during which the OSS team rescued 432 American airmen, and eighty personnel from British, Canadian, French, Italian, and Russian units. As Robert Wilson, Mike McKool, and all the other downed airmen made their way to Pranjane under the protection of Mihailovich and his fighters through December 27, 1944, they learned of the ongoing mission and prepared for repeats of the same landing and takeoff dramas that preceded them. The total number of men rescued was 512, with not a single life lost in the effort.

Operation Halyard, an audacious response to a desperate radio call for help and the query of a curious young woman in the States, turned out to be the most successful rescue ever of downed airmen behind enemy lines and one of the largest rescue missions of any type in World War II or since.

## Chapter 17

# *Gales of the World*

**The long ride back to Bari was joyous but tense for Tony** Orsini and Clare Musgrove, cold and loud as they sat on hard metal seats built around the rim of the plane's interior. The higher the plane climbed, the colder the air became and many of the men shivered in nothing but the thin shirts they were left with after leaving their overcoats behind for the Serb villagers. The crews of the C-47s handed out a few blankets and offered a spare jacket when they could, but the cold bit into the men's skin as the roar of the propellers stymied any attempts at conversation. The rescued airmen did their best to just settle in and ignore the cold, some closing their eyes and dozing off, others distracted by their fantasies of a hot shower and a hot meal.

Orsini, like others on his plane, had his fingers crossed that the plane could make it back to the base in Italy without being intercepted by the German fighters. He knew the C-47 was no match for the *Luftwaffe*, and even with the American fighter planes as escorts, it would take only one lucky hit to send the rescued airmen right back down again.

When they landed in Bari, the airmen onboard let out a loud cheer as the wheels touched down. Finally they were back. Their weeks and months behind enemy lines were over. When the first plane landed, George Vujnovich was standing with a broad grin on his face, clapping his hands, overjoyed at the success of such an audacious mission. Standing next to him was General Nathan Twining, commanding general of the Fifteenth Air Force, who was equally overjoyed and eager to personally greet his returning airmen. Vujnovich and Twining, along with many of the other OSS leaders who had made the mission possible, stayed at the airfield for hours to welcome the men back, congratulating them on a job well done, but there was no fanfare or publicity about Operation Halyard. The press wasn't told, and there was no newsreel cameraman waiting at the airport.

Twining lauded the returning airmen for their service and perseverance while in enemy territory, and then he issued a stern order.

"Do not talk to anyone about this. Do not reveal even the most insignificant information about your experience and adventures to anyone except the officers of the intelligence service," Twining told the men. "The war is still going on and we don't want to jeopardize any future evacuations."

Felman understood the reason for the order. Operation Halyard was not finished, and any security leaks could jeopardize the efforts to bring more men out. Plus, word of the mission's success might prompt the Germans to retaliate against the Serb villagers. Felman reiterated the orders to his men, but he also suspected there was a secondary reason for keeping quiet about the rescue.

Orsini had a shock when he first returned to the base in Italy. Amid all the jubilation of returning from Yugoslavia, a friend at the base took him to see the posted list of KIA—airmen killed in action. Orsini's name was on the list. He and his friend laughed, the other man telling Orsini that they had never given up hope for his return.

"We knew you'd come back. We knew you must still be out there," the man said, slapping Orsini on the back.

"Then why'd you put my name on the list?" Orsini asked, his smile starting to slip away.

"Well . . . we were hoping, you know," the man muttered. "But you were gone a while, so . . ." The two looked at each other for an uncomfortable moment and then laughed again at the irony of Orsini standing there looking at his name on the KIA list. Orsini shrugged it off for a while, but then he worried that his mother had been told he was dead. She hadn't, but it would be some time before he could get a message home to her assuring her that he was alive and relatively well.

Orsini and some of the other injured men were taken immediately to the sick bay, where X-rays revealed that his collarbone was very badly broken. He wasn't surprised, having lived for more than a month with the dull pain, which became truly bad only when he had to jump over a fence while fleeing the Germans or do something similarly physical. But still the X-ray of misaligned bones startled him. The doctor explained, however, that despite the severity of the break, there was little that could be done. Even with a fresh break, doctors could do little to help a collarbone heal except provide a brace that would keep it from moving around too much, and after five weeks without any care at all, the broken bone had already begun mending. The injury would heal, the doctor told him, but there may always be some pain and difficulty moving.

For the men without serious injuries, the first stop in Bari was for delousing. The airmen were taken to a specially equipped room, told to strip, and handed spray guns with delousing powder. The men in charge left and closed the door behind them, and then the airmen took turns spraying every nook and cranny on each other to kill the lice, fleas, and whatever other vermin they might have brought with them from Yugoslavia. While the chemical deluge was unpleasant, the men welcomed the opportunity to finally clean themselves of the grime and fleas that had plagued them the whole time they were in Yugoslavia. The delousing was followed by long hot showers and lengthy time in front of a mirror as they shed their scraggly beards.

Vujnovich, meanwhile, was doing his best to support Lalich, Jibilian, and Rajacich as they continued their evacuation of the airmen who made their way into Pranjane. As the winter of 1944 progressed and the snow grew deeper in the mountains of Yugoslavia, Lalich sent a message to Vujnovich pleading for more supplies. Medicine was especially needed, he said. The poor villagers had absolutely none, and no way to travel to a doctor in the heavy snows.

Even in the security of his office in Bari, Vujnovich had no trouble imagining the scene described by Lalich, and he wanted to write the requisition orders immediately. But he was stopped by the standing order that the Allies were not to provide any material support to Mihailovich or his supporters. The Operation Halyard mission was strictly for the purpose of bringing out the downed airmen, not to aid Mihailovich in any way. Vujnovich thought about the request for a day, seeing no way he could refuse but no way he could say yes without explicitly violating orders. It wasn't long before he came down solidly on the side of doing the right thing, orders be damned. Vujnovich instructed the supply depot to put together two large containers of medicine and lied on the paperwork ordering an airdrop over Pranjane, saying it was food for the OSS team.

In December, as the end date for the mission approached, Lalich contacted Vujnovich again and pleaded for shoes. He and his team could get by, Lalich told Vujnovich, but it was unbearable to watch the Serbian villagers walking about in rags, sometimes with their bare feet turning black against the white snow. The OSS agents had been tempted to give away their own boots and jackets when they saw the local people suffering, and Lalich begged Vujnovich for help. Again, it didn't take Vujnovich long to decide that he would do as Lalich asked. He drove the short distance from the OSS post in Bari to the air force base, where he walked into the supply officer's office and asked for six hundred pairs of shoes.

"Six *hundred* pairs of shoes?" the man replied, looking up from his desk.

"Yes, six hundred. I'll take less if that's all you have," Vujnovich said. He knew that the air force was under standing orders to comply with any request from the OSS, so the supply officer wasn't going to resist no matter how odd the request sounded.

"Well, we don't have anything close to that. If you want that many, you'll probably have to try the British. They should have it," the man said. "I can write the order for you, and if you take it to them they'll give you the shoes."

So Vujnovich took the requisition for six hundred pairs of shoes from the air force to the British base, where an officer filled the order with only a quick raise of the eyebrows and a "hmmmph, six hundred . . ." The shoes were trucked back to the air force base and on December 27, 1944, Vujnovich had them loaded onto a B-25 that was to be the last flight of Operation Halyard, the plane that would pick up Lalich, Rajacich, and Jibilian and bring them home.

The plane was to be flown by George Kraigher, the Serb who had flown for the Yugoslavian army in World War I, before heading Pan Am in Africa and helping Vujnovich as he fled the Germans. Kraigher, by this time, was flying for the air force and making special runs into the Balkans for the OSS. Vujnovich knew Kraigher would be the one going in to pick up the OSS team and the last few airmen, so he thought he would be able to convince him to take the shoes. Kraigher, however, was shocked when he went to the plane and found the entire floor covered with boxes of shoes, to a height of about three feet.

"George, what the hell is this?" he asked. Vujnovich knew he should be at the plane, ready with an explanation.

"Shoes. Let's just call it a belated Christmas present," Vujnovich said. He gave Kraigher a friendly grin and hoped he would just go along. Kraigher paused and looked at the fully loaded plane, then back at Vujnovich.

"You know I can't do this. I'm not allowed to carry that kind of cargo into that area." Kraigher was right; it was completely against the rules. But Vujnovich could tell his friend felt the same way he did, and he urged him to just take the shoes. "No one will know," Vujnovich said. "And when you get there and see those poor people with no shoes, you'll be glad you did this."

Kraigher finally relented and climbed over the boxes to get into the cockpit. Vujnovich watched the plane depart, comfortable that they were doing the right thing. When Kraigher reached Pranjane and the villagers lined up to receive a pair of shoes, he felt like Santa Claus and had no regrets. Lalich supervised the shoe giveaway and at first worried that the effort might be for naught because most of the shoes were a size 8, when the big Serbs, especially the men, needed something more like a size 12. It was pitiful to see the desperate men trying to shove their cold feet into the too-small shoes, but many made do by splitting the heel in back and forcing the shoe on like a very snug slipper.

Vujnovich was waiting at the airport when Kraigher brought Lalich, Rajacich, and Jibilian back from Pranjane. He couldn't have been more pleased with the success of Operation Halyard.

**When Jibilian finally returned from** Yugoslavia after helping rescue hundreds of airmen, he didn't ever want to see another bit of goat cheese. His first morning back, he wolfed down eight eggs, close to a pound of bacon, six slices of toast with butter and jam, and he drank more cups of coffee than he could count. He couldn't help indulging after months of barely surviving in the hills of Yugoslavia, though he felt bad when he thought of the villagers he had left behind, struggling to feed themselves.

As Felman had suspected, the cover-up was well underway by the time the airmen returned to free territory. A conspiracy was already in place to keep the world from knowing that the Allies had just pulled off the biggest rescue ever of airmen in enemy territory, a complete success made all the more amazing by the audaciousness of the mission. While the initial gag order had made sense while the rescue missions were still underway, after its completion the airmen began to wonder why the military still refused to acknowledge their incredible story. The reason, the airmen soon learned, was that the rescue could not be publicized without giving credit to the Serb guerilla leader who had harbored the men and made the whole operation possible. Mihailovich was officially ostracized for his supposed weakness and collaboration with the Germans, and even faint praise for his assistance with the downed airmen would have ruffled feathers in the State Department and the British government. While Operation Halyard was still going on and men's lives were at risk, no one wanted to jeopardize the rescues by trying to give Mihailovich credit. And after the rescues were completed, it just didn't seem worth the risk to career and interoffice harmony to challenge the

State Department and the Brits in order to let the world know what had happened. Vujnovich, Musulin, and others were willing, even eager, to put their careers on the line to ensure those men were rescued, but afterward there was little motivation to tell the story if it meant bucking the whole military and diplomatic hierarchy.

So the fantastic story wasn't told. There was no report back home in the newspapers of a huge operation that had saved so many lives, only the occasional item in a hometown paper noting that a local boy had been found and was no longer missing in action. With the initial orders to keep quiet forgotten once the rescues were complete, the men involved in Operation Halyard talked about it in the chow line, in the barracks, on the bus, in the cafés—anywhere they met up with other servicemen—because they were so thrilled to be back in Italy and so thankful to the Serbs who had harbored them. They wanted the other airmen to know what had happened to them, that the Serb people were astonishingly kind and helpful to American airmen, even though the briefings for bomber crews still included warnings that the Serbs would cut off their ears and turn them over to the Germans. Orsini, after returning from several weeks convalescence for his injury, returned to duty and had to sit through briefings in which an officer told him and his fellow crewmates that if they bailed out over northern Yugoslavia they should seek out Tito's forces and run from Mihailovich's fighters and the local villagers. It took all of Orsini's self-control to sit there and listen without earning himself a court-martial by telling the senior officer how wrong he was, and his voice was shaking when the briefing ended and he gathered the rest of the crew around. He would make sure the senior officer was out of earshot and then set the record straight.

"Don't believe a word of that crap about Mihailovich and Tito," he told the other men, including some young replacements who didn't know any better. "I've been there. I've been *on the ground* with these people, and the fact is that the Serbs will give you the shirt off their backs and every bit of food they have. If we bail out, just come with me and I'll walk right up and introduce myself again."

The continued warnings about Mihailovich, and offhand comments by other airmen who had heard only the official story, incensed Orsini and Musgrove and every other man who had experienced the truth first-hand. A few drinks were thrown and tables overturned in Bari as the returning airmen set the record straight on what happened in Pranjane.

After the initial warning, the army did not make much effort to keep the hundreds of returning airmen from talking, but the OSS agents who conducted Operation Halyard were on a shorter leash. Jibilian, like the airmen, wasn't looking for attention for his participation, but he also wasn't shy about telling people that Mihailovich and the Serbs deserved thanks. That stopped one day when an OSS officer pulled him aside and said, "Don't tell anyone. This will just create a big fuss with Tito and Mihailovich, so keep this under wraps." And after that he did, following his orders and telling almost no one about the rescue mission.

**Many of the rescued airmen** returned to the United States sooner than they would have if they had not spent so long in enemy territory. Richard Felman and his crew returned to the United States soon after being rescued, and they were told that the early return was partly due to fears that they would be executed as spies if they were caught behind enemy lines again. Two sojourns on the ground could make you a spy in the enemy's eyes, not just an unlucky flier, the theory went.

When Felman returned to New York, the Red Cross came aboard his ship and handed out coffee and doughnuts to the returning servicemen before they disembarked. They also distributed local New York newspapers, and Felman was pleased to find an article about the destruction of a major ammunitions warehouse and railway station in Gornji Milano-vac by guerilla forces resisting the German occupation in Yugoslavia. The only problem was that the paper attributed the guerrilla action to Tito's Partisans. Felman knew better because he had actually participated in that raid with Mihailovich's men, with not a single red star of the Partisans around for miles. Felman was livid to see Tito get credit for the work of Mihailovich's men, but it fit the pattern he had already started piecing together.

Orsini flew another thirty-three missions after recuperating from his shoulder injury, and then he was wounded again. While lying in the hospital, a doctor stopped by and asked him how many missions he had flown. Orsini replied that he had flown thirty-four, meaning he still had another sixteen to go before hitting the magic number of fifty, which usually was the point where the military said you'd done your duty and could go home. The doctor thought Orsini had made enough missions through hell for one man, so he authorized his return to the States. He was scheduled to return home on a hospital ship in April 1945, but one evening he found a note on his bunk that said, *You are returning to the States by plane in the morning.* With no time to notify his family that he would be home within days instead of months, Orsini flew back to the United States and made his way to the family's three-story apartment building on Beacon Street in Jersey City, New Jersey. Once he had reached the States, he decided not to call home first so he could surprise his mother.

When he reached home, he rang the bell for his mother's apartment, but there was no answer. He rang the bell for his aunt, who lived on the second floor and enjoyed a jubilant reunion with her for a moment before being able to get the excited woman to hear his question. "Where is my mother?" he asked. Orsini's aunt explained that his mother was at church, which didn't surprise Orsini much because he knew she went almost every morning. With another kiss for his aunt, Orsini dashed out of the building and onto the street, first walking quickly and then barely able to stop himself from breaking into a run as he headed toward the church. He hadn't gone far when he spotted his mother far down the street, about four blocks away, walking toward him with another woman. The two were returning from church and they didn't see Orsini yet. He kept walking toward them, his eyes fixed on the mother he had thought he would never see again, waiting for the moment when she recognized her son.

They kept walking toward each other, Orsini's heart beating faster and faster as they closed the distance, but his mother saw only another young serviceman walking toward her. He kept his eyes on her, wanting so much to scream out to her, but he waited, wanting to see the look on her face when she realized it was him. When they came to within a block of each other, Orsini saw his mother pause briefly, stopping on the sidewalk as she looked more closely at the man in uniform coming toward her. Then she put her hands to her face and cried out as her companion looked at her quizzically.

"Anthony? *È quello voi?*" his mother cried, at first questioning, and then as Orsini started running toward her, she knew. "*Il mio Anthony! Il mio Anthony! È il mio Anthony!*"

His mother ran toward him, her arms reaching, trying to get her son back in her arms faster than her feet could carry her. Orsini could run faster and came to her quickly, scooping his mother up in his arms and hugging her tightly as she sobbed, saying his name over and over and kissing him on the cheek.

"*Sono indietro, Mama,*" he told her. "*È giusto, io sono indietro.*" *I'm back, Mama. It's okay, I'm back.*

**The first hint in the** press of the remarkable success of the rescue mission came on February 20, 1945, more than six months after the first C-47s landed in Pranjane. A five-paragraph story on page 2 of the *Washington Post* carried the headline RADIO SIGNAL AIDS RESCUE OF 250 FLIERS. The story reported that, "A mystery radio message, picked up and recorded by RAF radio operators in Italy, led to the rescue recently of two hundred fifty Allied airmen, mostly American, who had bailed out over the Balkans." The article went on to explain that the airmen sent a specially coded message that eventually led to the rescue operation. "Translation of the messages indicated that a large number of Americans, some of whom were sick, were stranded in Yugoslavia. They were awaiting rescue anxiously, for enemy troops were not far distant." There was no mention of Mihailovich.

The rescue itself was described succinctly: "Full arrangements were soon completed and the airmen congregated at a secret airfield. There they were all picked up and brought back to their bases."

Two days later the newspaper ran a lengthy letter to the editor from Konstantin Fotić, former Yugoslavian ambassador to the United States, in which he said that, because of the report of February 20, apparently there was no more need to keep the rescue secret. Fotic provided a more complete account of the operation, the scope of the rescue, and the key role played by Mihailovich. He closed by noting that:

> Even this action did not prevent a continuation of slanderous accusa-
> tions against General Mihailovich and I am not aware what recognition
> was given him for this contribution to the Allied cause. Probably the
> general did not expect any recognition, because he felt that he was
> merely carrying out his duties as an ally. Nevertheless, today, when the
> story of this rescue is disclosed, credit should be given to those who de-
> serve it, and should not be presented as an anonymous action which oc-
> curred somewhere in the Balkans.

**Tito, meanwhile, was completing his** takeover of Yugoslavia and do-ing exactly what many feared he would do: He all but gift wrapped Yugo-slavia for Stalin and ensured that Communism would threaten Eastern Europe for decades. Churchill and Roosevelt already were acknowledg-ing, mostly privately, that they had made a grave error in siding with Tito over Mihailovich, but the full truth about how Communist moles and spies had misled them would not come out until long after Roosevelt's death on April 12, 1945.

By then, Churchill knew that Tito could not be trusted and that Sta-lin controlled Yugoslavia from Moscow. On February 9, 1945, Churchill and Roosevelt met with Stalin in an effort to encourage at least limited democracy in the portions of postwar Europe controlled by Russia, and though he did not promise much, Stalin did assure the world leaders that he would persuade Tito to recognize all prewar political parties—including Mihailovich's and his followers—and to have a freely elected Constituent Assembly. Churchill did not trust Stalin, and on February 21,

1945, it was clear to his closest staff that he was "rather depressed, thinking of the possibilities of Russia one day turning against us, saying that [former British Prime Minister Neville] Chamberlain had trusted Hitler as he was now trusting Stalin." Churchill was disillusioned with the Russian leader and regretting his decision to abandon Mihailovich.

Churchill's fears were well grounded. On April 5, 1945, scarcely a month after Stalin's assurances and a week before Roosevelt's death, Tito signed an agreement with Russia to allow "temporary entry of Soviet troops into Yugoslav territory." Though Tito would come to have serious disagreements with Stalin, Yugoslavia was for all intents and purposes an arm of Communist Russia.

Once Tito won the leadership of Yugoslavia, backed by the force of the Red Army, he committed all of the Partisan military to capturing Mihailovich, his hated enemy. Mihailovich committed himself to a path of voluntary martyrdom. He could have saved himself by accepting offers to leave Yugoslavia and exile himself in another country, his absence probably satisfying Tito and ending the manhunt. By the time the last American officers left Yugoslavia in December 1944, they were reporting that Mihailovich had an aura of saintliness about him, which seemed to grow stronger as the Partisan manhunt closed in on him. Indeed, his people already treated him nearly as a saint. Wherever Mihailovich went, the peasants came from miles around to see him. Old women knelt and kissed his hands, while children brought him eggs and apples.

Mihailovich was able to evade capture for seventeen months. When Mihailovich contracted typhus and was near death, Chetnik soldiers carried him on a stretcher from village to village and through the mountains, always running from the Partisans. Friends in Switzerland contacted him in 1946, urging that he leave the country at least long enough to recover, but Mihailovich refused.

**Jibilian was discharged from the** military in 1945 and found a job as a purchase-order writer at the Veterans Administration headquarters in

Washington, DC. A year had passed since Tito had established Communism in Yugoslavia, and like the rest of America, Jibilian was busy getting on with his postwar life. Reading the *Washington Post* on the morning of March 25, 1946, he found a small article with the headline MIHAILOVICH UNDER ARREST, BELGRADE SAYS. He was stunned, especially since the article only described Mihailovich as "accused by the regime of Marshal Tito of traitorous collaboration with the Germans during the war, is listed by Yugoslavia as a war criminal." There was no mention that Mihailovich had been a staunch ally of the United States, much less his role in saving downed fliers. The article predicted a swift trial for Mihailovich, followed by an immediate execution by firing squad.

Jibilian soon decided he had to do something to let the world know what Mihailovich had done for American airmen. He marched down to the newspaper to tell his story, sitting down with a reporter to explain his involvement in Operation Halyard and what he personally knew of Mihailovich.

"If he's a collaborator, I am too," Jibilian told the reporter. "Draza Mihailovich is a friend of this country and Tito is about to execute him before anyone hears the truth."

Jibilian left the newspaper office feeling better, satisfied that he had at least told the story. But the newspaper article that ran the next day was brief and gained little attention. *Washington is a tough town,* Jibilian thought at the time. *It takes a lot to get anyone's attention.*

Felman saw the same news report in a New York newspaper and, like Jibilian, was stirred to action in defense of Mihailovich. Furious that the airmen's savior had been captured like a common criminal and that the Western press was reporting Tito's lies about Mihailovich being a war criminal, Felman wrote letters to all the New York newspapers in an effort to correct the record. Nearly all of them ignored his pleas, but then he went to the *New York Journal American*, a staunchly anti-Communist newspaper, and found an interested editor. An article written by Felman appeared in the *Journal American* and other Hearst newspapers on March 31, 1946. That article drew the attention of others involved in Operation Halyard, and within a few weeks Felman had letters from more than three hundred airmen who had been rescued and wanted to help Mihailovich. Jibilian received a similar response to the article in Washington, and soon the airmen from Pranjane were all back in touch with one another.

Orsini also found himself in the odd position of trying to defend a world leader halfway around the globe. One evening at a small party thrown by some friends, a man started talking about the current events involving Mihailovich, not realizing Orsini's personal connection. The man expounded at some length on how Mihailovich had once been an ally but then collaborated with the Germans, adding that his soldiers and the villagers supporting him were known to be particularly brutal with captured Americans. Orsini felt like he was back in Italy, sitting through a mission briefing. He clenched his drink tighter and tried to ignore the windbag, but finally he couldn't stand it any longer.

"That's not true," Orsini said, a tinge of anger drawing attention from the clutch of people who had been listening to the diatribe against Mihailovich. "I was there and what you're saying is just not true. I'm visible evidence that they were helping rescue airmen. I bailed out and they helped me."

The other man refused to believe Orsini, insisting that if his story were true, he was the exception. The propaganda demonizing Mihailovich had reached all the way to Jersey City.

Orsini's experience was repeated across the country as airmen who had returned to their civilian lives found themselves trying to explain to friends and neighbors how the claims they heard against Mihailovich just weren't true. When Mihailovich was captured, the media coverage mostly portrayed him as a traitor to the Allied cause, with few reports acknowledging the complex history and competing motivations of those involved.

**News reports describing Tito's triumph,** and the arrest of Mihailovich, helped reunite the rescued airmen who had scattered to their respective communities after the war. Jibilian, Felman, Orsini, and many others involved in Operation Halyard started communicating, commiserating in their outrage at the treatment of Mihailovich and wondering what they could do. The airmen knew they had to do something to help Mihailovich, but what? How could they affect events in Yugoslavia?

The veterans all knew what was at stake. In the struggle for control of postwar Yugoslavia, Tito had won out over Mihailovich, with considerable help from the United States and Britain. Tito would put Mihailovich on trial, but it would all be a Communist dog and pony show. There was no hope that Mihailovich could actually defend himself in Tito's courtroom, and after being convicted of collaborating with the enemy, Mihailovich would be executed. The very thought of it caused such anguish in the hearts of these men who knew they would not be back home now with their wives and children if not for the benevolence of Mihailovich. They determined that they could not stand by and watch Mihailovich be executed by a Communist government without even trying to help him.

Most of the airmen, like Robert Wilson, knew they were attempting the impossible, but still they had to make the effort. "Even if we can't save him, we just want him to know that we remember what he did for us, that somebody appreciates how much he risked," Wilson said. "Maybe that will bring him a little comfort."

The Bishop of the Serbian Orthodox Church in New York, a close friend of Mihailovich, thanked Felman for writing the article that brought the men together and for the willingness of the airmen to stand up for an accused war criminal.

"It does not matter that Draza Mihailovich will live or die. Some other Draza will be born in the mountains to lead the nation," he told Felman. "What does matter is the effort to clear his name."

**Repeating his role in Pranjane,** Felman became the de facto leader of the downed airmen again and led their attempt to save Mihailovich from a Communist execution, or at least to let the world know what he did for Americans before he died. The group formed the National Committee for Defense of Draza Mihailovich and the Serbian People, setting about an organized effort to spread the word of their own experience with the supposed war criminal. The group rallied around the slogan "He saved our lives. Now we'll save his." They distributed pamphlets, wrote letters to the State Department and their congressmen, and told their stories to anyone who would listen. Building on each newspaper article and radio interview, the men worked hard to change public opinion and influence world events. Felman and the other organizers created a stunningly successful public relations machine, writing press releases to news outlets and taking advantage of the fact that there were more than five hundred men scattered across the country who could give dramatic, sometimes heart-wrenching firsthand accounts of their experience with the Serbs led by Mihailovich. Most of the men had not met Mihailovich personally, but they knew his people and they knew what the general had done for the lost Americans. They consistently vouched for his dedication to American servicemen, based on their own experience and the fact that they came home. Soon they found that all over the country, hometown newspapers were eager to run stories detailing a local boy's connection to a sensational postwar trial in Europe.

The headline in the *Press* in Cleveland, Ohio, was CLEVELANDER AIDS GEN. MIHAILOVICH. The story quoted local Western Reserve University student George Salapa, one of the rescued airmen, saying, "I think he is getting a boot in the pants." In the *Telegraph* of Pittsburgh, Pennsylvania, the headline read STATE TROOPERS HAIL MIHAILOVICH AS "FRIEND." The story quoted Paul F. Mato of South Connellsville and Carl J. Walpusk of Jenners, both state troopers and former airmen, as saying that the Chetnik leader "is getting a raw deal from the Allied nations." The upcoming trial would be a "treason of justice," they said. The *New York Journal American* quoted former OSS agent Eli Popovich as saying, "We have sold Mihailovich down the river to Tito. Now Tito is selling us and sitting in Trieste waiting to fire on American soldiers at the drop of a hat with American guns and American ammunition." The headline in the *Times* in Detroit, Michigan, read DRAZA BETRAYED, CLAIMS DETROITER.

Felman proved to be a persuasive, articulate, and most of all, passionate representative of the rescued airmen. In an article he wrote for the *New York Journal American*, headlined YANK VETS AID MIHAILOVICH, Felman described why he and the other airmen were so intent on helping a Yugoslav accused of aiding the Nazis:

> I am traveling to Washington today, well fed, well clothed, comfortable in body but not very comfortable in mind.
>
> I am going to meet some of my buddies, well fed, well clothed. When I last saw them we were dirty, bearded, ragged, and death was always behind the next boulder or tree. It should be a pleasant journey today, you think? Well yes, except . . .
>
> We shall be thinking, the other guys and me, of the soft-spoken, scholarly man who saved us from the shadow behind the boulder or tree.
>
> The same shadow now hovers over him, and we shall be thinking of that, too.

Felman went on to describe how the airmen hoped to influence the U.S. government to "assure a fair trial for the man who is still a hero to us, although a traitor to Tito and the man in the Kremlin who yanks the strings." Of Mihailovich, Felman said, "He was about as much of a Nazi collaborationist as I am. His great, unforgivable crime was that he didn't like Communists either."

Buoyed by growing public sympathy, Felman and nineteen other rescued airmen, along with two Canadians, chartered a DC-3, the civilian version of the same C-47 that had rescued the men in Pranjane. On April 28, 1946, they flew to Washington, DC. They dubbed their trip the "Mission to Save Mihailovich," which was stenciled on the side of the plane. They made stops in Detroit, Cleveland, and Pittsburgh to pick up more airmen from their communities, posing at each airport for the local press. The papers ran pictures of sharply dressed young men in suits and fedoras, waving to the camera from the steps leading into the airplane, with captions such as TEN FLIERS RESCUED BY CHETNIK LEADER STOP IN DETROIT.

Having skillfully publicized their journey to Washington ahead of time, the delegation's plane was met at the Washington airport by more than two thousand supporters who cheered and waved signs supporting Mihailovich. Police motorcycles escorted the group to their hotel in Washington, and there the men immediately set off on their rounds. Splitting up and visiting as many politicians and bureaucrats as they could, the airmen tried to convince Washington leaders that Mihailovich should be acknowledged for his efforts in saving the forgotten 500. Felman and other members sought a meeting with acting Secretary of State Dean Acheson but were refused. They visited with other State Department officials and asked for help in going to Yugoslavia to testify on behalf of Mihailovich, insisting that the story of Operation Halyard must be heard if Mihailovich had any chance at all of getting a fair trial. Dozens of airmen were willing to get on a plane at any moment and fly back to Yugoslavia to testify, but they could not go without an invitation from Tito, and the only way to get that was through the State Department.

Not surprisingly, considering its past involvement with Tito and Mihailovich, the State Department said no. Even sending information about Operation Halyard to Tito, or publicizing it for the whole world to see, was out of the question, the airmen were told. The State Department refused to forward the documentation offered by the committee, consisting mostly of the airmen's own personal accounts in Yugoslavia, to Tito. All government records documenting Operation Halyard were classified, so the only credit for Mihailovich's actions would come from the airmen themselves, and the State Department would do nothing to help them get to Yugoslavia.

The airmen did receive considerable press coverage of their trip to Washington, which helped raise public awareness that the case against Mihailovich was, at a minimum, not as certain as Tito claimed. In one article Nick Lalich delivered a copy of his own Legion of Merit citation to the *Washington Post* to prove that he had performed heroically in

Yugoslavia during Operation Halyard and arguing that in his five months with Mihailovich he had never seen any evidence of betrayal. Lalich described the Yugoslav general as a "good-humored, regular guy and accomplished scholar." The reporter, however, noted that the citation said Lalich was with Tito's Partisans during this time, not Mihailovich. Lalich explained he had vigorously protested that inaccuracy when presented with the citation, but senior officers told him to "forget it or he'd get into trouble."

"I'm not going to forget it," Lalich told the reporter. "And I'll do all I can to get Mihailovich a decent break. He's getting a raw deal. He is not and never was a Nazi collaborator. The proof is in the frontline intelligence reports, if the army will make them public."

The army wouldn't.

**Before the visit to Washington** ended, acting Secretary of State Acheson changed his mind and agreed to meet with a representative of the airmen's group. Mike McKool, the Dallas, Texas, airman nicknamed Tom Mix by the Serbs, and by this time a law student at Southern Methodist University, was chosen to meet with Acheson. After talking for thirty-seven minutes, Acheson assured McKool that the United States would make a strong appeal to Yugoslavia to give Mihailovich a fair trial.

While in Washington, the committee members also sought a meeting with President Truman. The president declined. Working through their senators and congressmen, they had to be satisfied with having a resolution entered into the congressional report of May 1, 1946:

> As we, the official delegates of the National Committee for Defense of Draza Mihailovich and the Serbian People, representing at the same time some six hundred Allied airmen whose lives as ours were rescued by Mihailovich and his people, came to the capital of our country from all regions of the United States, at our personal expense in order to submit full evident proofs in favor of Draza Mihailovich from Yugoslavia to

the President of the United States of America and to the acting secretary of state;

As we tried in vain to submit to the authorities at the highest level [meaning the president and the acting secretary of state] the reliable documentary negation evidence of charges that Draza Mihailovich has been a traitor and enemy collaborator as announced by Marshal Tito in Yugoslavia;

As we, being formally denied the right to ask directly our supreme commander to intervene personally with Yugoslav authorities and arrange for us and for other Allied personnel to be summoned as defense witnesses of material facts to appear in the court;

As we, being denied the right to ask personally our president and the acting secretary of state to have all the documents of the State Archives and of the Ministry of War submitted for the presentation at the trial to General Mihailovich, we therefore have decided that:

We, the representatives of the National Committee of American Airmen to Aid General Mihailovich and the Serbian People, in spite of the failure of our president to meet us and personally listen to us, in spite of the direct refusal of Mr. Acheson to personally see us, accept and further forward the documentation, in spite of the hesitant and evidently insincere approach of the USA government towards Tito's regime in Yugoslavia, shall prove unyielding on the fight for the fair trial and absolute justice for General Mihailovich.

Having said this, we make known that, no matter where we are, in our homes in the States where we live, or through our senators and congressmen of the USA, we shall persistently continue to insist on the fair international trial to Mihailovich. We, the American veterans, will consider that international justice and morality do not exist anymore if the fair trial is not provided.

**Though the delegation returned to** New York disappointed, the airmen continued their campaign, asking for three things: Let the airmen speak at the trial, allow OSS personnel to testify about Mihailovich, and move the trial to another country where he could get a fair hearing. Felman, Jibilian, Wilson, Orsini, and all the other men were just simple citizens or military personnel at this point, with no power but what they might muster under a democratic society. They persevered because they had faith that citizens of a free nation could stop an injustice being perpetrated halfway around the world. Their experience in the war had taught them exactly that.

The effort did yield results. Shortly after the trip to Washington, the State Department followed through on Acheson's promise and sent a letter to Tito stating:

> A certain number of those individuals [American airmen] who were in close contact with General Mihailovich have firsthand proofs that may deny allegations for collaboration with the enemy, of which Draza Mihailovich is indicted, as it was announced by Yugoslav authorities. The government of the United States believes in such circumstances that the Yugoslav government will in the interest of justice behave in an adequate way, accepting proof of each individual who wishes to submit it, and taking it into consideration at the trial of General Mihailovich.

Tito's reply was swift and clear. He had no interest in hearing from the American airmen. The *Christian Science Monitor* on April 13, 1946, reported that, "Belgrade has curtly turned down Washington's request that these men in the interest of justice be allowed to present their evidence. Its reason: It does not want to influence the court." The reason was laughable to anyone who knew how much the court was already influenced in the extreme by Tito and Stalin. The report went on to explain that, "The Tito government caps its rejection of Washington's request with the amazing statement that General Mihailovich's crimes are too terrible to permit the question of his innocence to be raised." The message from Tito stated that, "The crimes committed by Mihailovich are too great and terrible for any discussions to take place on whether or not he is guilty."

Aided by such blatant confirmation that the trial was merely a formality before execution, public sentiment was building in favor of the airmen and Mihailovich. Americans were already leery of the growing Communist presence in Europe, and no one in the United States seemed to have a good feeling about Tito, not even the State Department, which failed to embrace him even as it officially shunned Mihailovich. Anti-Communist feelings, coupled with respect for the returning war veterans who were sometimes moved to tears in their defense of this foreign leader, created a growing concern that Yugoslavia was being allowed to railroad an innocent man. A long list of prominent citizens, including numerous state governors, senators, congressmen, and judges formed the Committee for the Fair Trial to General Mihailovich, building on the airmen's own efforts to push for U.S. intervention before Mihailovich was executed by his sworn enemy. The executive vice president of the committee was Ray Brock, previously a foreign correspondent for the *New York Times*, and one of those who, years earlier, defended Vujnovich from the Ustashe guard who wanted to execute him if he didn't produce his passport. Soon after its formation, the committee announced that prominent attorney Morris L. Ernst had volunteered to defend Mihailovich, intending to fly to Europe immediately in an effort to contact Tito.

By this time, the British role in the betrayal of Mihailovich also was emerging. In the *New York World-Telegram* on April 19, 1946, a headline read CHURCHILL WAS TAKEN IN BY TITO, WRITER CLAIMS. The writer was David Martin, already known as the foremost scholar on Yugoslav history and active in the movement to save Mihailovich. He told the newspaper that although Churchill did not conspire to hand Yugoslavia over to Communism and acted in good faith, "His mistake was in treating Tito as an English gentleman." Martin also quoted Churchill as telling a Brussels, Belgium, newspaper that his handling of Yugoslavia was his biggest mistake of the war. In 1946, the influence of Communist spies and moles like James Klugmann was yet to be discovered or fully appreciated.

As public outrage grew at the prospect of a show trial in Belgrade, the State Department sent another letter to Tito, requesting that the airmen's story be allowed into evidence. Stanoje Simic, the Yugoslav minister of foreign affairs, responded by informing the State Department that the airmen would not be heard. Any further communication on the matter would be ignored, Simic reported.

Realizing that Tito would not allow the Americans to participate in Mihailovich's trial, the Committee for the Fair Trial organized the next-best thing—an investigation commission that would hear all the evidence in the United States and then forward it on to Tito whether he wanted it or not. The airmen eagerly lined up to testify before the commission, knowing that it might be the only way they could ever get their story on the record. In the interest of time, however, the commission heard from twenty airmen and OSS officers who had direct contact with Mihailovich and his guerillas. The airmen included Felman and McKool, and the written testimonies of three hundred more airmen also were accepted. Then the commission heard from six OSS officers who personally had worked with Mihailovich, including Musulin, Lalich, Rajacich, and Jibilian. To a man, every single person testified that they had never seen any indication that Mihailovich collaborated with the Germans.

After a week of testimony, the commission forwarded a six-hundred-page report to Tito. As expected, Tito's government completely ignored it.

**The trial of General Draza** Mihailovich began on June 10, 1946, in a makeshift courtroom, the auditorium of an infantry school in the Belgrade suburbs that had been rigged with floodlights. The outsized venue was necessary to hold the more than one thousand spectators and one hundred foreign and Yugoslav journalists. Tito returned from a trip to Moscow in time to be present for the trial of his rival. Mihailovich entered the courtroom unaided but looking weary and weak, stepping carefully to the defendant's dock because his nearsightedness had recently grown much more severe, nearly to the point of blindness. Thirteen other defendants stood in the dock with him, also on trial for collaborating with the enemy during the war. Ten more were tried in absentia, including Fotić, the former Yugoslav ambassador to the United States who had recently detailed Operation Halyard in the *Washington Post*. The indictment accused Fotić of organizing "large-scale propaganda, fully aware that Mihailovich and his Chetniks, with their organization, were collaborating with the occupiers."

Collaborating with the enemy was the main charge against Mihailovich. The indictment claimed that in August 1944, the same month that the Operation Halyard rescues began, Mihailovich met with an American officer and the chief of the administrative staff of the Nazi military command in Serbia. That meeting was but one example of ongoing collaboration with the Germans and Italians in an effort to defeat the Partisans led by Tito, the indictment claimed. And in a clear example of how the victors write history, the indictment went on to condemn Mihailovich for the very act of fighting the Partisans, describing the Chetnik resistance to the Communists as if it were treason *per se*. The Americans and the British were not spared criticism in the indictment even though Tito probably would not have been in a position to try Mihailovich without the support of the Allies during the war. The American and British governments, Tito claimed in the indictment, conspired with Mihailovich and King Peter's exiled government to defeat the Partisans, again describing resistance to the Communist movement as inherently criminal.

Mihailovich maintained a quiet dignity as the indictment was read and responded to preliminary questions with a firm voice. When the prosecutor asked his occupation, Mihailovich replied, "General of the army."

As the trial began, the prosecutor did not mention the possibility that Mihailovich could receive the death penalty, but he said he would "expect the court to pass severe and just sentence over these traitors and criminals." No one doubted that Mihailovich would be executed if found guilty, and hardly anyone doubted that either. That Stalin was directing the trial through Tito was obvious to most people in the West, and besides, it was clear that Tito harbored more than enough hate for Mihailovich to guarantee a guilty verdict even without Stalin's urging. Western observers already were forming a clear picture of Stalin and Communist Russia, including the campaigns of political repression and persecution orchestrated by Stalin in his own country beginning in the late 1930s. Stalin purged the Communist Party of the Soviet Union of anyone suspected of disloyalty and persecuted unaffiliated persons, while cowing the populace with omnipresent police surveillance, widespread suspicion of saboteurs, show trials, imprisonment, and nearly random killings.

In an editorial on June 17, 1946, the *Washington Post* acknowledged that Tito was railroading Mihailovich to extract a personal vengeance on his former competitor for postwar Yugoslavia and also to denigrate the West. "Now it becomes apparent that the propaganda is being directed not so much against Mihailovich and the Chetniks as against Great Britain and the United States. For this we have our own statesmen to blame." The editorial went on to address the most concrete of the charges brought out in the trial, that Mihailovich had secretly met with German commanders, noting that an American officer had already declared publicly that he organized the meetings on the orders of the American high command for the purpose of discussing the terms of a German surrender. The newspaper denounced the Partisans for having been more interested in taking over Yugoslavia after the war than defeating the Germans during it, and it said the country's experience did not bode well for a future in which Communists were growing more powerful every day. The *Post* concluded by noting that neither the British nor the American governments had explained the "sudden shift of policy whereby Mihailovich was abandoned to the vengeance of his enemies. Consequently there is no American who can read with any easy conscience about how this 'first organizer of the resistance,' as he proudly and rightly calls himself, now stands deserted and friendless, weakened by confinement and perhaps by torture, to face his vindictive and remorseful judge."

In a surprise to no one, including Mihailovich, the leader of the

Serbian resistance was found guilty of all charges on July 15, 1946. The official transcript of the show trial includes the closing comments of the President of the Court: "By pronouncing this verdict the Court considers itself to be a faithful interpreter of the national feeling for justice and equity, and that by the stigmatization of treason against the fatherland it has remained consistent to the agelong freedom-loving traditions of our peoples, who from time immemorial esteemed liberty above everything, and treason against the fatherland as the gravest crime. Death to Fascism. Liberty to the people."

The transcript ends with a notation typical of the way Communist governments claimed to always have the complete support of the people: "At the conclusion of the speech of the President of the Court, there was enthusiastic applause, and shouts of 'Long live the People's Courts.'"

**Mihailovich was executed** on July 17, 1946, and buried in an unmarked grave. The next day, a four-paragraph story on page 6 of the *Washington Post* reported what everyone who had followed the trial knew would happen immediately after. MIHAILOVICH EXECUTED BY FIRING SQUAD, the headline read.

> Gen. Draza Mihailovich died at dawn today before a firing squad.
>
> The bearded 50-year-old Chetnik leader, who electrified the Allied World in 1941 by organizing the first Yugoslav resistance to the Nazi invaders, was executed less than 48 hours after a Yugoslav military court found him guilty of treason and collaboration with the Germans.

Mihailovich's last words to the world were, "I strove for much, I undertook much, but the gales of the world have carried away both me and my work."

Tony Orsini wept when he heard the news, and he was not alone. All over the country, men who owed their lives to Mihailovich broke down in tears of sorrow and anger, some pounding the table in frustration, others trying to comfort children frightened by their fathers' show of emotion. The execution of Mihailovich was so unfair, Orsini thought, a stain on the honor of all freedom-loving countries.

The gales of the world left young American men stranded behind enemy lines in Yugoslavia, and now the gales of the world left them wondering how the man who had watched over them could be executed in a Communist country while the free world did nothing.

# Chapter 18

## Secrets and Lies

Once Mihailovich spoke his last words and took his last breath, the press and concerned citizens of the Western world forgot him as quickly as they had learned of his plight. His show trial and ignoble death faded from the headlines within days. The world moved on to other troubles, other international threats and controversies, and Draza Mihailovich became just another casualty of World War II. Only in the years to come would he be seen as one of the first casualties of the Cold War.

The only Americans who continued to think of Draza Mihailovich were those of Serbian descent and the more than five hundred airmen and OSS agents who felt they had lost a dear friend. The rescued airmen never forgot Mihailovich, and they never gave up on the effort to clear his name. Their effort was even more difficult than before. Felman wrote more articles and letters to the editor, as did scores of other airmen, but they quickly found out that the press was no longer interested in their stories. As headlines go, LOCAL MAN STILL UPSET ABOUT DEATH OF MIHAILOVICH SIX MONTHS AGO just wasn't the same as the ones that ran on so many stories in papers across the country while Mihailovich was on trial and there still seemed to be some chance that the airmen could influence world events. They gave it a good try, the country seemed to think, but there wasn't any more for them to do and the world moved on.

Within two years of Mihailovich's death, he and the rescued airmen were all but forgotten. Felman, Musgrove, Orsini, Wilson, Musulin, and Jibilian all immersed themselves in their civilian lives, followed eventually by Lalich and Vujnovich. Though they had little or no audience anymore, they continued to tell their stories whenever they could, to family and friends, to church groups, to school classes who asked what they had done in the war. They always emphasized that a great man had been the victim of a great injustice. They held out hope that one day the name of Mihailovich would be cleared and he would get the proper recognition for aiding the airmen in their time of need, but in moments of honesty, they were not optimistic.

What the airmen did not know was that the Mihailovich name was still spoken in the halls of the Pentagon. There were still active-duty military personnel, as well as OSS agents and directors, who felt as strongly as the airmen that Mihailovich had been treated unfairly not just by Tito and Stalin, but by the U.S. government. They pushed, discreetly but persistently, for the American government to somehow right this wrong. One of these advocates for Mihailovich was General Dwight D. Eisenhower, supreme commander of the Allied forces in Europe, with responsibility for planning and supervising the successful invasion of France and Germany in 1944 and 1945. He would become president of the United States in 1953.

Eisenhower strongly urged President Harry Truman to correct the historical record and formally acknowledge that, despite being abandoned by the Allies in the midst of the war, Mihailovich was a true friend of the United States. In 1948, Eisenhower and the army convinced Truman that Mihailovich had done the country a great service and deserved recognition. Truman posthumously awarded Mihailovich the highest award possible for such service to the country by a foreign national—the Legion of Merit. This was no small decision, and it could not be construed in any way as throwing a bone to Mihailovich supporters. The Legion of Merit is a significant military decoration, awarded for exceptionally meritorious conduct in the performance of outstanding services and achievements. It is one of the few medals that can be issued both to U.S. military personnel and to military and political figures of foreign governments. Seventh in the order of precedence of military decorations, the Legion of Merit also is one of only two U.S. decorations to be issued as a "neck order," meaning it is worn on a ribbon around the neck. The other is the esteemed Medal of Honor.

Created on August 5, 1942, the Legion of Merit required that the president personally approve its award to any foreign national, and noncitizens can receive the Legion of Merit in one of five degrees, the top award being "chief commander" when awarded to the head of a foreign government. Several of the OSS agents involved in Operation Halyard had received the Legion of Merit, including Musulin, whose award was presented personally by OSS director Wild Bill Donovan.

So by the time Truman was convinced that Mihailovich should be recognized for his service to the United States, the choice was obvious. At the urging of the army, Truman decided that the country would posthumously award the Legion of Merit to Draza Mihailovich as official recognition for his aid to American airmen and as an apology of sorts. In a subtle rebuke to Tito and Stalin, the Legion of Merit would be awarded at the highest level, recognizing Mihailovich as the chief commander of Yugoslavia.

On April 9, 1948, almost two years after his death, the United States of America posthumously awarded the Legion of Merit to Mihailovich. The accompanying citation stated that Mihailovich

> . . . distinguished himself in an outstanding manner as Commander-in-Chief of the Yugoslavian Army Forces and later as Minister of War by organizing and leading important resistance forces against the enemy which occupied Yugoslavia, from December 1941 to December 1944.

Through the undaunted efforts of his troops, many United States airmen were rescued and returned safely to friendly control. General Mihailovich and his forces, although lacking adequate supplies, and
fighting under extreme hardships, contributed materially to the Allied
cause, and were instrumental in obtaining a final Allied victory.

Interestingly, Truman gave Mihailovich the Legion of Merit not just
for rescuing the airmen but for his overall effort in the war. Essentially
the citation said that Mihailovich did everything the British and Americans accused him of not doing—fighting valiantly against the enemy.
The award was signed personally by President Truman.

**Years after accusing Mihailovich** of failing to fight the enemy and
possibly even collaborating with the Nazis, the United States acknowledged that Mihailovich was, in fact, loyal to the end and had acted heroically in helping rescue the forgotten 500.

The award would go a long way toward assuaging the anger and frustration felt by the airmen and OSS agents—if only they could know that
it was given to Mihailovich. But they did not.

No one outside of the Pentagon and a few government offices would
hear about Mihailovich receiving the Legion of Merit. When State Department officials got wind of the effort to award the medal, they immediately expressed concern that the award could be detrimental to current
relations with Yugoslavia. Showing the same attitude toward Mihailovich that it had shown four years earlier, the State Department strongly
suggested to Truman that if the Legion of Merit was awarded, it should
be kept quiet. One cable from the State Department post in Rome,
dated April 1, 1948, urged Truman to consider how any positive recognition of Mihailovich could antagonize not only Tito but the Italian government as well. The cable stated that, "We do not believe it would be a
positive factor in Italian preelection period and might in fact be harmful
to U.S. prestige in Italy. Non-Communist Italians have no great sympa-

thy for any Yugoslav and any pro-Mihailovich elements here would be inclined to view cynically posthumous recognition of a patriot whom they might feel the Allies had abandoned in life." State Department officials in Belgrade sent similar discouragement, and Truman agreed not to rock the boat.

A telegram from the State Department to the American embassy in Belgrade on April 21, 1948, assured the ambassador that, "No steps will be taken at this time to give publicity to this award."

Instead of being publicized and Mihailovich's family or other representative invited to the White House for a formal presentation, the State Department insisted that the whole matter be stamped SECRET. It was officially awarded to Mihailovich, but for the first time in history the Legion of Merit was kept secret from its recipient and nearly everyone else, including the forgotten 500. The army forwarded the violet, blue, green, and gold medal, with its violet neck ribbon and citation signed by the president, to the State Department, which put it in a drawer for safekeeping "until such time as arrangements for presentation may be made."

No one without official clearance from the army or the State Department even knew that the Legion of Merit had been awarded to Mihailovich. Meanwhile, Tito's Communist government continued to tell the world that Mihailovich was a traitor for collaborating with the Nazis.

The Legion of Merit awarded to Mihailovich sat in the drawer at the State Department, officially secret, for almost twenty years. It might have remained a secret if not for the work of Congressman Edward J. Derwinski of Illinois, who intervened in 1967 at the urging of airmen who had heard rumors. Derwinski insisted that the State Department make the text of President Truman's citation public and for the first time the airmen and the rest of the world learned that the country had thanked Mihailovich for saving more than five hundred American servicemen with a grand gesture made halfhearted by the State Department's timidity.

The revelation helped rehabilitate Mihailovich's name, albeit in a small way and without the impact that the award would have had if made public in 1948, or even better, in 1946, before Mihailovich was executed. As the years passed, the world continued to forget who Mihailovich was, and whether he was friend or foe was relegated to arguments between historians and Americans of Serbian descent.

Avowed anti-Communist Ronald Reagan, then governor of California and about to become president in the next year, paid respect to Mihailovich on September 8, 1979. He wrote to the California Citizen's Committee to Commemorate General Draza Mihailovich:

> *I wish that it could be said that this great hero was the last victim of confused and senseless policies of Western governments in dealing with Communism. The fact is that others have suffered a fate similar to his by being embraced and then abandoned by Western governments in the hope that such abandonment will purchase peace or security. Thus, the fate of General Mihailovich is not simply of historic significance—it teaches us something today as well. No Western nation, including the United States, can hope to win its own battle for freedom and survival by sacrificing brave comrades to the politics of international expediency.*

Reagan went on to say that the betrayal of Mihailovich showed "beyond doubt that both freedom and honor suffer when firm commitments become sacrificed to false hopes of appeasing aggressors by abandoning friends."

Another step toward clearing Mihailovich's name, this one far more significant than the secret medal, came in 1997 when the British declassified wartime reports on one of the most controversial British undercover operations of World War II. With those documents, it was revealed that the suspicions of many were true: The Soviet mole James Klugmann was largely responsible for the British switching their support from Mihailovich to Tito. Not only did Klugmann's lies ensure Mihailovich's defeat and execution, they helped sway the Allies' support to Tito and cemented Communist control over Yugoslavia.

Many Americans were appalled to learn that not only was an ally betrayed, but that the American and British governments had helped Communism gain a foothold in Europe after the war that would take decades to dislodge. The world was learning the treacherous, deceitful ways of the Communists, something that Vujnovich, Musulin, and the forgotten 500 already knew from firsthand experience.

# Epilogue

**With every passing year, the airmen rescued in Opera-**tion Halyard and the OSS agents who saved them were forgotten, just as the world forgot Mihailovich. The airmen and their rescuers could never forget the experience, thinking about it every day of their lives, and many continued to campaign for clearing the name of the Serbian fighter who had saved them. Their pleas were largely ignored by a world that was moving on, uninterested in a controversy that seemed to die with a supposed Nazi collaborator executed in 1946.

As they got on with their lives, many of those involved in Operation Halyard grew disillusioned with international relations, convinced from their own experience that nations exhibited a disturbing willingness to trust those who shouldn't be trusted and to sacrifice those who had demonstrated great loyalty. They struggled to reconcile that conclusion with their own patriotism and love of country, and their frustration grew more pronounced as Communism's grip on the Balkans and Eastern Europe grew tighter in the 1950s, 1960s, and on.

George Vujnovich left the OSS in 1946 and wanted to go back to medical school, but he found that with so many servicemen returning to school, the one school that accepted him, Boston University, wanted to place him in the second year of studies even though he had completed four years of school in Yugoslavia. He would have to live on one hundred twenty dollars a month provided by the GI Bill meant to support returning servicemen, and he decided he couldn't support Mirjana and his daughter, Xenia, on such a pittance. He reluctantly gave up on becoming a doctor and he and Mirjana moved to New York, where he went back to work for Pan American as a purchasing agent. Within a few years Vujnovich opened his own business selling aircraft parts. Mirjana studied art history and for three years worked as a librarian at The Metropolitan Museum of Art. She also worked for Voice of America radio and Grolier Publishing, retiring in 1972. Ahead of her times with her view that women should not content themselves with housework, Mirjana encouraged her daughter, Xenia, to go to college and develop a profession. (Xenia excelled academically and enjoyed a successful career in, of all places, the State Department.) At home, Mirjana was an accomplished classical pianist and weaver, loved by her friends and family for being loyal and a good listener who knew how to draw people out with a carefully considered question. She never got over her disappointment at how the Allied victory led to Communism instead of a representative democracy in her native country.

Mirjana died on April 19, 2003, at the age of ninety. She and George had been married for sixty-two years, and he still misses his dear Mirjana terribly. Now ninety-two years old, Vujnovich lives on his own in New York, only semiretired from the aircrafts parts business and still easily riled when the subject turns to Communism and the mistreatment of Mihailovich.

George Musulin passed away in McLean, Virginia, in February of 1987 at the age of seventy-two, having lost touch over the years with the rest of the men involved in Operation Halyard. Those who had any contact with him after the failed effort to save Mihailovich remember him as being disillusioned and bitter about the war experience. Nick Lalich worked for the CIA in Greece for five years, and then he became an account executive with an advertising agency in New York. In the 1960s he joined the U.S. Department of Commerce and retired in 1984. Lalich died in May of 2001 at the age of eighty-five.

Frustrated with his inability to more effectively influence the events leading to the death of Mihailovich, and more than a little bitter, Arthur Jibilian decided he needed more of an education so that he might be better prepared for any future challenges. He returned to the University of Toledo, where he had studied for a year before the war. In the next three years he met his wife and obtained a degree in business administration. After college, he worked with Wonder Bread and then as safety director for an industrial manufacturing company while raising three children. He and his wife still live in Toledo.

Richard Felman never gave up his effort to honor Mihailovich and all those involved in Operation Halyard. Felman retired from the United States Air Force in 1968 and spent his time speaking fervently about the debt owed to Mihailovich. In 1970, he sought federal approval for a statue on Capitol grounds honoring Mihailovich. After being rebuffed, he tried again in 1976 and again in 1977, when finally the bill was introduced into the Senate by Strom Thurmond and Barry Goldwater. The legislation died because of the State Department's continued reluctance to do anything that might jeopardize current relations with Yugoslavia. The bill was reintroduced several times more in the coming years but without success.

In 1995, Felman and Lalich, along with a number of other Operation Halyard vets returned to Serbia for the fiftieth anniversary of V-E Day. They were met on a mountain in Ravna Gora, near Pranjane, by fifty thousand Serbian people who cheered them as returning heroes. Felman died in November 1999, at the age of seventy-eight.

Clare Musgrove studied agriculture and forestry at Michigan State College of Agriculture and Applied Science after the war, going on to a long career in the Michigan state cooperative extension service. He retired in 1980 and currently lives in Berrien County, Michigan, with his wife. Musgrove has never forgotten the people of Serbia and often thinks of the family that sheltered him that first night on the ground in Yugoslavia, hiding him under a bed while a Nazi officer stalked through the house looking for him.

Tony Orsini returned to working at a local bank after the war and then went to college, earning a degree with honors and enjoying a long career in finance. Having lost his beloved wife to Alzheimer's disease recently, he still lives in New Jersey and has seven grandchildren.

Robert Wilson also returned to school after the war, going back to the University of Illinois, and obtained a degree in mechanical engineering. He worked as an engine designer and analyst with Caterpillar for eighteen years and then left to work in the stock market full-time. He married during that time and lives in Peoria, Illinois, with his wife, still working full-time. In 1966, Wilson returned on his own to Communist Yugoslavia, still under Tito's control, to visit Bunar, one of the small villages that harbored him before his rescue in Pranjane. The people of the village recalled the American airmen with great warmth, which only underscored the fact that Americans barely remembered them at all. Though proud to have contributed to the defeat of the Nazis and unwavering in his loyalty to his country, he recalls the betrayal and execution of Mihailovich as one of the great disappointments of his life.

Nick Petrovich, the young Serbian fighter who helped protect the airmen in Pranjane and watched from his guard post as the American planes swooped in for the rescue, is now a successful businessman in Mexico City, Mexico. He still considers himself a great friend of the American people.

**On September 24, 1945,** Major General William J. Donovan made a final address to a gathering of OSS employees at the headquarters in Washington, DC. Donovan told the men and women of the OSS that they were coming to the end of "an unusual experiment. This experiment was to determine whether a group of Americans constituting a cross section of racial origins, of abilities, temperaments, and talents could meet and risk an encounter with the long-established and well-trained enemy organizations." As the OSS agents and staff went on to other chapters in their lives, Donovan told them, "You can go with the assurance that you have made a beginning in showing the people of America that only by decisions of national policy based upon accurate information can we have the chance of a peace that will endure."

Having served its purpose in helping win World War II, the OSS was disbanded along with many other war operations. Key government leaders, however, had learned the value of clandestine work. Before President Roosevelt's death, Donovan proposed to him the idea of creating a new espionage organization that would be similar to the OSS Donovan had created years earlier, but with one major difference: This spy group would be directly supervised by the president. Sensing a threat to their own power and influence, the military establishment, the State Department, and the Federal Bureau of Investigation opposed the idea without success.

President Truman created the Central Intelligence Agency in 1947 by signing the National Security Act of 1947. The work of the OSS would continue.

**Tito ruled Yugoslavia as dictator** until his death on May 4, 1980. Representatives of 122 states attended his funeral and most eulogized him as the last great World War II leader, praising him for successfully challenging Stalin's efforts to control his country after the war. He was considered the creator of modern Yugoslavia and credited with uniting the country's diverse ethnic and religious factions. He did so by using the iron fist of a Communist police state, of course, and his long rule over Yugoslavia was instrumental in ensuring that Communists maintained control over Eastern Europe through the end of the Cold War.

**The forgotten 500 never forgot** who helped them survive the war. They were eternally grateful to the OSS agents who came to their aid, and they held a special place in their hearts for the Yugoslav people who harbored them at great risk to themselves. Sixty years after their rescue, on May 9, 2005, the downed airmen presented the Legion of Merit—

kept secret for so many years—to Mihailovich's daughter Gordana. Though they struggled with the limitations of age, George Vujnovich, Arthur Jibilian, Clare Musgrove, and a number of other veterans involved in Operation Halyard were proud to return and do what should have been done decades earlier.

The surviving airmen and OSS agents, much older and even more aware of how much Mihailovich had done for them, gathered around Gordana Mihailovich and expressed their gratitude. Some of the old men cried openly as they told her how much their father had done for them, and how much they regretted the way he had been treated. A retired medical doctor, Mihailovich's daughter was seventy-eight and a bit of an enigma. Over the years, little was known about her except that she had joined Tito's Partisans after her father's death, probably against her will, and had almost never appeared in public since.

Nervous and excited, her hands trembling, Gordana broke into tears when the Americans handed her the Legion of Merit medal. She kissed her father's photograph, whispering to her long-gone father.

The tears from the Americans flowed partly in gratitude, but also because Gordana Mihailovich reminded them of all the women who ran to greet them as they parachuted down and all the villagers who helped them along the way.

Jibilian, still spry and quick-witted as ever, was happy to see the Legion of Merit in the hands of the Mihailovich family, where it belonged, but he still thought it was only a step toward justice for the man who had saved so many Americans. As pleased as he was to be in Yugoslavia honoring the memory of Mihailovich, he could not help feeling frustrated that his country still was not willing to come clean with the story of Mihailovich and Operation Halyard. He was quick to anger when informed that the medal presentation ceremony, originally scheduled as a public event with media coverage, was changed to a small affair in a private home. Jibilian was sure the State Department had stepped in yet again, reluctant to allow publicity favorable to Mihailovich even after sixty years. *There's still a conspiracy to keep this story from being told.*

His anger was tempered upon meeting another American attending the small ceremony. The young man introduced himself as Clare Musgrove's grandson and remarked that, if not for Mihailovich and Operation Halyard, he never would have been born. The sight of the young man who had traveled all the way to Serbia to honor a man from his grandfather's past helped restore Jibilian's faith.

Jibilian choked up and tears came to his eyes as he realized that, though good men may pass without the world's recognition, they can live on in the hearts of young people who know the truth.

# Partial List of Airmen
# Rescued in Operation Halyard

This is a partial list of the 345 Americans, four British, four French, seven Italians, and twelve Russians rescued in the Operation Halyard mission between August 9, 1944, and September 1, 1944. Another 167 were rescued before the mission ended on December 27, 1944.

(B) - British
(F) - French
(I)  - Italian
(R) - Russian

| | | |
|---|---|---|
| Lloyd J. Adams | J. W. Barrett | G. F. Blackburn |
| Harold M. Adee | F. Bartels | Vladimir Bobrov (R) |
| Carl P. Anderson | N. M. Baughman | R. S. Boren |
| P. D. Angleberger | R. E. Baum | Roy J. Bowers |
| B. Antoine (F) | C. Baumann | Tom Bradshaw |
| C. E. Astifan | Charles Beall | T. R. Bradshaw (B) |
| Howard Baetjer | T. L. Beard | Herbert S. Brinell |
| Paul Baker | A. R. Berger | G. J. Broadhead |
| Hugh Balfont | B. H. Berger | L. C. Norman Brooks |
| D. Barna | Bernie Berggren | Leonard M. Brothers |
| Russell W. Barney | Edmund Bernice | Robert L. Broun |
| F. Barrett | C. T. Beyer | Donald P. Brown |

E. J. Brown
Gus T. Brown Jr.
J. F. Brownell
W. B. Brubeck
G. T. Bryan
H. W. Brynildsen
Jack A. Buchanan
J. E. Buchler
Anthony Buckner
K. W. (Roy) Buckner
R. W. Buckner
Billy B. Burnett
Ennis Burns
John A. Burton
F. Byfield
F. J. Byrne
W. K. Callam
V. S. Callicutt
J. L. Camara
C. M. Card
J. F. Cardone
Thornton Carlough
J. P. Carlson
A. C. Carrico
J. B. Carroll
P. E. Carroll
Damon L. Carter
L. W. Carver
R. Cassity
B. C. Cator
J. W. Chambers
F. J. Chappell
A. Chesbowitz
S. T. Ciotti
D. Clark
Victor Clarke
Bruce H. Clifton
F. H. Clos
Floyd S. Cofer Jr.
Bertram Cole

R. Cole
J. V. Crandall
Frank S. Crawford Jr.
J. Cribari
Martin Cudilo
Boris Cugionski (R)
J. W. Cunningham
Willard Curtis
P. Dansercour (F)
Charles L. Davis
Richard L. Davis
Anthony Degaetawd
Donald DeLauca
John P. Devlin
A. J. Dewa
T. N. Dixon
H. L. Dodgen
C. E. Drigger
E. Dunn
Robert Eagan
Wilbur Earl
D. Edmundson
John B. Edwards
John T. Eldridge
W. Elvin
W. R. Ely
N. L. Elzeer
Robert English
Julian Entreken
Everett C. Estys
D. L. Fairbanks
W. F. Farley
Lee Farris
Richard Felman
R. B. Ferris
Sameuel Ferris
C. R. Flower
Robert T. Foley
E. W. Ford
Edward Ford

H. D. Foreman
J. Foster
J. T. Fox
Ervin Frekco
A. Friedberg
M. Friend
Kenneth C. Fulier
_ Gannaro (I)
W. Gantt
C. B. Gerrish
S. A. Gibson
V. Gibson
R. D. Gilson
G. E. Goad
R. H. Goldman
Viktor Golukokov (R)
C. F. Gracz
J. F. Granger
R. Greene
Willy Griffin
Beluga Grigorije (R)
P. C. Grinnell
Stephan Hanick
R. L. Hansen
R. R. Harper
William B. Harrell
W. R. Harris
W. J. Harter
L. L. Harvey
R. J. Hefling
G. A. Heinicke
W. M. Henley
H. D. Henton
C. B. Hickman
Richard B. Hobby
H. S. Hock
J. P. Hoffman
J. T. Holcomb
J. G. Holtz
J. E. Honsinger

R. L. Hooper
Allan H. Hoover
Lawrence H. Horne
J. R. Horner
R. I. Howard
V. Hunt
G. R. Hurd
J. Indrisek
Fred Irwin
Rudolph M. Janci
N. S. Janosky
M. W. Jarvis
D. B. Jeffers
V. E. Johnson
C. R. Johnston
E. D. Jones
F. V. Jones
Forrest N. Jones
W. E. Jones
Charles R. Kear
W. L. Keepers
Menly Kent
R. C. Kent
Glenn Kerris
William Keys
J. I. Kidd
M. L. Kiel
F. N. Kincaid
James E. King
W. J. Kirkpatrick
Clarence E. Knight
R. Knowlton
G. G. Koch
F. S. Koffel
Vladimir Komiskalov
(R)
Peter Kovacovich
Petar Krikun (R)
D. E. LaBissioniere
A. F. LaCom

John Lane
O. H. Larson
Bernard J. Larvin
A. LeBoulie (F)
Clarence R. Ledford
William Lee
R. Leger
W. T. Leslie
John Lindstrom
Donald E. Loehndorf
T. O. Looney
C. S. Lovitt
C. Luciano (I)
F. Lukas
E. D. Lynch
Al Maas
Nikolaj Mahinjko (R)
Konstantin
  Mamasuk (R)
K. B. Manley
W. K. Mann
F. Mario (I)
H. Marker
Robert L. Marshall
D. Y. Martin
Frederick Martin
J. P. Martin
R. A. Martin
C. Masellis (I)
Frank Mathews
Paul F. Mato
B. V. Mazzara
Lee McAlister
Michael E. McDonnell
Dale L. McEhaney
Thomas McElroy
W. O. McGinn
G. N. McGuire
Mike P. McKool
R. P. McLaughlin

O. Menaker
G. F. Messick
S. J. Methvin
L. Meyer
G. Mitchell
Robert D. Molina
R.D. Moore
J. Morris
J. Mortimer
Simeon Moskalemko (R)
H. Muckow
J. F. Mueller
K. Munn
Irving S. Muny
L. K. Murray
Clare M. Musgrove
M. Nierman
F. Nino (I)
Lawrence T. Norton
Robert J. Norwood
O. Nouska
D. O'Connell
Michael O'Keefe
J. T. Oliver
Thomas K. Oliver
J. F. O'Grady
G. O'Neal
Anthony J. Orsini
D. B. Osborne
J. D. Owens
K. L. Owens
John W. Pace
D. Parkerson
K. Patten
D. T. Patterson
T. F. Paul
L. Pavlovich
A. L. Pearce
F. Pederson
L. W. Peller

S. N. Pensabena

A. E. Peterson

T. Pettigrew

K. A. Pfister

D. Pierino (I)

Aleksander Plahotnikov (R)

Robert L. Powers

Leonard. E. Pritchett

D. D. Radabaugh

C. G. Rechtin

N. C. Reid (B)

Norman Reid

P. L. Reinhardt

Joe Renkowitz

D. F. Rice

T. C. Richards

H. J. Ripper

Howard Robert

Hupert Robert

Paksmur Robert

Dale F. Rodgers

A. D. Romans

Anthony Russo

W. C. Rye

George Salapa

Delbert F. Salmon

A. Saucer

J. H. Scharnitsky

Baxter C. Scott

J. E. Scroggs

Floyd F. Shanley

R. S. Sheehy

J. Sickels

Donald Siegfried

S. Sika

E. E. Simon

A. Simone (I)

D. J. Smith

L. L. Smith

Philip Smith

W. R. Smith

H. J. Snyder

R. Somers (B)

H. Souter

R. L. Spence

P. A. Stearns

C. L. Stevenson

H. R. Stillman

R. Straub

Edward E. Stringham

M. Sucharida

D. W. Sullivan

Joseph P. Sullivan

Frank Sutton

Georgij Taminsin (R)

W. Taylor (B)

M. A. Tennison

Anthony P. Thalmann

John H. Thibodeau

R. J. Thies

G. Thomas

J. Thomas

Rodger Thomas

C. H. Townsend

Kenneth M. Turnquist

Sergije Valar (R)

G. Vandervall (F)

M. Vasquez

A. P. Verdi

Joe Verecher, Jr.

F. Vernon

R. N. Vlachos

R. C. Volk

V. A. Volrath

A. P. Waldschmidt

James A. Walker

M. W. Walker

C. J. Walpusk

R. M. Walton

R. J. Weber

Robert Weiss

R. L. Wellborn

N. C. Werner

W. Whelan

Richard P. White

Glenmore R. Wickum

R. R. Wiese

R. W. Williams

Robert I. Wilson

W. Wink

Robert E. Winmill

Harvey C. Witman

Leslie Wolfe

W. E. Wright

D. Yaun

A. Zion

F. A. Zuerchet

# Acknowledgments

Writers always owe a huge debt of gratitude to people who were willing to share their intensely personal stories with a stranger. I must thank the veterans involved in Operation Halyard for sharing their stories with me and allowing me to craft their memories into a singular narrative that portrays a bigger picture. George Vujnovich, in particular, was extremely helpful in walking me through the history of the OSS and Operation Halyard, not to mention the fascinating story of his own adventure in Yugoslavia with Mirjana. My thanks also go out to Arthur Jibilian, Tony Orsini, Robert Wilson, Clare Musgrove, and Nick Petrovich for taking the time to share their stories and for trusting that I would treat them with respect.

My research assistant, Drew Mosley, must be credited with much of the legwork and background studies that help frame the stories of the men involved in Operation Halyard. Drew was a terrific asset, and I appreciate his dedication to researching this story.

Mel Berger is exactly what every writer wants in an agent. Thank you, Mel. Thank you, Mark Chait, my editor, for your thoughtful input. My appreciation also goes out to the research assistants and staff at the Library of Congress, National Archives, and the Air Force Academy. My good friend Wes Hardegree made a significant contribution with his review of an early version of the book and by suggesting the title.

Thank you, Caroline and Nicholas, for being at my side throughout this project. When I think of why stories like this matter, and why men and women throughout history have been willing to risk everything for those they love, I think of you.

—GAF

# Notes

A note about the Mihailovich name: Because of the vagaries of translating Balkan names to English, the name of Draza Mihailovich is found under various spellings, sometimes varying even within the same government document or press report. The most common usage is Mihailovich, but Mihailovitch, Michhailovic, Michailovich, Michailovitch, Mikhailovic, Mikhailovich, Mikhailovitch, Mahailovic, Mihajlovic, and Mihajlovich also have been used. For consistency, this book uses Mihailovich regardless of how the original source document spelled the name.

## Chapter 2

Page 11 "Soviet advances from the Ukraine" Baker, Addison Earl, Lloyd Herbert Hughes, John Louis Jerstad, Leon William Johnson, John Riley Kane. "Ploesti: When Heroes Filled the Sky." www.homeofheroes.com/wings/part2/09_ploesti.html

Page 11 "seven major refineries, storage tanks, and related structures covering nineteen square miles" "Ploesti Oil Raid: Operation Tidal Wave." www.ww2guide.com/oil.shtml

Page 11 "accounting for 40 percent of Romania's total exports" Ibid.

Page 16 "an ingenious piece of machinery" Kennedy, Joseph. "Sperry Ball Turret." freepages.military.rootsweb.com/~josephkennedy/sperry_ball_turret.htm

## Chapter 4

Page 46 "not just to herd the flock but also to keep the wolves away" Pesic, Miodrag D. *Operation Air Bridge: Serbian Chetniks and the Rescued American Airmen in World War II* [English translation from the original Serbian]. Belgrade, Yugoslavia: Serbian Masters' Society, 2002, p. 171.

Page 48 "they had bailed out much later and farther away than the other crew" The pilot and copilot of Wilson's B-17 were aided by a separate group of Chetniks but never joined up with the other crew. They made it out of Yugoslavia safely.

Page 48 "was a machine gunner on a B-17 when he bailed out over Yugoslavia on July 4, 1944" Pesic, p. 164. Mike McKool's story is a summary of the account he provided in *Operation Air Bridge*, along with newspaper articles from 1946, in which he described his experience while campaigning to save Mihailovich.

Page 49 "was flying a borrowed plane" Oliver, Thomas. *Unintended Visit to Yugoslavia.* Unpublished manuscript donated to the United States Air Force Academy, 1990, p. 1. Thomas Oliver's story is a summary of the account he provided in his unpublished manuscript.

Page 50 "Another pilot blamed Dinah Shore when he found himself in trouble over Yugoslavia" Pesic, p. 164. Richard Felman's story is a summary of the account he provided in *Operation Air Bridge*, along with multiple speeches he gave about his account, and various newspaper and magazine articles in which he described his experience.

Page 53 "Felman was immediately struck by Vasić's appearance" Ibid.

## Chapter 5

Page 63 "known as Captain Milankovic, spoke English" Pesic, p. 166.

Page 65 "afternoon on horseback, accompanied by three soldiers" Oliver, p. 2.

Page 74 "joined Mihailovich's forces in conducting sabotage against the Germans" Felman, Richard. "Mihailovich and I." Serbian Democratic Forum, October 1972.

Chapter 6

Page 80 "Please advise the American Air Ministry that there are more than one hundred American aviators in our midst" Martin, David. *The Web of Disinformation: Churchill's Yugoslav Blunder.* Orlando, Florida: Harcourt Brace Jovanovich, 1990, p. 232.

Page 83 *"Are you involved in trying to get them out?"* These are not the exact words from Mirjana's letter, which is no longer available, but George Vujnovich recounts this version as the gist of what she wrote to him.

Page 83 "One agent reported finding a half-starved B-24 tail gunner who had been shot down in the first raid on Ploesti" Ford, Corey. *Donovan of OSS.* Boston: Little, Brown and Company, 1970, p. 205.

Page 94 "When Hitler first heard of the coup d'état and the country's attempt to withdraw from the Axis, he thought it was a joke." Testimony of Hermann Goering at Nuremburg Military Tribunals, *Proceedings of the International Military Tribunals at Nuremburg,* p. 344.

Page 94 "Winston Churchill described what happened next" Winston Churchill, *The Second World War, Volume 3: The Grand Alliance.* Boston: Mariner Books, 1986, p. 175.


Chapter 7

Page 110 "'It's Mrs. Goebbels!'" There is no way to verify that it actually was Magda Goebbels on the plane, but George and Mirjana Vujnovich both thought it was her and said that she acted as one would expect the powerful wife of a top Nazi officer to act. George and Mirjana responded accordingly at the time and remained confident after the war that Magda Goebbels had saved them from a likely arrest.


Chapter 8

Page 123 "individual commanders who were accustomed to working independently" Ford, Kirk, Jr. *OSS and the Yugoslav Resistance 1943–1945.* College Station, TX: Texas A&M Press, 1992, p. 6.

Page 124 "Mihailovich took a firm position that he could not expose the people of Yugoslavia to such risk unless the outcome was great enough to justify the inevitable deaths . . ." Ford, Kirk, Jr., p. 7.

Page 125 "chief of the Yugoslav prime minister's military cabinet and the former Yugoslav military and air attache in Washington" Knezevic, Zivan. *Why the Allies Abandoned the Yugoslav Army of General Mihailovich, with Official Memoranda and Documents*, First Part. Unpublished manuscript donated to the United States Library of Congress, 1945, p. 4.

Page 126 "the deaths of seventy-eight thousand Serbians between the ages of sixteen and fifty" Ibid.

Page 127 "many of those joining the Partisan movement had no such dreams" Ford, Kirk, Jr., p. 8.


**Chapter 9**

Page 130 "'grand finale against the Axis'" Deakin, F. W. *Embattled Mountain*. New York: Oxford University Press, 1971, p. 152.

Page 131 "he announced that for every German soldier killed by Mihailovich, one hundred Serbs would be shot" Martin, p. 34.

Page 131 "In a telegram sent from Mihailovich on March 2, 1943 . . ." Knezevic, First Part: p. 7.

Page 134 "The English are now fighting to the last Serb in Yugoslavia" Knezevic, Second Part: p. 2.

Page 134 "'I appreciate that words spoken in heat may not express a considered judgment. . .'" Knezevic, Second Part: p. 5.

Page 135 "'much worse things would be heard than that speech by General Mihailovich,' he told Churchill" Knezevic, Second Part: p. 6.

Page 135 "'I avoid battle with the Communists in the country and fight only when attacked'" Knezevic, Second Part: p. 9.

Page 135 "detailing an 'operational decision' concerning Mihailovich" Knezevic, Second Part: p. 10.

Page 136 "'who was killing the most Germans and suggesting means by which we could help to kill more'" Ford, Corey, p. 206.

Page 137 "If Hitler invaded Hell, I would make at least a favorable reference to the Devil in the House of Commons!" Churchill, Winston S. *Never Give In: The Best of Winston Churchill's Speeches*. New York: Hyperion, 2003, p. 289.

Page 138 "Some OSS agents felt that the British were every bit their enemy as the Germans, at least when it came to their intelligence activities" Tompkins, Peter. *Italy Betrayed.* New York: Simon and Schuster, 1966, p. 253.

Page 139 "the heaviest American soldier to make a successful parachute jump in World War II" Ford, Kirk, Jr., p. 29.

Page 139 "could mobilize more than four hundred thousand if he had arms for them" Musulin, George. "Report on the Michailovic's Cetnik army; suggestions of some Allied support." Central Intelligence Agency 1944. Reproduced in Declassified Documents Reference System, Farmington Hills, Michigan: Gale Group, 2006.

Page 139 " 'a fairly well-organized army' " Interestingly, an American woman was one of Mihailovich's better-known fighters. Ruth Mitchell, the sister of William (Billy) Mitchell, the outspoken Army Air Forces general who was court-martialed in 1925 for accusing superiors of incompetence in not focusing more on air power. His red-haired, headstrong sister volunteered to serve with Mihailovich, acting as liaison officer of the Chetniks with the British army. She was captured by the Gestapo after several months and spent thirteen months in German prisons. She was finally released in 1942 as a result of pressure from the Swiss government and returned to the United States, where she helped report on German atrocities and torture.

Page 141 "virtually all communications in and out of Yugoslavia had to go through British channels" Ford, Kirk, Jr., p. 14. George Vujnovich also confirmed in personal interviews that the British were difficult to work with and sometimes seemed to intentionally interfere with OSS operations.

Page 141 "We can't fight Jerry with bare feet, brave hearts, and Radio London" Ford, Kirk, Jr., p. 31.

Page 142 "The documents included transcripts . . ." Brown, Colin, and John Crossland. "How a Soviet Mole United Tito and Churchill." *The Independent,* June 28, 1997: 1A.

Page 143 "that the time should be called the 'Klugmann period' " Martin, *The Web of Disinformation: Churchill's Yugoslav Blunder,* p. 94.

Page 144 " 'Klugmann was a mole whose great accomplishment . . .' " Martin, *The Web of Disinformation: Churchill's Yugoslav Blunder,* p. xix.

Page 144 "'the pure intellectual of the Party'" Woodward, E. L. *British Foreign Policy in the Second World War*. London: Her Majesty's Stationery Office, 1962, p. 346.


Chapter 10

Page 148 "by October 1944 that number would reach forty" O'Donnell, Patrick K. *Operatives, Spies, and Saboteurs: The Unknown Story of the Men and Women of WWII's OSS*. New York: Free Press, 2004, p. 86.

Page 149 "'Listen, you bastards! You think I went in and risked my life for almost a year for nothing?'" Ford, Kirk, Jr., p. 51.

Page 149 "I came to Bari and saw Partisans all over the damn town" Ford, Kirk, Jr., p. 51.

Page 150 "Yugoslav refugee girls working as waitresses who made no effort to conceal their pro-Communist politics, even wearing Partisan uniforms around Bari on their off hours." Martin, *The Web of Disinformation: Churchill's Yugoslav Blunder*, p. 107.

Page 153 "they hadn't completely vacated the premises by the time the OSS moved in" Ford, Corey, p. 122.

Page 154 "'absolute discretion, sobriety, devotion to duty, languages, and wide experience,' Ian advised" McLachlan, Donald. *Room 39*. London: Weidenfeld and Nicolson: 1968, p. 233.

Page 154 "'calculatingly reckless' and trained for 'aggressive action'" Smith, Richard Harris. *OSS: The Secret History of America's First Central Intelligence Agency*. Guilford, Connecticut: The Lyons Press, 1973, p. 31.

Page 154 "The most important qualification, Donovan declared, was strength of character" Ford, Corey, 1970, p. 134.

Page 155 "A columnist for the *Washington Times* wrote of the new OSS . . ." Brown, Anthony Cave. *The Last Hero: Wild Bill Donovan*. New York: Vintage Books, 1984, p. 301.

Page 156 "and a Catholic missionary who had lived with the Kachin tribesmen in northern Burma" Ford, Corey, p. 135.

Page 157 "'The major part of our intelligence was the result of good old-fashioned intellectual sweat'" Ford, Corey, p. 148.

Page 157 "Largely because of the number of upper-class, Ivy League–graduates in the ranks, OSS agents at desks in Washington and in the field around the world tended to share a social idealism, the same unwavering faith in the common man espoused by Donovan." Smith, p. 26.

Page 158 "'I don't know if he's on the Communist honor roll, but for the job he's doing in Italy, he's on the honor roll of OSS'" Ford, Corey, p. 135.

Page 160 "an explosive that looked remarkably like regular flour and could even be used to bake muffins and bread" Lovell, Stanley. *Of Spies and Strategems.* Englewood Cliffs, NJ: Prentice Hall, 1963, p. 17.

Page 161 "The Beano activated and exploded when he caught it on the way down" O'Donnell, p. 17.

Page 161 "Of the 831 members of the OSS decorated for gallantry during World War II . . ." Ford, Corey, p. 145.

Page 162 "impale members of the resistance on meat hooks in the public square" Ford, Corey, p. 186.

Page 162 "Biting down on the pill would spill its contents and bring nearly instant death" Roosevelt, Kermit. *The Overseas Targets: War Reports of the OSS.* Vol. I. Washington, DC: Carrollton Press, 1976, p. 159.

Page 163 "the agents risking their lives in the field developed a disdain for the 'bourbon whiskey colonels' in Washington and other OSS posts who thought they could tell them how to do their jobs" Smith, p. 6.

Page 163 "'men for the higher echelons of the organization who by background and temperament were unsympathetic with Donovan's own conception of the necessity of unstinting cooperation with the resistance movements'" Goldberg, Arthur. Review of *Sub Rosa: The OSS and American Espionage. The Nation*, March 23, 1946, pp. 349–350.

Page 165 "a larger discussion about how Donovan and his subordinates were not happy about losing their presence in the territory controlled by Mihailovich" Donovan, William J. Letter to President Franklin D. Roosevelt. July 4, 1944. Reproduced in Declassified Documents Reference System, Farmington Hills, Michigan: Gale Group, 2006.

Page 166 "'Screw the British! Let's get our boys out!'" This exchange is not officially recorded, but the anecdote was passed down among OSS veterans and participants in Operation Halyard. Both George Vujnovich and Arthur Jibilian report hearing of the exchange during or soon after the rescue. It is possible that the comment is apocryphal, but it is entirely consistent with William Donovan's personality and conversational style.

## Chapter 11

Page 169 "'You are requested, therefore, to act on this soonest . . .'" Ford, Kirk, Jr., p. 100.

Page 169 "managed to rescue ninety downed airmen over a four-month period" O'Donnell, p. 84.

## Chapter 12

Page 183 "randomly assigned code name Operation Halyard . . ." The Serbians know the mission as Operation Air Bridge. "Air bridge" was a generic term in the military for connecting distant points through the use of airdrops or frequent flights. The rescue mission is well known in Serbia, much more than in the United States, because the Serbian people are particularly proud of their efforts in aiding American airmen during World War II.

Page 184 "'any military or political commitments on behalf of the United States of America . . .'" Ford, Kirk Jr, p. 101.

## Chapter 13

Page 191 "sending the first message from the downed airmen" Felman, Richard. "Mihailovich and I." Serbian Democratic Forum, October 1972.

Page 192 "Oliver volunteered to work with some other airmen to develop a code" Oliver, p. 5.

Page 195 "'That's Oliver's crew and Buckler's crew!'" Martin, *The Web of Disinformation: Churchill's Yugoslav Blunder*, p. 235.

Page 197 "'Take good care that nothing happens to these men.'" Martin, David. *Ally Betrayed: The Uncensored Story of Tito and Mihailovich*. New York: Prentice Hall, 1946, p. 292.

## Chapter 14

Page 205 "'Captain George! Captain George!' they shouted . . ." Felman, Richard. "Mihailovich and I." Serbian Democratic Forum, October 1972.

Page 207 "Mihailovich often would tease the boys in the group by saying he had heard that one of them was a Partisan . . ." Martin, *Ally Betrayed: The Uncensored Story of Tito and Mihailovich*, p. 283.

Page 208 "In Kraljevo, only thirty miles away, a *Luftwaffe* unit was stationed at an airfield . . ." The downed airmen, Chetniks, and OSS men involved in Operation Halyard sometimes disagreed about why the Germans never attacked the airmen in Pranjane. Some thought the Germans were fully aware of the airmen's presence but unwilling to launch an all-out battle with the many thousands of Chetnik fighters. Others thought the efforts at secrecy had been a complete success and the Germans never knew they were there, at least not until the rescue flights were well underway.

Page 209 "The minimum distance required for landing a C-47 is seven hundred yards" Casey, H. J. Office of the Chief Engineer, Southwest Pacific Area, United States Army. *Engineer Estimating Data*, June 1, 1945, p. 9. The official manuals of the army during World War II state seven hundred yards as the minimum landing distance for a C-47, but that allows no margin of error. It also does not take into account the risk of trees and other obstructions directly beyond the landing strip, as was the case in Pranjane. The original field at Pranjane has been reported in varying lengths between six hundred and seven hundred yards, but whatever the original size, it was extended by the airmen and villagers.

Page 210 "sixty oxcarts . . ." Ford, Corey, p. 210.

## Chapter 15

Page 213 "He was playing it safe by assigning only twelve men to each C-47 . . ." Some reports, including Felman's recollections, indicate that Musulin assigned twenty men per plane, but Musulin's report of the initial rescues indicate that he selected seventy-two men for six planes. It is likely that he increased the number of men per plane after the first night, once he had more confidence that the C-47s could safely use the improvised landing strip.

Page 217 "The cows waddled up into the field . . ." Martin, *The Web of Disinformation: Churchill's Yugoslav Blunder*, p. 237.

Page 221 "Then, at exactly ten p.m., they heard the drone of a plane" Ford, Corey, p. 211. Other reports state that the planes arrived at eleven p.m. or midnight, but all state that the planes arrived exactly when they were expected. Musulin's report after the rescue includes a direct quote saying they arrived at ten p.m.

Page 222 "This time he used the lamp to blink a predetermined code word: -. .–. *Nan*" Ford, Corey, p. 211.

## Chapter 16

Page 227 "The planes were on the ground, and now he had to get back in the air" Some accounts describe the four planes landing one at a time, loading up with airmen, and then taking off before the next plane landed. That was Musulin's intention, to avoid the planes crowding each other on the small airstrip and possibly colliding, but the C-47 pilots apparently were eager to land and get back up again because they were carrying a minimal fuel load. Musulin's report indicates that the planes were on the ground together and then took off again.

Page 235 "'is LaGuardia airfield anything like this?'" Martin, *The Web of Disinformation: Churchill's Yugoslav Blunder*, p. 237.

Page 236 "He had overindulged in plum brandy during the night and almost missed his flight" Martin, *The Web of Disinformation: Churchill's Yugoslav Blunder*, p. 237.

Page 237 "Musulin soon had orders to get on one of the rescue planes and return to Italy" Some participants recall that Musulin was ordered back to Italy on the same day, returning on one of the last flights out of Pranjane on August 10. Though that version of events makes a better anecdote, Musulin actually stayed in Pranjane for more than two weeks after sending the Serbian men to Italy. The rebuke from Bari did come on the same day, but Musulin spent two weeks arguing with his superiors and insisting that he be allowed to stay. When he saw that the dispute was holding up any further rescue flights and nearly one hundred more men were ready to leave Pranjane, he relented and angrily returned to Bari.

Page 239 "the most successful rescue ever of downed airmen behind enemy lines and one of the largest rescue missions of any type in World War II or since" In fact, by just one man the Operation Halyard mission was the largest rescue behind enemy lines in World War II—if the multiple rescues over several months are counted as a single mission. A total of 512 American airmen and Allied personnel were rescued in Operation Halyard from August 19, 1944, to December 27, 1944. A month later on January 30, 1945, United States Army Rangers and Filipino guerillas liberated 511 American and Allied personnel from a prisoner-of-war camp near Cabanatuan in the Philippines. (King, M. J. Leavenworth Papers No. 11, Rangers: Selected Combat Operations in World War II. U.S. Army Command General Staff College.) The number of prisoners thought to be at the camp was higher by at least two or three, but 511 were successfully rescued. It should be noted that unlike Operation Halyard, the Cabanatuan rescue took place all at once and under enemy fire. A full account of the Cabanatuan rescue can be found in *Ghost Soldiers* by Hampton Sides (Doubleday, 2001).

Readers also may be familiar with the story of Royal Air Force officers who escaped from Stalag-Luft III, Germany's most secure prisoner-of-war camp, in March 1944. The story is told in *The Great Escape* by Anton Gill (Review, 2002) and other books, as well as the 1963 movie by the same name. By comparison to the 512 rescued in Operation Halyard, the Stalag-Luft III escape involved seventy-six men, of which seventy-three were recaptured.

## Chapter 17

Page 249 "The first hint in the press of the remarkable success of the rescue mission came" "Radio Signal Aids Rescue of 250 Fliers." *The Washington Post*, February 20, 1945, p. 2.

Page 250 "Two days later the newspaper ran a lengthy letter to the editor from Konstantin Fotić . . ." Letters to the Editor: Credit Where Due. *The Washington Post*, February 22, 1945, p. 6.

Page 251 " 'rather depressed, thinking of the possibilities of Russia one day turning against us . . .' " Gilbert, Martin. *Churchill: A Life*. New York: Henry Holt and Company, 1991.

Page 252 "Reading the *Washington Post* on the morning of March 25, 1946, he found a small article . . ." "Mihailovich Under Arrest, Belgrade Says." *The Washington Post*, March 25, 1946, p. 2.

Page 254 "It does not matter that Draza Mihailovich will live or die" Pesic, p. 122.

Page 255 "The headline in the *Press* in Cleveland, Ohio, was CLEVELANDER AIDS GEN. MIHAILOVICH." National Committee of American Airmen to Aid

Gen. Draza Mihailovich and the Serbian People. Press Clippings, Book II. Chicago, 1946.

Page 255 "In the *Telegraph* of Pittsburgh, Pennsylvania, the headline read STATE TROOPERS HAIL MIHAILOVICH AS FRIEND" Ibid.

Page 255 "The *New York Journal American* quoted former OSS agent Eli Popovich . . ." Ibid.

Page 256 "The headline in the *Times* in Detroit, Michigan, read DRAZA BE-TRAYED, CLAIMS DETROITER." Ibid.

Page 256 "In an article he wrote for the *New York Journal American* . . ." Ibid.

Page 257 "In one article Nick Lalich delivered a copy of his own Legion of Merit citation to the *Washington Post* . . ." "Ex-OSS Agent Uses Citation in Effort to Aid Mihailovich." *The Washington Post*, May 1, 1946, p. 14.

Page 261 "In the *New York World-Telegram* on April 19, 1946, a headline read CHURCHILL WAS TAKEN IN BY TITO, WRITER CLAIMS" Ibid.

Page 262 "The trial of General Draza Mihailovich began on June 10, 1946, in a makeshift courtroom . . ." "Draza Aided Reich, Italy, Court Told." *The Washington Post*, June 11, 1946, p. 2.

Page 264 "In an editorial on June 17, 1946, the *Washington Post* acknowledged that Tito was railroading Mihailovich . . ." "Mihailovitch Trial." *The Washington Post*, June 17, 1946, p. 6.

Page 265 "MIHAILOVICH EXECUTED BY FIRING SQUAD, the headline read" "Mihailovitch Executed by Firing Squad." *The Washington Post*, July 18, 1946, p. 6.


## Chapter 18

Page 271 "It might have remained a secret if not for the work of Congressman Edward J. Derwinski of Illinois, who intervened in 1967 at the urging of airmen who had heard rumors" The State Department telegrams that led President Truman to agree to classify the Legion of Merit were themselves classified. The telegrams were not declassified until 1973.

# Bibliography

Baker, Addison Earl, Lloyd Herbert Hughes, John Louis Jerstad, Leon William Johnson, John Riley Kane. "Ploesti: When Heroes Filled the Sky." www.homeofheroes.com/wings/part2/09_ploesti.html.

Brown, Anthony Cave. *The Last Hero: Wild Bill Donovan.* New York: Vintage Books, 1984.

Brown, Colin, and John Crossland. "How a Soviet Mole United Tito and Churchill." *The Independent,* June 28, 1997: 1A.

Carroll, Tim. *The Great Escape from Stalag Luft III: The Full Story of How 76 Allied Officers Carried Out World War II's Most Remarkable Mass Escape.* New York: Pocket Books, 2004.

Casey, H. J. Office of the Chief Engineer, Southwest Pacific Area, United States Army. *Engineer Estimating Data,* June 1, 1945.

Churchill, Winston. *The Second World War, Volume 3: The Grand Alliance.* Boston: Mariner Books, 1986.

Churchill, Winston *Never Give In: The Best of Winston Churchill's Speeches.* New York: Hyperion, 2003.

Davis, Larry. *P-51 Mustang in Action.* Carrollton, TX: Squadron/Signal Publications, 1981.

Davis, Larry. *P-38 Lightning in Action.* Carrollton, TX: Squadron/Signal Publications, 1990.

Davis, Larry. *C-47 Skytrain in Action.* Carrollton, TX: Squadron/Signal Publications, 1995.

Deakin, F. W. *Embattled Mountain.* New York: Oxford University Press, 1971.

Donovan, William J. Letter to President Franklin D. Roosevelt. July 4, 1944. Reproduced in Declassified Documents Reference System, Farmington Hills, Michigan: Gale Group, 2006.

"Draza Aided Reich, Italy, Court Told." *The Washington Post,* June 11, 1946, p. 2.

Draskovic, Wuk. Letter from Serbia and Montenegro Minister of Foreign Affairs to Mr. and Mrs. Arthur Jibilian. April 7, 2005.

Drendel, Lou. *Walk Around: B-17 Flying Fortress.* Carrollton, TX: Squadron/Signal Publications, 1998.

"Ex-OSS Agent Uses Citation in Effort to Aid Mihailovich." *The Washington Post,* May 1, 1946, p. 14.

Federal Bureau of Investigation. Freedom of Information requests regarding Burgess, MacLean, and Philby. foia.fbi.gov/foiaindex/philby.htm.

Felman, Richard. "Mihailovich and I." Serbian Democratic Forum, October 1972.

Ford, Corey. *Donovan of OSS.* Boston: Little, Brown and Company, 1970.

Ford, Kirk Jr. *OSS and the Yugoslav Resistance 1943–1945.* College Station, TX: Texas A&M Press, 1992.

Franklin D. Roosevelt Library. President's Personal File: Correspondence related to William J. Donovan. Hyde Park, NY.

Garland, Greg, and Frederick N. Rasmussen. "Nick A. Lalich, 85, leader of OSS team that rescued downed air crews in WWII." *The Sun,* May 15, 2001, p. 6B.

Gilbert, Martin. *Churchill: A Life.* New York: Henry Holt and Company, 1991.

Gill, Anton. *The Great Escape: The Full Dramatic Story with Contributions from Survivors and Their Families.* London: Headline Book Publishing, 2002.

Goldberg, Arthur. Review of *Sub Rosa: The OSS and American Espionage. The Nation,* March 23, 1946, pp. 349–350.

Interagency Working Group. "Records of the Office of Strategic Services 1940–1946 (Record Group 226)." Washington, DC: National Archives.

Goldich, Robert L. "Yugoslavia: World War II Resistance Operations and Their Implications for the Current War." Washington, DC: Congressional Research Service, The Library of Congress, 1999.

Jeffrey-Jones, Rhodri. *Cloak and Dollar: A History of American Secret Intelligence.* New Haven: Yale University Press, 2002.

Jibilian, Arthur. Personal interviews and correspondence with the author.

Kelly, Richard M. *The Halyard Mission. The 461st Liberaider* 1995; 12:28–37.

Kennedy, Joseph. "Sperry Ball Turret." freepages.military.rootsweb.com/~josephkennedy/sperry_ball_turret.htm

Knezevic, Zivan. *Why the Allies Abandoned the Yugoslav Army of General Mihailovich, with Official Memoranda and Documents.* Unpublished manuscript donated to the United States Library of Congress, 1945.

Letters to the Editor: Credit Where Due. *The Washington Post,* February 22, 1945, p. 6.

Lindsay, Franklin. *Beacons in the Night: With the OSS and Tito's Partisans in Wartime Yugoslavia.* Stanford, CA: Stanford University Press, 1993.

Lovell, Stanley. *Of Spies and Strategems.* Englewood Cliffs, NJ: Prentice Hall, 1963.

Marquette, Sandy. "Goodbye to a tireless warrior." *Liberty.* January 10, 2000.

Martin, David. *Ally Betrayed: The Uncensored Story of Tito and Mihailovich.* New York: Prentice Hall, 1946.

Martin, David. *Patriot or Traitor: The Case of General Mihailovich.* Stanford, CA: Hoover Institution Press, 1978.

Martin, David. *The Web of Disinformation: Churchill's Yugoslav Blunder.* Orlando: Harcourt Brace Jovanovich, 1990.

Mauer, Mauer, Ed. *Combat Squadrons of the Air Force: World War II.* Washington, DC: U.S. Government Printing Office, 1969.

McLachlan, Donald. *Room 39.* London: Weidenfeld and Nicolson, 1968.

"Mihailovitch Trial." *The Washington Post,* June 17, 1946, p. 6.

"Mihailovitch Executed by Firing Squad." *The Washington Post*, July 18, 1946, p. 6.

"Mihailovich Under Arrest, Belgrade Says." *The Washington Post*, March 25, 1946, p. 2.

Musgrove, Clare. Personal interviews and correspondence with the author.

Musulin, George. *Report on the Michailovic's Cetnik army; suggestions of some Allied support*. Central Intelligence Agency 1944. Reproduced in Declassified Documents Reference System, Farmington Hills, Michigan: Gale Group, 2006.

National Committee of American Airmen to Aid Gen. Draza Mihailovich and the Serbian People. Press Clippings, Books I, II, III. Chicago, 1946. Unpublished collection donated to Library of Congress, 1946.

O'Donnell, Patrick K. *Operatives, Spies, and Saboteurs: The Unknown Story of the Men and Women of WWII's OSS*. New York: Free Press, 2004.

Oliver, Thomas. *Unintended Visit to Yugoslavia*. Unpublished manuscript donated to the United States Air Force Academy, 1990.

Orsini, Tony. Personal interviews and correspondence with the author.

Pesic, Miodrag D. *Operation Air Bridge: Serbian Chetniks and the Rescued American Airmen in World War II* [English translation from the original Serbian]. Belgrade, Yugoslavia: Serbian Masters' Society, 2002.

Petrovich, Nick. Personal interviews and correspondence with the author.

"Ploesti Oil Raid: Operation Tidal Wave." www.ww2guide.com/oil.shtml

"Radio Signal Aids Rescue of 250 Fliers." *The Washington Post*, February 20, 1945, p. 2.

Rebic, Aleksandra. "The Living Spirit of Ravna Gora." *Liberty*, July 25, 2003. www.snd-us.com/Liberty/sm_1843.html.

Roberts, Walter R. *Tito, Mihailovic and the Allies: 1941–1945*. Durham, North Carolina: Duke University Press, 1987.

Roosevelt, Kermit. *The Overseas Targets: War Reports of the OSS*. Vol. I. Washington, DC: Carrollton Press, 1976.

Roosevelt, Kermit. *The Overseas Targets: War Reports of the OSS*. Vol. II. Washington, DC: Carrollton Press, 1976.

Savich, Carl K. "Draza Mihailovich and the rescue of U.S. airmen during World War II." Serbian Unity Congress. www.serbianunity.net/culture/history/Draza_Mihailovich/rescue.html.

Smith, Richard Harris. OSS: *The Secret History of America's First Central Intelligence Agency*. Guilford, Connecticut: The Lyons Press, 1973.

*The Trial of Dragoljub-Draza Mihailovic: Stenographic Record and Documents from the Trial of Dragoljub-Draza Mihailovic*. Salisbury, North Carolina: Documentary Publications, 1977.

Tompkins, Peter. *Italy Betrayed*. New York: Simon & Schuster, 1966.

United States Department of State. Telegrams related to awarding Legion of Merit to Draza Mihaliovich. April 1, 1948, to April 9, 1948.

United States Department of War. Western Union Telegram to Angiolina Orsini, Jersey City, NJ: August 3, 1944.

Vujnovich, George. Personal interviews and correspondence with the author.

Vujnovich, George and Mirjana. As told to Theodore Wilkinson. *Memoirs of a Marriage: Oral History of George and Mirjana Vujnovic*. Washington, DC: Five and Ten Press, 2001.

Vuksic, Velimir. *Tito's Partisans: 1941–1945*. Botley, Oxford, United Kingdom: Osprey Publishing, 2003.

Wilkinson, Xenia. Personal interviews and correspondence with author.

Wilson, Robert. Personal interviews and correspondence with the author.

Woodward, E. L. *British Foreign Policy in the Second World War*. London: Her Majesty's Stationery Office, 1962.

# Index

# Contact the Author

For more information about Gregory A. Freeman and his work, go to the author's Web site at www.GregoryAFreeman.com.

If your book club is interested in having the author participate in a discussion of *The Forgotten 500* by phone, send your request to author@ GregoryAFreeman.com.

Photo by Eric Beach

**Gregory A. Freeman** is an award-winning writer with more than twenty years of experience in journalism. He is the author of *Sailors to the End: The Deadly Fire on the USS* Forrestal *and the Heroes Who Fought It* and *Lay This Body Down: The 1921 Murders of Eleven Plantation Slaves.*